BLACK FOUNDERS AT WORK

Journeys to Innovation

Edited by

DELA WILSON & HADIYAH MUJHID

HBCUvc
Black Founders at Work: Journeys to Innovation
© 2021 by HBCUvc (fiscally sponsored project of Social Good Fund
EIN: 46-1323531)

Editors: Deloris "Dela" Wilson and Hadiyah Mujhid
Copy Editor: J.D. Ho, Kathleen Tracy
Transcriptionist: Alissa Johnson
Cover Designer: Desmond Wilson
Layout Designer: Najdan Mancic
Proofreaders: Cynthia Dixon, Chelsea Roberts, Elshadye Bussie

First printing 2021
ISBN: 978-1-7369521-0-8

CONTENTS

ACKNOWLEDGMENTS

We would like to acknowledge the partners and supporters who have contributed to HBCUvc in various ways.

Foundation Partners
Surdna Foundation, Alabama Power, Techstars Foundation, Gucci Changemakers, Concrete Rose Foundation, Annenberg Foundation, Mark Cuban Foundation, Morgan Family Foundation, Anchor Point Foundation.

Organization Partners
Google for Startups, Intel Capital, American Family Insurance Institute for Corporate and Social Impact, Redpoint Ventures, Echoing Green, Praxis Labs, Silicon Valley Bank, True Ventures, DoorDash, Legacy Venture, Munich Re Ventures.

HBCUvc Staff and Team
Cynthia Lopez-Dixon, Chelsea Roberts, Charlton Cunningham, Lavonya Jones, Jameela Bahar, LaVaughn Jones, Amira Ouji, Elizabeth Tente, Nathan Jones.

Special Mentors and Advisors to HBCUvc
The following mentors and advisors have been instrumental in the start and development of HBCUvc: Uriridiakoghene (Ulili) Onovakpuri, Brian Dixon, Monique Woodard, Bryce Roberts,

Marlon Nichols, Arlan Hamilton, Jorge Torres, Austin Clements, Jonathan Jackson, Megan Holston-Alexander, Terik Tidwell.

HBCU VC Fellows

A special thank you to our HBCU VC Fellows (Classes 1–4). Thank you for believing and contributing to the mission: Cameron Kipper, Paul Lockett, Richard Clay, Saleah McFadden, Chrystal Cantrelle, Tobi Plumpter, Kiley Williams, Jessica Tarin, Jose Flores Gomez, Frederick Uy, Biruk Abate, Timileyin Adebisi, Phiwinhlanhla Ndebele-Ngwenya, Kayla Boyd, Courtney Johnson, Garrett Coley, Dakota Price, Shannon Brown, Adrianna Seeney, Trea'jure Dahl, Jordan King, Judy Silva, Bryanna Barnett, Olumide Longe, Elijah Porter, Shondace Thomas, Whitney Griffith, Malcolm Beason, Lyndon Bowen, Anthony Edwards, Dorian Holmes, David Jeffries, Austin Jeter, Zaira Jacome-Meza, Denkenesh Dobbins, Raquel Permaul, Khrys Hatch, Baffour Osei, Briana Davis, De'Havia Stewart, Lamarr Nash, Micah Hall, Nia Scott, Ime Essien, Carlos Murguia, Kendall Camp, Daryl Riley, Justice Sims-McCray, Kiante Bush, Kristen Bailey, Kareem Michel, Jerry Ford II, Nia Baker, Yolanda Stephens, Tobi Shannon, Edward Nwaba, Shelby Hicks, Alyiah Ellsworth, Martin Adu-Boahene, James Shonubi, Deveraux Mackey, Geo Albert Mirador, Elizabeth Hardy, LaKendra Harden, David Hulett, Khadijat Aboderin, Chibuzor Martins, Darren Butler, Betangabeh Khumbah, Blanca Burch, Nava Levene-Harvell, Martin Chaplin, Elon Stein, Gazette Thompson III, Enrico Scott, Alanah Mack, Kevin Mwangi, Shuhab Elhag, Oluchi Chukwunyere, Desiree Jones, Jared Tate, Madison Stewart, Miniya Williams, Louis Deas, Delsa Guerrero-Castillo, Damian Murray, Ali Aly.

ON GENIUS AND AFFIRMATION

Deloris "Dela" Wilson

The inequities of the venture capital (VC) industry, similarly embedded across sectors, were brought to broad awareness in 2020. A contemporary movement for civil rights questioned the longstanding design and operations of almost every facet of our lives, with direct focus on a primary source of wealth concentration—and creation—for those privileged enough to break into its folds. Through a historically closed network of dim pathways, VC crafts a space where one learns by association and through doing. Only until the last few years, venture capital's coveted roles were held for carefully selected Ivy League grads, legacy hires, or through a potion of pure luck.

What naturally follows this thread of conversation is typically a landscape analysis of the VC industry. Articles often cite that 20 percent of public companies were started with venture capital backing, or the record high of $150 billion in financing that circulated within 2020 alone, despite a global pandemic and economic crisis. Existing publications may also note that this feat was primarily driven by just a few fundraising rounds and unicorns.[1] The narrative then typically compares the fraction of financing flowing to Black founders vis-à-vis White founders, encapsulated within a dearth of Black control of investment dollars. They may then highlight how less than 1 percent of that $150 billion were directed to companies with Black founders.[2]

My approach intentionally departs from this. Our deficits are widely reported, researched, extrapolated, and articulated to paint a clear picture of what we don't have—due to histories of lawful discrimination and learned behavior, out of intention and design. This context helps set the stage, though I refuse to let it determine our outcomes. To understand the context, however, I encourage you to explore publications like *Building Supportive Ecosystems for Black-Owned US Businesses* by McKinsey & Company; Crunchbase's Diversity Spotlight report, Funding to Black & Latinx Founders; and Black Women Talk Tech's *The New Face of a Founder: Uncovering Black Women as the Next Billion Dollar Founders*, which help illuminate the intricacies of

---

[1]   Andrea Hoffman, *Why New Black Venture Capital Funds Will Generate Outsized Returns and Help Close the Racial Wealth Gap* (Culture Shift Labs, 2021).

[2]   Gene Teare, *Highlighting Notable Funding to Black Founders in 2020*, *Crunchbase News*, February 12, 2021.

Black disruption into concentrated capital. Where we as a society have invested far less attention, however, is in the examination of our assets: in the analysis of our achievements, our greatness, and Black genius at scale. Such framing is much more beneficial for self-actualization.

In March 2020, I wrote an article announcing HBCUvc's selection of emerging Black professionals in venture capital.[3] Designed to amplify and connect, the recognition cultivated an ecosystem of relationships to open access to shared resources, deal flow, and community support. It framed the current venture capital landscape from a singular lens: a Black lens. I drew market insights from the reference point of Black CEOs and Managing Partners, research published by Harlem Capital Partners (a venture fund whose founders met through Management Leadership for Tomorrow, a program equipping African Americans, Latinos, and Native Americans for careers in business), Delane Parnell's Series C raise, as well as Goodr, Naza Beauty, and PopCom's fundraising feats as Black women CEOs. I oriented promotion and primed readers with an expectant lens towards excellence. Some, like Arlan Hamilton of Backstage Capital, noticed, citing that it was "one of the best things she's read all year," while others may not have realized the not-so-subtle nod and skipped down the page to the feature of their homegirl (which is cool too).[4] In either case, though, it helped set a tone that I hope becomes the norm across

---

3   Dela Wilson, "HBCUvc's 31 Under 31: The Future of Venture Capital," *HBCUvc*, March 3, 2020.

4   Arlan Hamilton (@ArlanWasHere), Twitter, August 9, 2020.

the industry: where "firsts" aren't newsworthy since excellence is expected, and our achievements, processes, and experiences become primary sources in the database of success.

Our leadership pathways are largely unrecorded, and countless inventions uncredited, remnants of a system ripe for dismantling. Innovation and invention have been critical to America's progress, with intellectual property policies among the first formed in this country. But just as Black bodies were commodified, so were our ideas, siphoning the wealth, influence, and impact of innovators unnamed and unknown. Legal barriers prevented the earliest Black inventors from obtaining intellectual property rights since they were precluded from qualifying as citizens.[5] Even after citizenship rights were granted, patterns of intentional misinformation and misattribution continued, where Black men and women were intentionally separated from the benefits of their intellectual contributions. For example, Katherine Johnson's contributions in mathematics earned her name's removal from reports she authored, despite discovering a design flaw in the technology that would propel Americans into space. Jack Daniel's infamous whiskey was actually formulated by Nathan "Uncle Nearest" Green, a formerly enslaved whiskey distiller who used a special charcoal filtering technique learned in West Africa to craft the well-known brew. Today, Green's technique is known as the "Lincoln Method."

Misappropriation of credit and explicit barriers to entry have also limited Black leadership's progression into C-Suite roles.

---

[5]   David Baboolall, Kelemwork Cook, Nick Noel, Shelley Stewart, and Nina Yancy, *Building Supportive Ecosystems for Black-Owned US Businesses* (McKinsey & Company, 2020).

Chad Sanders, author of *Black Magic*, found himself emulating whiteness in order to achieve success in Silicon Valley. Once "integrated," he only later realized that a recommitment to his Black identity held the true catalyst to his—and others'—success. Many of us aren't as vulnerable as Sanders in our pursuits of truth, however, as some fear losing progress, and preclude public vulnerability as a result. For others, ambitions of grandeur are curtailed by the need to survive. Risk is a privilege. The Toigo Foundation explains that "because so few African Americans have reached senior levels of leadership in global enterprises, few of their peers have a road map for how interactions with these (and upcoming) leaders should unfold."[6] The vulnerabilities that inform the guides that follow do more than provide direction; they affirm existence. They promote self-actualization. They ground identity and translate our power for generations to come.

You'll see yourself in the founders who forged some of the earliest advances in contemporary technology developments, new industry creation, historic industry disruption, and, of course, the control and influence of capital in the infamous Silicon Valley. You'll witness vulnerability, self-awareness, confrontation, and reflection as these leaders navigate the complexities of innovation. You'll grapple with their personal and familial sacrifice. You'll witness their failures as integral components to later success. These mechanics of business and realities of product development, team

---

[6] Nancy Sims, Sue Toigo, Maura Allen, and Toni Cornelius, "From C-Suite to Startups: The Illusion of Inclusion," in *Race Work & Leadership: New Perspectives on the Black Experience,* ed. Laura Morgan Roberts, Anthony J. Mayo and David A. Thomas (Boston : Harvard Business Review Press, 2019), 209–22.

sourcing, and fundraising are woven in-between the thoughts, feelings, and context of decisions that are often limited to personal relationships, years of mentorship, or kitchen-table talks. It is our hope to make this advice palatable, relatable, and widely available.

Through *Black Founders at Work*, we share their genius to catalyze yours.

We open the text with the stories of **Hadiyah Mujhid, Monique Woodard** and **Chris Bennett**, who mobilized communities of Black founders together before innovating independently—launching transformational nonprofits, venture funds targeting changes in population demographics, and startups that solve systemic issues in early childhood education. **Angela Benton** defines the ecosystem builder in action, weaving foundational networks of Black Silicon Valley that continue to power the startup and venture capital landscape today. Through **Charles Hudson**, we witness an honest journey through awareness of privilege and multiple bets on self to ultimately launch Precursor Ventures, while **Melissa Hanna** demonstrates how a lifelong commitment to problem solving could correct market inefficiencies in maternal health - even if still defining her path. **Frederick Hutson** navigates life post-incarceration to build technology and influence policy that reforms our broken criminal justice system, and **James Jones, Jr., Esq.** shows how a husband and wife team scaled a legal tech startup to multiple enterprises aligned with their passions and purpose. Through **Juanita Lott**, we recognize the power in patience and the mechanics of leveraging in-house expertise to lead her enterprise software company through a multimillion-dollar acquisition. **Erik**

Moore and **Kirby Harris** talk teams and how their individual paths converged to become one of the earliest first Black VC funds in Silicon Valley, with legendary investments in Blavity, Mayvenn, StyleSeat and more. We then chart the new school with Delane Parnell, who unapologetically leads a revolution in high school esports competitions, raising the largest ever Series-A round by a Black founder in consumer Internet—all before age twenty-eight. To close, we hear the story of **Michael Seibel** who shows us how *literally* being along for the ride can change everything about your intended future.

These accounts, shared in their own words, are designed to be starting points for your journey through a brief stopover in theirs. Collected in transit and in-between meetings, all amidst a global pandemic and collective realization of the Black experience, these stories are meant to spur further discovery into the progress of entrepreneurship. They're collected to prompt your own potential as an innovator. What resounds through each account is an awareness and ascription of value to Black identity, and an unrelenting commitment to reinvest in Black innovation at scale.

HADIYAH MUJHID

Founder and CEO, HBCUvc

HBCUvc's mission is to direct how capital is formed and distributed so that it increases opportunities for Black, Indigenous, and Latinx innovators. We accomplish this by increasing the number of successful Black, Indigenous, and Latinx venture capital leaders in communities where entrepreneurs face barriers in accessing investment capital, and by empowering institutions to employ race-conscious investing practices. Since 2017, HBCUvc has supported 185 undergraduate and graduate students, entrepreneurs, and emerging professionals across four programs: HBCU Fellowship, City Ecosystems, Emerging Manager, and the HBCUvc Lab Fund. HBCUvc is a fiscally sponsored project of Social Good Fund (EIN: 46-1323531), a 501(c)(3) nonprofit organization.

Hadiyah Mujhid is the CEO and Founder of HBCUvc, a nonprofit that is dedicated to changing how investment capital is formed and allocated to benefit historically underestimated groups. She has experience as both a tech founder and software engineer and is obsessed with leveraging technology entrepreneurship for economic inclusion. She is also an Echoing Green and Praxis Fellow. Hadiyah earned her MBA from Drexel University and holds a BS in computer science from the University of Maryland Eastern Shore, an HBCU.

Twitter: @hadiyahdotme
Website: hbcu.vc

Tell us about your personal background. What was it like growing up?

Hadiyah Mujhid: I talk a lot about how my origin story relates to our mission at HBCUvc. If anyone has ever seen me at a conference or anywhere, I always share how I grew up in an immigrant household. My grandmother moved here to the United States from Jamaica, leaving her entire family behind—including her seven children. When she came here, she hustled. She hustled so that she could save up enough to sponsor her children to come over, one by one.

And that was a shift because she was married, and coming to the US meant leaving her husband and seven kids for a long time. There's still some family drama that stems from this huge risk she took.

By the time I came into the picture, my mother had only been in the United States for a few years. My early childhood memories are all around us being in one household in Philadelphia, Pennsylvania. I grew up in a house with my grandmother, my mother, and many of my aunts and uncles. My mother was the third child out of seven, so I believe my uncle is only, like, fifteen years older than me. I remember him and a few of my aunts being teenagers, and then going off to college. In hindsight,

My grandmother had a number of businesses, and in my early years, I didn't think that this was anything to really be proud of then. But now I see: Through entrepreneurship, she took care of us and also other members of our family.

seeing their journey played an impactful role in my own journey.

What I didn't understand until later was that our household survived off of entrepreneurship. I didn't name it "entrepreneurship" then, but there were a number of businesses run by our household. My grandmother had a number of businesses, and in my early years, I didn't think that this was anything to really be proud of then. But now I see: Through entrepreneurship, she took care of us and also other members of our family.

My grandmother had a cleaning business and cleaned offices at night. The family, including my aunts and uncles, would join her in the evenings. Since I had a couple of cousins who were a few years older than me, I sometimes was the one to stay home and watch my younger siblings. I was old enough to watch the kids, but not old enough to go and clean households [*laughs*]. Whereas, my cousin, who was fifteen in high school, went with my grandmother at night, and then to school in the morning.

[My grandmother] also owned a Jamaican restaurant, which was down the street, and I remember playing on the cash register and experiencing the tactile feeling of making money—the sounds of the old school cash register: *Ding, ding, ding, ding, choo* [*laughs*]! I know you're laughing, but, yeah, there's a tactile feeling to making money for me. So I watched my grandmother hustle. You know, she did all of this—the restaurant, the cleaning business—and she still held a full-time job during the day at the Philadelphia School District as a bus aide.

I remember overhearing some conversations about my family pooling money together at times to bring over other relatives. Sometimes, the relative would stay with us for a little bit—you know, there were a lot of people in that house, yet we always had room. There was always an opportunity to work with one of the businesses, and stay with us until they landed on their own.

Of course, sometimes there would be drama, but there would always be family. I remember a kitchen conversation about bringing another aunt to the United States for her to attend college. She was my grandfather's child, but not my grandmother's child. My grandmother played a role in helping her get to the United States. It's layered, complicated, but I've watched my grandmother do for others in situations where others would only criticize. These threads still show up in my life: this constant presence of entrepreneurship and making your own way; and this concept of having a strong community despite the drama and conflict.

So, from Philadelphia you go off to college at University of Maryland Eastern Shore. Was that always the goal?

Mujhid: Sometimes I feel like my life is a little bit aligned with Forrest Gump. Where things have happened, and it wasn't intentional, but it ends up becoming a huge part of your journey. It was always told to me that I would go to college because part of the reason why everyone was here [from Jamaica] was to have access to a good education. But it was also told to me that there wasn't any money for college. *I was going to go, but I had to find a way to go.*

I went to a magnet high school in Philadelphia. It was small, and the principal at the time pushed a lot of students to [go to] the University of Pennsylvania. I'm pretty sure 50–80 percent of my graduating high school class applied to Penn. I was one of them, and I was really confident that I was going to get in: We had a pipeline; our principal had connections there, and she encouraged us all to apply for early decision. Well, I did [apply], and was extremely disappointed to be waitlisted. *Extremely* disappointed because that was the only university I had applied to. That's how confident I was.

And keep in mind that I didn't have people at home to guide me through the college application process. But what did keep arriving in the mail was offers for HBCUs. I don't know if they still do this, but when I was in high school, universities would send automatic acceptance letters (with no application) based on SAT scores, demographics, and other factors. I kept getting accepted to HBCUs and small, rural colleges. To be honest, at the time, I hadn't thought much about either—especially HBCUs. Neither I nor my family knew anything about them. I knew that they were a thing but my thoughts at the time were: *Why would I go to a Black school when the rest of the world doesn't look like that? Why would I prepare myself for a false reality?* And to be honest, I think that was a concept I had gotten from my school counselor at that time.

So acceptances to Hampton and Howard came in the mail. Followed by Grinnell College in the middle of Iowa [*laughs*]. And then one came from the University of Maryland Eastern Shore. And I was like: *Oh, I know the University of Maryland! That's not an HBCU!* I know this sounds really naive, but keep in mind this was the late nineties. I graduated high school in '97, and the way we researched colleges was by going to the counselor's office and flipping through a thick book, a college directory. Schools had one-page profiles, and you'd ask your guidance [counselor] questions to fill in details based on their experience. Yes, there was Internet at that time, but it was very seldom used...and the Internet just looked horrible. So I was working with somewhat limited knowledge when I went on my acceptance visit to the University of Maryland Eastern Shore. As I looked around, I was like: *Wow, there are a lot of Black people on campus.* Come to find out, it was a Black college.

And I wasn't that disappointed, you know? It was a free college experience. I do remember calling my aunt who was a UPenn alum, and remembering her feedback was like: "Oh, well, you know, I think you'll have a good time and a good experience there. Don't be so disappointed that you weren't accepted into Penn. No one really cares about undergraduates anyway; it's all about your grad school." I think a lot of HBCU students still think about it this way. Undergraduate: Get the Black experience. Graduate: Get the brand name degree from an Ivy.

So I went to University of Maryland Eastern Shore, an HBCU, which, at the time of acceptance I didn't know, but looking back, it probably was one of the most transformative years of my life. Coming from a Caribbean American background, it gave me the opportunity to experience just how different Black people were across the United States. Seeing the differences in Black culture between Philadelphia, Baltimore, and DC, for example, and the different languages that we use. If I say, "I'm going to get my sneakers," people will look at me crazy and ask, "Your tennis shoes?" But I'm not playing tennis!

Since I ran track in college, I arrived on campus early, with the athletes, before the rest of the students started the school year. The only folks on campus early were the athletes and students participating in PACE, a program supporting students who normally would not have been accepted into college. Basically, PACE students would take a lot of non-credit courses

It was later in life that I realized just how much HBCUs were an equalizer for a lot of us. Seeing Black excellence at a young age was important.

their first year and, based on their performance, would be formally accepted. What stood out to me later in life is that I met so many people in that PACE program who, unlike me, didn't come from a very academic high school, or walk in with good grades, but we all graduated with the same degree. We all held the same paper. And, at the same time, I watched as my graduating class became doctors, lawyers, and engineers. It was later in life that I realized just how much HBCUs were an equalizer for a lot of us. Seeing Black excellence at a young age was important.

I'll add that I was also a computer science major, and at that time, about half of the Department of Computer Science's graduating class was comprised of Black women. I went back and tabulated this after the fact because, later in my journey, when people kept telling me statements like, "Oh, wow, you're a Black woman and you're an engineer? You're in computer science, that's so unheard of!"—it was all very foreign to me. Like: *What do you mean?* There were fifty graduates in my program, and about half of them were Black women. So the anchoring and start of my career is different from a lot of people entering tech and engineering.

With a computer science degree in hand, where did you head next?

Mujhid: My first job out of college was at Lockheed Martin as a software engineer. Though I loved my university experience, I don't know how much it actually prepared me for the job search—and that's just the reality of things. I still had no idea what to do with that degree or what it meant. This is 2001, so again, there wasn't a lot of information out there on what the day-to-day responsibilities of a computer scientist or a software engineer would look like. So I found myself randomly applying to a lot of companies not knowing if that was a role that actually applied to my degree.

I was at this career fair, and a Black woman spotted me and asked me to come over. Looking back, I think a lot of things happened because I just always looked really young for my age. So imagine seeing this person who probably looks fourteen walking around a career fair. She asks me, "Hey, what are you doing here?" I told her I was looking for a job, and she took a look at my resume. "Oh, you're a computer science major?" *Yeah*. She basically then marked up my resume and said, "I need you to change these things and come back."

And so I did. I changed it up and then came back. "Okay, I have four teams that I'm going to have interview you. These are the things they are looking for that you should make sure to talk about." I so wish I could remember her name, but I'm grateful for having this woman look out for me. She honestly probably stepped up because she saw another Black woman. I don't know if she was in cahoots with the managers at the time, but in the division where I interviewed, the Center of Software Excellence, there was a director who was a White man, and he had three managers underneath him who were all Black. She had me interview with each of these Black managers.

What was your experience like at Lockheed Martin?

Mujhid: So Lockheed Martin is generally a majority White company, and [it] represented what the tech industry looked like overall at the time (and arguably still today). But there's this department that had three Black managers, the Center of Software Excellence, that oddly sat off campus in another building. We used to call it the United Nations when you walked in the building [*laughs*]—which isn't funny, but it is. There were some two hundred people that sat in that building, and it was probably the most diverse environment I've ever been in.

I remember one incident in particular as being significant to the way I think about things today. I was twenty [or] twenty-one at the time, and working late one evening on a deadline with a few team members, three White men. We took a dinner break and got on the topic of race. I don't remember what exactly was said now, but I remember feeling really uncomfortable and really offended about a particular comment. In their eyes, they were just making a joke, but it really affected me. The next morning, I purposefully got to the office at the crack of dawn to meet my manager who worked on a 5 a.m. to 2 p.m. schedule. I might have been feeling myself just a little bit because I remember feeling like I had air cover. *If anyone was going to understand how hurtful this comment was, it was going to be my Black manager.* And at the same time, I kind of felt like: *Oh, you guys picked the wrong one. You do know I have a Black manager, right?*

So I went in early in the morning to discuss the incident. I told him what happened, that I'm offended, and sought his advice on reporting them to HR. He was like, "What? I mean, yeah, it's a messed up comment, but I want to point some things out to you. You are a Black woman who is working in a predominantly White male industry, right? And I'm here to support you either way, but I want to tell you that taking a comment like this to HR may be seen as threatening someone's job. And do you know what that could mean in your relations with the rest of the team and your career?" He pretty much told me straight up that, "Hey, we can do this. HR's going to investigate. It may be uncomfortable for you, though, because people are going to come back and feel like you're threatening their job. You're twenty. You have a long journey ahead of you as a Black woman in a male-dominated field. You're going to have to understand the battle from the war, you know?" He left the decision up to me to think about. "If this is something that you want to die on, and you want to go ahead and report them, then you can do that. Or, if this is something where I can help you navigate these conversations so that you can create your own space in the workspace, we can do that as well."

I chose, obviously, the second option: to learn how to handle these conversations in the future. And we worked on that together. That was a really important conversation to have, and I don't think that it would have happened if I didn't have a Black manager. I'm not sure if a White manager would have been able to navigate the nuance, to know what it might mean for me to damage my career before it even started.

As you're developing your career at Lockheed Martin, when did you begin to pivot towards entrepreneurship? Was your initial plan to work your way up through the ranks of corporate leadership, or did you always intend to venture out on your own?

Mujhid: I think I was more of a double mind. Based on my economic situation, entrepreneurship was always an economic driver. Like: *We need to get money.* So if getting money meant doing this corporate thing to get as much as I could, then do that. At the same time, though, how was I *hustling*? I always had. Even while at Lockheed Martin, I was always freelancing, building websites, or doing different things on the side for a large part of the journey. The itch and desire for entrepreneurship definitely grew stronger the more I stayed at Lockheed Martin, though, and this desire for more learning opportunities than the roles immediately around me could provide.

By this time, 2009 or 2010, I was already based in California and had asked to be transferred from the San Diego office to the office in Sunnyvale. I was hearing about all these companies that were starting up in Silicon Valley, and just became really curious. I'd asked to be transferred up to Sunnyvale because that was the closest that I could get. That was also the first time I really immersed myself in startup culture, even while still working at Lockheed Martin.

I had this background in entrepreneurship, but I didn't have a background in high-tech entrepreneurship. At the time, I didn't really know what it meant to grow a high-tech company, or how it was different from the other varieties of entrepreneurship that I'd known. It was also the first time that I saw wealth up close and personal.

So if I'm sitting across from someone and ask the right question, they'll tell you everything. I was thriving in that environment. Everyone I met was a warehouse of knowledge and was willing to share as much as they could.

I remember going to a small networking event at the Computer History Museum and meeting a guy there named Adam [D'Angelo]. (I later discovered [he] was the founder of Quora). He wasn't a co-founder but was one of the first employees at Facebook, and had left Facebook to create another company. I remember thinking like: *Wow, he's on something else.* The way he was talking about things, the way he was thinking about things...it was so very different for me. I was meeting all of these people starting up companies, growing them fast, and hiring their friends. This had a strong influence on me.

Silicon Valley was very different from other cities, if you could find yourself in the right rooms, the access is amazing in terms of knowledge transfer or access to people. People don't feel that they have proprietary access to knowledge. So if I'm sitting across from someone and ask the right question, they'll tell you everything. I was thriving in that environment. Everyone I met was a warehouse of knowledge and was willing to share as much as they could.

Was it during this time of networking and knowledge exchange that the idea for Black Founders came about? How did you connect with Monique Woodard, Chris Bennett, and Nnena Ukuku (co-founders of Black Founders)?

Mujhid: So at this time, I don't know if I had left Lockheed Martin yet, but I was getting ready to leave Lockheed Martin. I had already started working on a company, Picturely, with two other co-founders, and [we had] a goal to develop what we called "an image analytics company." My focus at the time was to build this tech company. As I was moving across Silicon Valley with this goal in mind, it felt weird because I felt like I was with my people in terms of technical people, and people who loved entrepreneurship and startups. But at the same time, I was actually the farthest from my people, having grown up with Philadelphia being a Black city, attending an HBCU, and starting my career within a group with strong, Black leadership. My community was always a key element, and it took me a minute to notice it was missing in Silicon Valley.

When I'd attend networking events and see another Black person, I would just gravitate to them and give them the nod [laughs]. That's how I met the co-founders of Black Founders.

When I'd attend networking events and see another Black person, I would just gravitate to them and give them the nod [*laughs*]. That's how I met the co-founders of Black Founders. They were feeling the same thing, in an environment where they felt as though they were among their people, but at the same time, they were missing Black people in that space. At the same time, we were hearing conversations about companies not being able to "find" Black people to hire, and not funding Black people. So we realized that we were in a position of access. We knew that there was a greater community who wanted this access.

What were your initial steps after the idea was conceived?

Mujhid: We asked ourselves: *How do we create a space for Black people to share this type of knowledge and access across lines? Who are you meeting with? What investor are you meeting with? What are you building?* We weren't even trying to be an official organization at the time, but really just focusing on connecting our own networks. When we first started meeting, Monique, Nnena, Chris, and myself, we all sat down, and the first conversation was like: *How about you call all of your Black friends, I call all my Black friends, [and] let's get in a room and talk about what we're doing, and just start sharing.* We had a list of maybe ten people, and [we] held our first event at a Black-owned bar in San Francisco, which unfortunately is no longer there. Close to fifty people showed up, and it was just mind-blowing to us. We literally took over the bar.

We soon realized: *Wait a minute, there's something here.* Everyone kept asking: *When's the next event? When are we going to do this? When are we going to do that?* So many people felt the need that we were feeling—this excitement of being in a place but missing your people! So we began organizing and growing and expanding our reach. As we grew, the community shifted. When we started, it was a space for people who were actively building companies. Those folks would tell their friends, and the next thing you know, people were showing up like, "I haven't started yet but I heard that this is the place where I can meet other entrepreneurs and learn from them." We then began supporting aspiring entrepreneurs too. From that, we put together educational content and transitioned from a networking organization to more of an educational one. We listened to what the community wanted, and [we] were happy to help and serve them in that way.

At the time, hackathons were really popular in San Francisco, and colleges like Stanford and Berkeley would host them regularly. Why aren't they doing this on our campuses? So Black Founders then became one of the first groups to bring hackathons to HBCU campuses.

How did you shift to serve the HBCU community, specifically current HBCU students? Was it an expansion of the existing work with Black Founders?

Mujhid: Since attending and experiencing an HBCU, I've had this huge affinity, this love and loyalty for them. Even while building Black Founders, I began thinking about who was up next, who would be next up in the pipeline. At the time, hackathons were really popular in San Francisco, and colleges like Stanford and Berkeley would host them regularly. *Why aren't they doing this on our campuses?* So Black Founders then became one of the first groups to bring hackathons to HBCU campuses. And I really shepherded this in the most bootstrap of ways [*laughs*]. I really just flew to campuses and was like: *We're going to do this on your campus.*

I was walking around Clark Atlanta University one day, distributing flyers about hackathons. Funny enough, I got kicked off of campus—well, not kicked off, but asked to leave. "You can't promote things on campus. Do you go here?" I'm like: *No...* But instead of leaving, I just walked around the building. We called it HBCU Hacks. I'd seen entrepreneurs at Stanford and Berkeley starting up so early, and I wanted that for our community—that spirit of tinkering and building things. The industry was growing at such a rate that you could now just be in your dorm room and build a whole company. There were tools becoming available—like

It was definitely the right time, and I knew HBCUs were going to produce the next set of founders, and I wanted to have a part in that.

GitHub and Heroku—where you could just build something, put it on the web, and get people playing with it within two hours.

So, you know, it was definitely the right time, and I knew HBCUs were going to produce the next set of founders, and I wanted to have a part in that.

What was difficult about the shift in focus from Black Founders to HBCUvc?

Mujhid: There was a time when Black Founders wasn't as active, and we all kind of had other things going on. Well, we always had other things going on, and I think that is one of the reasons why it became not as active. Truthfully, we never created it to be an organization; it was this little baby, this love child that got created. And we got tired of watching the baby. It was like: *No, I was supposed to be doing this, you watch the baby.* I hate to say this, and my co-founders may disagree—we disagree on some things a lot—but it was never supposed to be a real thing, although the baby just grew and grew. We didn't plan for it. We didn't realize that, if we were going to run an organization, it's going to take up our time, we've got to raise money for it, etc. We were all growing in our different understanding of running a nonprofit.

Monique [Woodard] was very influential in how we thought about our growth: *If we're going to grow Black founders and their companies, how are we thinking about access to capital for them?* From the very beginning, she always talked about access to capital. We would be in a Black Founders meeting, and she'd be like, "Hadiyah, let's meet with the VCs," and I'm like, "Well, what about the students?" So it's very interesting to see how our careers shifted but, at the same time, came back together. She went on to the other side of the table and became an investor, and I've worked on a couple of other startups since then, and began freelancing since then. I had left Lockheed Martin for a few years now, but the problem of supporting Black Founders and accessing capital was still a theme in my head. I'd read an article by Richard Kerby [of Equal

I began to look at the nuances of building relationships in venture capital, and a lot of them were anchored in experiences and mentorship at universities.

Ventures], where he breaks down capital, its role in the ecosystem, and basically who's making the decisions. He talks about not only the racial demographic but also the university demographic. When he surveyed all these VCs, he showed

that 40 percent of them either went to Stanford or to Harvard. It correlated with a Crunchbase report that also looked at the universities where startup CEOs were raising a million dollars or more—and Stanford and Harvard were always the top two. Always. And I was witnessing those strong university networks firsthand. So, for me, I began to look at the nuances of building relationships in venture capital, and a lot of them were anchored in experiences and mentorship at universities.

At the same time I'm thinking through this, I was also running my software development agency, Playpen Labs. I was known for Black Founders, but also [as] a software developer. So I'd work with different startups, and they'd ask me, "Hey, we're hiring. Where can I find other Black people?" And it got to the point where I was constantly shifting people back to HBCUs. I started doing more and more unofficial work in helping startups connect with HBCU students.

What other aspects of existing models inspired your approach?

Mujhid: Well, I saw this huge opportunity there, in supporting and introducing entrepreneurship and investment to students who are still on campus. I also saw the impact that Dorm Room Fund was having on college campuses—how student partners would fund student founders, which would, in turn, create micro-ecosystems that, even if not resulting in a successful venture, would result in experience. So I thought: *How do we take this model and leverage it a bit, anchor it into locations where our people are, and use it to shift the entire industry?* And that's how HBCUvc was founded.

> *How do we take this model and leverage it a bit, anchor it into locations where our people are, and use it to shift the entire industry? And that's how HBCUvc was founded.*

HBCUvc was already gaining traction before 2020, but this year undoubtedly accelerated its growth—catalyzed by a national conversation and confrontation of institutional racism and bias. What's been your experience paving a fundraising journey as a nonprofit CEO, which is quite different from the experience of other founders in this book?

Mujhid: I'm extremely thankful that, during the time of Black Founders, we developed some key contacts and relationships.

When I was developing this idea and thinking about funding, I reached out to Lesa Mitchell, who used to be at the Kauffman Foundation and now is at Techstars in Kansas City, to share my thoughts. *Hey, I have this idea and I don't know exactly what to do with it.* My experience with Black Founders was different. We started an organization without careful thought on how we would sustain the organization financially. This was a very painful journey, and I didn't want to repeat the same mistakes.

I talked with Lesa about it, and she was immediately supportive, very supportive. She was like, "Hey, I just left Kauffman Foundation, but this is the type of work that Kauffman Foundation gets behind. And I can introduce you to Philip Gaskin, who just started over there." I immediately connected with Philip about my idea, and I remember him saying, "Your timing is impeccable." *Why?* "Because, normally it would be a different process to get funding, but we just opened this Inclusion Open grant challenge where we're focusing on new ideas to think about inclusion in entrepreneurship. And the application opens up on Monday, so make sure you apply."

The thing about getting your first check, regardless of whether your company is for-profit or nonprofit, is that it signals to the rest of the industry that this is something to take seriously.

So, it was a bit of timing luck. Previous networks, access—all these things are very important. I applied, and we were one of the grantees selected for funding. That anchor of support really allowed me to focus full-time on HBCUvc with a $120K grant to support initial operations. So I drilled down and built out the program; I had the time, finally. I didn't have to only do this on nights and weekends. From that initial seed investment in 2017, things took off.

We are now in 2020, and our primary funders are foundations, many of which came on and supported us after Kauffman. The thing about getting your first check, regardless of whether your company is for-profit or nonprofit, is that it signals to the rest of the industry that this is something to take seriously. That initial round of funding supported our first year and allowed us to build up some significant momentum. We were beginning to be known in corporations and VC firms, and we started to partner with corporations who wanted to get behind this work.

2020 was an interesting year in that we had *just* developed this routine of how we get organizations to support us and provide value, and the model was largely an event sponsorship model—and then COVID-19 happened. And all across the world, anything that was in-person stopped. Any type of sponsorship for events stopped. So we were at a critical moment: *We just lost 30 percent of our budget. What does this mean for us as a team?* Money froze as companies tried to figure out what they were going to do—and it's actually quite funny to highlight that. It's funny how money ebbs and flows, how it disappears and reappears.

Immediately after stay-at-home orders were activated, money disappeared. And then, following the unfortunate murder of George Floyd, racial equity ripped into a lot of industries, and money made a reappearance. Similar to other industries, in venture capital there was this huge awakening, reckoning, and questioning of what the industry was doing to address its inequities. Those first couple of weeks after the murder, we received a lot of calls and [an] increase in donations. I think a lot of people were experiencing "White people guilt." Which is somewhat good, you know. Money is needed to address this problem. But one of the things that we wanted to be mindful of when bringing on new partners is (1) that this wasn't a knee-jerk reaction, and that they understand that we're combating systemic barriers, the nature of which is a 400-plus-year-old problem, and (2) yes, we need your money, but we also need your full awareness of what's happening and your intentions to do something about it. So we've had some of these conversations, sometimes difficult conversations, and sometimes some partners get it, and they've been supporting us. And then, some partners still don't get it, but still write a check. To be honest, I like the latter, too, but they may or may not stick around. Hopefully, they do, though. It's a process for a lot of people. Maybe once they're in proximity to working with us, they understand a little bit more, over time.

So, why this book, and why now?

Mujhid: My vision for this book began when we created Black Founders. I read Jessica Livingston's *Founders at Work* at that time. I geeked out while reading interviews of founders as they talked about their early days. I eagerly wanted a collection of stories from founders who represented the Black community, and to serve as inspiration for future Black founders and investors. There are so many people I've had the chance to work with at the start of Black Founders, and personally knew their journey. We worked closely with Angela Benton, and I remember having a phone call with her when she was going through the process of launching NewME in the Bay area. Angela Benton is someone who I think is a pioneer and has been instrumental in helping Black entrepreneurs and investors get their start. She is Black history in the making. I feel the same about Charles Hudson, who I jokingly call the godfather of Black VC. For many years, it felt like Charles was the only Black person in venture capital, and yet was always accessible and putting in work to grow the community behind the scenes. I think it's erroneous to have a conversation about venture capital and inclusion and exclude the work of Angela or Charles. But a lot of people do, because we haven't written our stories down. When we started the process of writing this book, I thought we were creating a collection of Black innovation stories, and I was excited to memorialize my living heroes. The book would document the successful accomplishments of some of my favorite founders and investors. During the interview process, I discovered there was more: I heard stories of failures along with the successes, pivots, and setbacks, but most importantly, I saw the continuous evolution of an innovator. Initially, I thought readers would read this book as inspiration, and identify benchmarks they could use in their own journeys in launching a startup. Now I hope that, in addition to the inspiration and encouragement, that future founders will see innovation as a journey. And it is in the journey, not the destination, where the innovation truly happens.

> *I think it's erroneous to have a conversation about venture capital and inclusion and exclude the work of Angela or Charles. But a lot of people do, because we haven't written our stories down.*

Black Founders launch event, San Francisco (2011).

The founders of Black Founders at launch. Left to right: Hadiyah Mujhid,
Nnena Ukuku, Monique Woodard, and Chris Bennett (2011).

MONIQUE WOODARD

Managing Director, Cake Ventures

Cake Ventures is a venture capital fund that invests in the future of technology being driven by major demographic trends.

Monique is an entrepreneur and venture capital investor at the intersection of technology and newly powerful consumer groups. She believes that shifting demographics will create the next big emerging markets, right here in the United States. As the founding partner and managing director of Cake Ventures, Monique invests in areas where she sees the future of technology being driven by three major demographic trends: an aging population, the shift to majority-minority, and the increased spending power of women.

Monique has invested in global startup ecosystems in the United States and Africa, and she presently invests in companies with global ambitions that are creating technology products to meet the needs of tomorrow's Internet users. Previously, as venture partner at 500 Startups, a global venture capital firm with $350 million-plus in assets under management, she invested in early-stage companies across several sectors, including consumer Internet and government technology. She also kicked off 500 Startups' investing and deal-flow pipeline in sub-Saharan Africa and led a group of investors, tech executives, and founders on a tour of the continent's most thriving startup ecosystems.

Following her time at 500 Startups, Monique became a venture scout at Lightspeed Venture Partners and a trusted advisor to foundations and venture capital firms like SoftBank, where she advised on their early-stage pipeline development focused on underrepresented entrepreneurs. Before moving on to the investor side of the table, Monique spent more than fifteen years in the tech industry and has been a startup founder, product-focused operator, founder of a national community of tech entrepreneurs, and advisor to cities on innovation and entrepreneurship.

Monique is the co-founder of Black Founders, a community of tech founders started by four friends in a San Francisco restaurant over shrimp and grits and jazz music. Their hackathons at historically Black colleges and universities (HBCUs), workshops, and conferences for founders are designed to move entrepreneurs from idea to execution. With a mission to increase the number of successful Black entrepreneurs in tech, the organization cultivated a new generation of tech founders from Silicon Valley to New York City, Atlanta, Austin, and several HBCU campuses.

Monique was one of the first innovation fellows for the San Francisco Mayor's Office of Civic Innovation, where she worked on initiatives to help a city at the epicenter of innovation to use technology to transform the workforce and other government services. During her fellowship term, she wrote the resolution on broadband and unlicensed spectrum, which was adopted at the US Conference of Mayors and contributed to the city's early strategy around municipal Internet access.

As an entrepreneur before entrepreneurship was the new normal, she has built things big and small, including the mobile shopping app Speak Chic, which gained a loyal fashion insider following and was featured in *Harper's Bazaar UK*, *Cosmopolitan*, *Essence*, and *InStyle*.

Monique has been an advisor to private companies and technology-focused organizations, including Women 2.0, Hackers/Founders, and Startup Policy Lab. She has been interviewed around entrepreneurship and investing for *USA Today*, MSNBC, the *New York Times*, *Buzzfeed*, NPR, CNBC Africa, and *Essence* magazine.

Twitter: @moniquewoodard

Website: monique.vc, www.cake.vc

Tell us about your background and where you grew up.

Monique Woodard: I grew up in Ocala, which is a really, really small rural town in Florida. Actually, Ocala isn't even the town that I grew up in; it's just the "bigger" town next to it. I think the small town I grew up in still only has about fifteen thousand people, so back then it was even less.

I didn't grow up knowing what a *venture capitalist* was, but I did know what an entrepreneur was because my grandfather was one. He owned his own farmland and was an independent farmer. My dad worked fire and rescue at NASA until he was hurt on the job and became disabled. After that, he owned a fish market, and our family always owned farmland that we sold crops from. So I definitely knew how to be entrepreneurial within the context of a small business. But I didn't have the concepts of *high-growth, Silicon Valley,* or *tech entrepreneur.*

What was your earliest exposure to technology?

Woodard: I was the first person in my neighborhood with an Atari. I definitely think video games were my gateway drug to computers and technology. Then I got my first computer when I was about seven, and was in computer programming classes when I was seven or eight. My parents drove me once or twice a week, about twenty miles, to this Apple programming class. And they did that because I was super interested in it. But like a lot of young girls, I didn't stick with it. There was no Black Girls Code when I was growing up. I sort of taught myself HTML in high school, and then continued to teach myself how to build. I always knew that I wanted to be an entrepreneur. I never had any vision of myself going to work at some company. Even as this little girl in the small, rural town I grew up in, I was like: Oh, I'm going to start my own company one day [*laughs*].

What university did you attend, and what did you study?

Woodard: I went to Hampton University immediately after graduating from high school. But then my dad became even sicker from the injuries he sustained at NASA, so I transferred to the University of Miami to be closer to home. He died my junior year in college. That experience gave me the sense that this life is short, and you can die at any moment. I knew from that point I would be the person who would have to earn, support, and thrive for myself and for my family.

After college I wanted to go into the music industry. I had been an intern for Luther Campbell, and booked shows for a club in Miami. I thought I would end up at a label, or in the mailroom at somewhere like CAA [Creative Artists Agency], and move up into becoming an agent. That's where I thought my life would end up. But I was still building a variety of media, subscription, and E/N—everything/nothing—sites on the Internet, which was still relatively nascent at the time. That's what kicked off a career in tech for me. I was incredibly scrappy. There wasn't anyone out there telling you how to do it. I definitely just fell into it and found my way. And I got really good at building because of that.

What did you do after college, and when did you start Black Founders?

Woodard: A company here in San Francisco knew that I was good at building products. They called and asked me to come out and talk to them about building a new video platform. I flew out and was there for one day. That was my first trip to San Francisco ever, and thirty days later, I moved. I've been in San Francisco ever since.

That was September 2008, which was an interesting time to move to Silicon Valley because the entire country was in the middle of a financial crisis and economic downturn. At that time, the tech industry, and San Francisco itself, had very few Black people and very few Black professionals in tech. So we were a small but close-knit community, but we still felt the sting of being outside the general Silicon Valley seats of power.

I was working at that company during the day but also attending all these tech events in the evenings. One of the things I noticed at the events was there were very few Black people in these rooms, and very few Black women. That's how I actually met Hadiyah [Mujhid], Nnena [Ukuku], and Chris [Bennett]. We coalesced together around an interest in technology, startups, and our big pain-point of never seeing enough Black people in this town and industry. So the four of us met up for dinner at this Black-owned soul food restaurant in the Fillmore called 1300. I think it's closed now.

Yeah, it's shut down now. I think there are very few, if any, Black-owned restaurants remaining in San Francisco.

Woodard: So we all had dinner that night, and we were all lamenting about the issues and challenges of being a Black founder. And then, just like entrepreneurs, we were like: Let's just do something about it.

It started with get-togethers for basically anyone who was Black and running a tech company in the Bay Area. Our initial objective was community building and potential collaboration. The goal was to get all the Black entrepreneurs that we knew, who likely didn't know each other, to come to a happy hour and get to know each other. We did one happy hour that was a total success and just thought: *Oh, let's do some more happy hours!*

Look, we all had day jobs and companies we were just starting, *and* we were trying to do this thing. Then we started posting about it on Twitter. And that's really when people from outside of our immediate networks started to see it. They were like: *Well, when are you coming to Atlanta? When are you coming to New York? And when are you coming here?*

Our initial thoughts were: *OMG, we have jobs. We can't be traveling around the country running meetups.* But that's exactly what we did. We made it work because there was such a demand for what we were doing. Black Founders expanded beyond the Bay Area to places like New York City, Atlanta, and Austin. We had a conference tour and were hosting hackathons at HBCUs.

Let's talk about the real hustle days of Black Founders. Could you share some of the financial realities and contradictions of being a struggling entrepreneur and creating a platform so that other entrepreneurs could succeed?

Woodard: We were trying to build Black Founders, and trying to do right by Black entrepreneurs, and also trying to bootstrap businesses or raise money, and also having to pay high-ass San Francisco rent [*laughs*]. The struggle was real. Back then, and still today to some extent, access to financial support was just closed off to us because of biases, structural inequality—all those things. Look, if the four of us had been White men in hoodies doing all the things that we were doing, we would have been perceived differently. We would have received the financial support and stability that we didn't have. We had to hack, create, and carve it out for ourselves.

> *We were trying to build Black Founders, and trying to do right by Black entrepreneurs, and also trying to bootstrap businesses or raise money, and also having to pay high-ass San Francisco rent [laughs].*

I was living in a studio apartment and juggling a ton of small consulting gigs at one point. And then some of those gigs were slow to pay me. It was crazy. Sometimes Nnena would have money, and I wouldn't have money. And she would be like: *Okay, I got you, girl.* And then sometimes Nnena wouldn't have money, but Hadiyah would have money, and Hadiyah would be like: *I got you, girl* [*laughs*]. Back then no one had money at the same time. No one [*laughs*].

I definitely feel that, if we had been different people who were better resourced, we could have been like Kevin Rose, [cofounder of Digg], or Tim Ferriss, [early investor in Uber], who were making similar moves at that time. We would have been founders and angels who would've been able to invest in the founders we were discovering, help them, and be financially rewarded with returns.

I think it's a conversation that has to be had: how the industry expects people of color—specifically Black people, Black entrepreneurs, and Black investors—to do with less and to get fewer rewards from it.

The Silicon Valley conversation around diversity and inclusion was different—and barely existed—around the time that you founded Black Founders. What was the reception to Black Founders then?

Woodard: It's so funny. We were super intentional about naming it Black Founders. The four of us had some internal back and forth around it, but we all agreed that [the name] set the right tone.

Then, when it came out publicly, the response was: *Well, why do you have to say "Black"?*

What? Because we Black [laughs]!

I remember having a whole discussion around whether we should change the name to something that was more palatable for the general public. I also remember being at this party with a CEO that everybody knows—I won't say their name—and I told him what we were doing with Black Founders. And his response was: *Well, I don't see color.* Nobody was woke [*laughs*].

And to have these conversations at that time from a VC perspective, the number of Black entrepreneurs who had been funded by Silicon Valley VCs between roughly 2008 to 2012 was almost zero. We were going into these offices and having meetings with Sand Hill Road VCs and talking about Black entrepreneurs that we knew and believed in. Black entrepreneurs were building companies, and we wanted to see them get investment, and the VCs just couldn't see the value in it. The hardline excuse at that time was: *The reason we don't have any Black founders in our portfolio, isn't because of race or inequality. We just invest in the best people.* Yeah, and it just so happens that none of those "best" people were Black.

I came around to realizing that if we were not personally controlling the capital, if we were not deploying the capital, then our access was always going to be limited.

Well, to our credit, we were calling bullshit early on. We had the ear of the press early on, even though I have mixed feelings about that because they often distorted the story. But we were able to get into these rooms to have the conversation. I came around to realizing that if we were not personally controlling the capital, if we were not deploying the capital, then our access was always going to be limited.

How did you make the jump from Black Founders to becoming a venture capitalist?

Woodard: You know, internally at Black Founders, we all had a role. One of the things I started to think about early [on] was how our impact was limited if we couldn't touch capital, right? We could create programs to train more entrepreneurs, but unless we were able to put money into companies and put money behind these great founders we were meeting, then it was all for nothing. It was going nowhere. We were limited in our mission. That's when I started trying to make my way into the investor side of the table.

In my Dropbox folder, I found a cover letter that I sent to Scale Venture Partners way back in 2013, stating my interest in a role at their firm. That's how long I'd been trying to move to the investor side of the table. I also talked to another venture fund earlier—I won't say who—about being an entrepreneur in residence (EIR). And they were like: *Uh, no, we don't do that.* But they absolutely did do that for other people [*laughs*].

I was knocking on doors, trying to get in for a while. Getting into venture feels like you're a little hedgehog burrowing around.

Is the opening here?

No.

Okay, is the opening here?

No.

And you just keep burrowing and trying to find that opening until you get in.

Interestingly enough, fast forward to 2020. I now know Kate Mitchell, the founding partner at Scale Venture Partners, very well. She's been a mentor, friend, and one of the first people to put money into my fund. It feels very full circle. I showed her that original cover letter I had sent to her firm in 2013 [*laughs*].

Okay, back to 2015. I was advising companies. I knew Dave [McClure] and Christine [Tsai], who were the founders at 500 Startups, and had previously sent companies to the team at 500.

How did you meet Dave and Christine?

Woodard: Through Black Founders. We were invited to a 500 Startups demo day. This may have been the demo day that Diishan [Imira] was pitching. I've known Diishan since day zero of Mayvenn. And one of the things that Charles [Hudson of Precursor Ventures] said to me was: You have to do the job before you have the job. That's one of the ways to get into venture: doing the things that come with the job of a VC before you are officially employed as a VC. Helping founders by introducing them to investors, giving them advice, helping them work on their pitch. In a lot of ways, I was doing the job before I had the job.

Well, Diishan was one of the founders I knew super early. So when I attended his demo day, that's the first time that I officially met Dave. That may have been in 2012.

How did you build a relationship with them that led to you joining 500 Startups?

Woodard: After meeting Dave, I would send founders to 500, and built a relationship with them over a number of years. I was going to different events and attending demo days. To be honest, that's a large part of how you actually get into venture. It just requires people constantly seeing you, and being present all the time [*laughs*].

I feel like the only reason I'm in venture now is because I just kept showing up. Eventually people were like: *Well, she's not going anywhere; we're just going to have to give her something to do* [*laughs*].

How were you showing up at these events and able to get noticed? As a venture capitalist, a lot of entrepreneurs and people want to get your attention. How were you able to create that interest, where no one said: Please leave me alone?

Woodard: [*laughs*] Right, so it's one thing to show up, but you have to deliver value. My superpower was always: I'm going to show up. And my value is these connections to founders that they probably don't know. And I knew a lot of founders well because we had built Black Founders.

Everyone has to find their edge; something that other people don't have. Maybe they have specialized expertise in an area, or they have some access to entrepreneurs that other people want. Whatever that is could be your edge. I think it's really the two steps: show up and deliver value. You can't just keep showing up and not delivering value because then you're just annoying. *Why is this person always in my face? They keep showing up, and they got nothing* [*laughs*]. So showing up and delivering value is how I've always been able to create relationships in the industry.

Everyone has to find their edge; something that other people don't have. Maybe they have specialized expertise in an area, or they have some access to entrepreneurs that other people want. Whatever that is could be your edge. I think it's really the two steps: show up and deliver value.

Sometimes I see other people who have something, and they treat it as if it's a golden nugget. They don't want anybody else to have it, and [they] are very quid pro quo with their relationships. I think about it quite differently. I'm there, and I may say: *You've got to meet this entrepreneur; they're building this amazing company doing X.* And I'm truly not expecting or asking for anything. Just delivering value. I know there is a fine line between delivering value and being used. I've always been quick to cut someone off if that's the case. There is a way to be collaborative with others, where we're both getting value from the relationship.

Let's get back to joining 500 Startups.

Woodard: Someone at 500 asked me to come in one day and talk to them about Black Founders. I was talking to another partner and, in a very offhand way, said something like: Yeah, I'm thinking about moving onto the venture side of the table and eventually raising my own fund. I threw it out there in a casual sort of way.

And they were like: Oh, tell us more about that. After a few more meetings with Dave and Christine, I was invited to join 500. So I joined.

When you joined 500, there was a major headline in USA Today about you joining the firm. Why was it a critical move for you, and why was it a big deal for the industry?

Woodard: When I was trying to make my way into venture, I knew I wanted to be in early-stage because I wanted to have an impact on those founders I was meeting, who were all early. I knew I had to be at a place where [VCs] were writing checks early and believing in founders at their earliest stages, which is another reason why 500 made sense for me. There were also very few visible Black people, even in later stage investments at that time—there was Lisa Lambert [of Intel Capital], and that's it.

I do remember the day the article was published. I was driving to the South Bay, and my phone started blowing up. And I was thinking: *What in the world is happening?* I really thought something was wrong, so I pulled over on the side of the highway, and it's the *USA Today* article circulating on Facebook and Twitter.

Well, I knew *USA Today* was doing a story. But the original story was supposed to be about my work with Black Founders. Jessica [Guynn], the journalist who wrote the story, was also highlighting Charles Hudson, NewMe co-founder Wayne Sutton, and some other Black folks in Silicon Valley. When Jessica was interviewing me for the original article, I felt I needed to tell her about my transition to the new role at 500. I thought it was weird and shady if I didn't. So I gave her the scoop.

She asked me: *Are you the first Black partner at 500 Startups?* And I was like: *Oh, right, yeah, I'm the first.* I actually didn't think that the comment would go anywhere. Then, the next day, the headline in *USA Today* was: "Monique Woodard Joins 500 Startups as First Black Partner."

I didn't know how to take it. It was a good headline for sure; I guess it got the attention it was supposed to. But I always have mixed feelings about public attention. I don't think I would have framed it that way for myself. I don't necessarily think of myself in terms of *first Black* anything. If I happen to be the first Black person to do something, I like to figure out how I can help the next Black person do the same thing. I have no interest in being the first Black anything for too long.

> I don't necessarily think of myself in terms of first Black anything. If I happen to be the first Black person to do something, I like to figure out how I can help the next Black person do the same thing. I have no interest in being the first Black anything for too long.

But it ended up being a stake in the sand, I guess.

Tell us about your work at 500.

Woodard: I invested out of their seed fund into companies that were in my network from Black Founders. The first deal I did at 500 was an investment into Blavity. I came in with that deal and was certain it was the right company for us to invest in. Other deals I did at 500 included Court Buddy and Silvernest. While there, I had the opportunity to open up their sub-Saharan African partnerships and deal flow, even though I had never been to Africa at all prior to this [*laughs*].

When I first came in, other investors would send me deals for Africa, and I was like: *I don't know anything about Africa. I'm from Florida.* Despite the fact that I'm African American—but not African—and had never been to the continent, I decided to take advantage of that. People like Maya Horgan-Famodu at Ingressive [Capital] and Yele Bademosi [CEO at Bundle Africa] were a huge help in helping me understand the ecosystem, and [they] became great friends.

At 500, I had the opportunity to work closely with Dave [McClure]. He was the one who extended a large amount of trust in my decision-making around companies, and [he] also helped me build a lot of new relationships in the industry. He really opened up his own network and extended those relationships to me. Both Dave and Christine are definitely the reason why I'm still working in venture today.

What were some of your successes and challenges while in this role?

Woodard: There were always challenges because I was coming into an organization [that] was different from a lot of other venture funds in that they had already done a number of investments into Black entrepreneurs. There were Diishan and Chris from Soldsie. They had done some investing in Black entrepreneurs. But imagine coming in and saying: Now, let's two-times that. Let's fund this

Black entrepreneur, and that Black entrepreneur, and that other Black entrepreneur [*laughs*].

Frankly, these were businesses and business models where there wasn't a lot of internal expertise. So Blavity wasn't an easy investment to get through. And I approached my role at 500 Startups with the attitude that I wasn't there to just take up space. *If I'm here, then y'all are going to have to seriously look at these deals. You're going to take them seriously and evaluate them as you would any other founder or market.* We [needed] to open our minds to what a good business model is and what a good business is.

A lot of that was hard, for sure. And there were certainly times where I had to draw a line in the sand and say: *This is a company you need to invest in, and if you don't, then it's bullshit.* It wasn't always easy to get those deals done, but as time went on, it got easier as people were trusting and believing in my expertise on these founders and companies.

Not too many people know what a VC looks for in a company and what makes a company fundable from a VC perspective. Could you share what it means to be fundable?

Woodard: So when you're a VC, and have a fund, there's an expectation that you return all the money—and more—from the investments that you make. If I raise a $25-million fund, then I want to return at least $75 million to my investors. And returning a fund is hard! Venture capital investors have to go into every deal with the expectation that this is the investment that will at least return the fund, and if it doesn't, I'm failing. So for venture capital funding, most investors aren't usually looking for small base hits; they're looking for the largest opportunity possible.

When I'm evaluating companies at the earliest stages, I'm looking at the team and their dynamics. Do I think this is the team that can execute in the long-term vision? Do they have a long-term vision that is big enough? And finally, I like to see early proof points of ability to execute, and proof of success. That could be revenue, early sales prospects, early customers—anything that shows proof it's working now and has potential for growth. Those are the top three things I like to see.

What are some of the biggest challenges for Black and Brown founders when raising money?

Woodard: I think the biggest thing that leaves Black and Brown founders out of consideration is the network. Look at some of these funding rounds. If you have some industry knowledge, you're able to look at a funding round and see: that person knows this person, those funds like investing together, and that investor knows that investor. You're able to connect the dots between these networks. You can play six degrees of Kevin Bacon with this company and this venture fund, and who led that round, and who participated or led the previous round. And, so often, Black entrepreneurs are not in those networks, so we don't get access to the type of capital that we should.

I think it's a couple of things. It's being able to get into those rooms and to infiltrate those networks. And it's also creating new networks that can move capital and provide a different type of access, creating the next Charles Hudson, the next Marlon Nichols [of MaC VC], the next Monique Woodard.

I think if you're a Sand Hill Road VC, and you've spent fifteen to twenty years looking at founders from Stanford and HBS [Harvard Business School], can you really effectively evaluate a founder from Howard or Jackson State? Do you even know where Jackson State is? You probably don't. And here's a hint: It's not in Jacksonville [*laughs*].

> I think if you're a Sand Hill Road VC, and you've spent fifteen to twenty years looking at founders from Stanford and HBS [Harvard Business School], can you really effectively evaluate a founder from Howard or Jackson State? Do you even know where Jackson State is? You probably don't. And here's a hint: It's not in Jacksonville [laughs].

It's almost impossible to think that your average Sand Hill Road VC is going to become really good at sourcing deals and accurately evaluating Black and Latinx founders. It's almost impossible to think they will be able to go from zero to 250 in any kind of reasonable time period. So they need to focus on hiring Black investing partners and general partners at their firms.

I don't get worried about my value in this industry, or my deal flow, because I know that a White guy who went to Stanford, and probably has a super homogenous network, won't be able to do what I do tomorrow. They're just not going to be as good at sourcing the most diverse portfolio of founders, and then helping all of them think about what it means to build a modern company where issues around inclusion could be the thing that tanks your company. Look at how long it's taken me to get good at it, and I'm still working on it every single day.

Investors who invest out of homogeneous networks are going to be disadvantaged as the world continues to change and shift around them. LPs [Limited Partners] should start asking investors these questions: *What does your personal network look like? Do you have any Black people who have been to your house in the last nine months? Do you know any women who are not related to you by birth or marriage—AND also run a company? Do you know any Latinx people who have been to your house, that you've played golf with, or have gone to dinner with?* If your answer to any of these questions is no, then you are at a disadvantage. And that's just real.

This framing, that traditional VCs—White, cishet VCs—are the ones who are disadvantaged when we take into consideration the shift of the world, is important. With that in context, could you share why it was important for you to start your fund after leaving 500 Startups?

Woodard: I always knew that I wanted to start my own fund. I always knew that was going to be a part of my journey. So I was working on it while I was at 500 Startups. Then they went through a GP [General Partner] breakup of their own, and it sort of derailed. I came out of that needing to just rest and regroup. But I always knew that a fund was the thing I was moving toward. It was always a part of the plan.

I also think that we've made some strides in having Black male fund managers who have raised their own funds. But we've done a really poor job of supporting and putting real money behind Black women fund managers. So starting a fund wasn't a decision

I made lightly. I think more of us have to be visible, in-market, raising and managing funds successfully, in order for the industry to move forward in an equitable way.

Trust me; I'm making a lot of sacrifices to get this off the ground. I mean, I'm back in those old hard days of us building Black Founders. I thought I was done with those days [*laughs*]. But I'm making these sacrifices because I know that if women like me don't, then Black women in this industry will continue to be afforded less and never have the same kind of access that other people do.

Now, will there be a lot of women and Black and Latinx founders that I invest in? Of course, because they're always going to be visible to me. But is it exclusive to traditionally underrepresented founders? No, because I don't think you can say: Networks and access are a problem, and then create yet another network with access to a homogeneous network. I'm never going to build a thing that just exacerbates the same problem I've already identified.

Even though we've done a lot to advance equity in the industry, I will say this about some LPs: I think they have an image of something they want, and if you do not fit perfectly in that box of what they want, then you're not as attractive to them. I think a lot of LPs want Black fund managers to only invest in Black entrepreneurs.

Are most of us going to naturally invest in a larger percentage of Black entrepreneurs than our non-Black peers? Yes. Making it a mandate is often not to the service of founders. Some of those portfolios are then viewed by the rest of the industry at a discount. For a founder to go from a fund that's viewed as a charity, or somewhat less than other venture funds, to try and raise a Series A, B, or C, and not be able to do it, that's not good for anyone. I don't think these LPs are thinking about it in that way.

My fund is thesis-driven. It's all about the areas where I see a demographic change happening, such as the massive aging market, companies that can get to billion-dollar outcomes based on the economic impact of women, and also the shift to majority-minority in the United States.

Now, will there be a lot of women and Black and Latinx founders that I invest in? Of course, because they're always going to be visible to me. But is it exclusive to traditionally underrepresented founders? No, because I don't think you can say: *Networks and access are a problem*, and then create yet another network with access to a homogeneous network. I'm never going to build a thing that just exacerbates the same problem I've already identified.

What are some of the points of indecision or mistakes you've made as an investor?

Woodard: Maybe this is obvious, but there have definitely been deals that I wanted to do but couldn't for some reason. I couldn't get them across the line, or I didn't have enough capital to do them. If anything, those are the ones that I feel most deeply. On the other hand, there are deals where I had the access and had the capital, but didn't invest for one reason or another. And I try to communicate transparently, but there will always be people who take that very personally. But, from my perspective, I'm usually super happy when I see them go out and raise money and succeed, especially when it's a Black founder.

Someone asked me this question on a panel: They wanted to know what was in my "anti-portfolio." I struggle so much with that question because I so rarely regret *not* doing a deal. Maybe I just don't personalize it so deeply. I very much believe there are a lot of good companies out there, and some are just not going to be the right fit for me. I have a clear view of the type of founder that I want to work with and the types of companies I want to help them build. Sometimes, even if it's a great company, I don't necessarily want to work with the founder. I can support you from afar, but I have to protect my peace [*laughs*].

As long as you're learning and pushing at the edges of your ability, mistakes are inevitable. And, in some ways, I welcome those.

There will always be mistakes that you make in life and in your career. Things you could have done better or differently, and I approach investing from a place of constantly learning. As long as you're learning and pushing at the edges of your ability, mistakes are inevitable. And, in some ways, I welcome those.

Were there times where you felt tokenized as a Black woman or put in a position to educate others?

Woodard: Yeah, I remember being invited to this very small, intimate dinner party. And there was a theme that was, like, inequality, or something like that. So I showed up, and I was the only Black person in the room. And I was like: Oh, it's me; I'm the theme [*laughs*].

So, yes, it can be hard. I was talking to Sian [Morson] about this when she was EIR [Entrepreneur in Residence] at Cross Culture [Ventures]. She was asking about my experience in venture and how I dealt with all the attention that sometimes comes with being a VC. And I was really honest and told her I don't really go anywhere. I still talk to the same seven people that I've been talking to for the last ten years. I don't really have many new friends. I think it's about knowing who your crew is, or the people who consistently have your back and have been there since the beginning. It's not that you can't create new relationships, but it's important to know how to get back to center and get back to the people who don't care if you were on TV today. People that you can just text and go to dinner with at the last minute. Having that is invaluable.

I've seen some younger VCs come to venture thinking they know all the things, and feel that they wield a lot of power, and, unfortunately, it can create an attitude that is probably not conducive to them having a long career in venture capital. I think coming to venture after really working for this—and even struggling for this—for a long time has given me a different perspective and a little bit of humility. My hope is that those experiences allow me to continue to have empathy with people—especially founders—and to create real connections, even as an investor.

CHRIS BENNETT

Co-Founder and CEO, Wonderschool

At Wonderschool, our mission is to provide high quality early childhood education to every child. Wonderschool is a network of early childhood programs that combine the quality standards of world-class educators with the warmth of an in-home program. We make it easy for educators to start and operate successful programs, and for families to find them. Wonderschool is a venture funded by Andreessen Horowitz, First Round Capital, the Omidyar Network, Cross Culture Ventures, Uncork Capital, Rethink Education, Edelweiss, Lerer Ventures, 500 Startups, FundersClub, and a number of angels.

C hris Bennet is the son of Honduran immigrants. He was the first in his family to graduate from college. He is a graduate of the Wharton School at the University of Pennsylvania, where he received a bachelor's degree in economics.

Chris resides in San Francisco, where he has lived since 2009. Chris is passionate about social justice, entrepreneurship, traveling, and spending as much time near the ocean as possible.

Wonderschool is a childcare marketplace with a mission of ensuring all children get access to high quality early childhood education to help them realize their potential. Wonderschool is venture funded by Andreessen Horowitz, First Round Capital, Imaginable Futures, Learn Capital, Cross Culture Ventures, Uncork Capital, Rethink Education, Edelweiss, Lerer Ventures, 500 Startups, FundersClub, and a number of angels.

Twitter: @8ennett

Website: https://www.wonderschool.com/

What was it like growing up, and what influenced you to become an entrepreneur?

Chris Bennett: So I grew up in Miami with my parents and a large extended family—I have thirty-one cousins. My parents are immigrants from Honduras, and most of my family members ran small businesses, so the thing in my family has always been to start your own company. It's what people always talk about. Growing up, I sold baseball cards, lollipops, and concert tickets. I actually didn't have my first job until after college because I always earned money from running my own businesses.

I grew up in a very diverse zip code—the fiftieth most diverse zip code in America—and my high school was actually made to desegregate the area. So it pulled students from a Black neighborhood, a White neighborhood, and a Hispanic neighborhood, making it a really diverse place inside of the school. That was a mind-blowing experience.

Once it was time to start thinking about college, a lot of my friends started applying to schools out of state. I assumed I was only going to go to school in Florida, so my out-of-state shot was the University of Pennsylvania (UPenn). I saw one of my really good friends get into Northwestern, and I was like: *Oh, if he could get into Northwestern, I can get into a good school too.* My college counselor coached me through my SATs and options for schools, but I was primarily following my friends. I don't think I even knew what an HBCU was at the time, even though I was in the International Baccalaureate (IB) program, which was incredibly rigorous.

So I applied to UPenn. I got in and became one of the first in my family to go to college, and the only one to go to an Ivy League, graduating in 2007. When I was there, I started another company with a classmate called LiquidBooks, which made it easy for students to sell their textbooks on the Internet. We were making, like, $100,000 a year—just the two of us. But at the end of college, it just ended. I never really thought about selling it. Up until that point, I'd never sold a company, so I didn't really think about selling the company. It was more like: *We're leaving school, so we're going to stop doing this.* When it was actually something we could have scaled to something even bigger.

What was the impetus for LiquidBooks?

Bennett: Well, while in school, I needed money. I qualified for work-study but I'd always get fired from it because I would never show up. I couldn't even keep a work-study job, so I knew I needed to start my own company [*laughs*]. I started selling my textbooks, and then I started selling my fraternity brothers' textbooks, and then I started selling more peoples' textbooks. Then I started a company. It was all just gut instincts, you know? People didn't think entrepreneurship was cool then. It was sort of, like, weird... You were "supposed" to get a job on Wall Street.

After college, I moved and tried a couple of things, really trying to find my fit. I worked for a real estate private equity firm called Heitman Investment Management in Chicago. After a few years, I moved back to Miami to start a post-baccalaureate (post-bacc) in preparation for medical school. But then I realized I didn't want to do that. I considered joining the US Foreign Service, explored it, and it still didn't appeal to me. One of my friends came to visit me during this time and was like, "Hey, man, you don't really seem happy down here. Have you considered coming to Silicon Valley? You've always been interested in companies; you could start a company out here." So, I moved to Silicon Valley.

I think a lot of my journey was just following my peers, listening to my friends, my close friends, and really taking notice of these inputs. I wasn't following the guidance of a professor; I didn't really have the social-emotional skills to be able to engage with a professor at that time, you know? I was still relatively raw when it came to that.

What was your family's response to these shifts in your journey—from private equity to medicine, and eventually, Silicon Valley–based entrepreneurship?

Bennett: My parents have been really influential. I remember when I was laid off from my first job in PE (private equity), during the financial crisis, I ended up getting another job in PE thereafter, and I turned it down. It was a big deal because, when I got laid off, I thought that maybe I wasn't good enough for it. When I got a job again, it was like: Actually, I just don't want to do this, I know I don't.

When I was doing the post-bacc for medical school, surprisingly, my parents weren't really excited about it. They were like, "You're not a doctor, we know you. We know you're not going to like that... Why are you doing this?" I was doing well, though, performing at the top of my class, and was on a clear path to becoming a doctor. But even my classmates in the post-bacc, who are doctors today, would ask me "Why are you doing it?" They knew too.

> When I told my mom I was moving to Silicon Valley to be an entrepreneur, I don't think I've ever seen her happier. "Finally," was her response. Having that support from my parents really helped give me confidence in doing what I was doing. To them, it was just sort of obvious. I was supposed to be an entrepreneur.

When I told my mom I was moving to Silicon Valley to be an entrepreneur, I don't think I've ever seen her happier. "Finally," was her response. Having that support from my parents really helped give me confidence in doing what I was doing. To them, it was just sort of obvious. I was supposed to be an entrepreneur.

Tell me about day one in Silicon Valley. What were you doing, working on, seeking?

Bennett: When I arrived, my friend Jonathan Manheim let me sleep in one of his rooms for a month. And with some housing secured, I got started on the networking circuit. The first thing I did was go to networking events. A lot of networking events. I remember taking the Caltrain down to Stanford or to Palo Alto, and walking to an event on the other side, near the 101, and just being like: I fucking love it here, this is it. Let's go!

I remember it really well. It felt like I was back in college, in a way. That's what Silicon Valley felt like then. I didn't know who I was going to be. I didn't know what was going to happen, and that's actually how I met Hadiyah Mujhid—at one of these networking events. Since I had always grown up in really diverse communities, I was naive to what most of America looked like. It was somewhat of a shock to me. Back in Miami, since my middle school, my elementary school, and my high school were all created to desegregate the area, I had always been around really diverse groups of kids. Then I go to UPenn, incredibly diverse. I show up in Chicago (to my first PE job), and there's no Black people on the north side where I lived. And if you wanted to be around Black people, there were no White people. That separation was super weird to me. I was like: *What is going on?* When I took the job in private equity, I was one of the only two Black people there—out of 400 people. I was like: *Where am I?*

And it turns out, that that's America. It isn't a unique experience at all; the separation is actually quite normal. It was my childhood that was unique. So when I moved to San Francisco, I knew I needed to have a Black community, and I need to have Black mentors, because if I don't, I'm going to experience Chicago all over again. In Chicago I felt like I was in a drying machine. I was

In San Francisco, I was committed to doing things differently. So I immediately tapped into the Black community.

just getting thrown around. I didn't really know what was going on. I didn't have as much context. I didn't know what the fuck was going on, actually. In San Francisco, I was committed to doing things differently. So I immediately tapped into the Black community.

What I found was that there are a lot of Black folks in Silicon Valley, but they weren't really connected. So we (me, Hadiyah Mujhid, Monique Woodard, and Nnena Ukuku) started Black Founders, an organization dedicated to diversity in tech. That network was super helpful. Through that, I found out about the NewME Accelerator. Through the NewME Accelerator, I got into 500 Startups. Through 500 Startups, I ended up raising my seed round for my first company, Central.ly. And it was all through those connections and information as my guide.

So you're in Silicon Valley, you've built and benefited from this network of Black founders, and with much in-between, you eventually land on Wonderschool. How?

Bennett: I first started a company called Central.ly, a one-stop web promotion shop for small- to medium-sized businesses who wanted to easily create websites. Central.ly was in the NewME Accelerator and 500 Startups. While in 500 Startups, we changed the company to Soldsie, focusing on the e-commerce experience, and in direct response to the needs of our customers. We sold Soldsie in 2019. But in 2016, we're like: We don't know if Soldsie is going to be the thing. We don't know how big it's going to be. We need to come up with another idea. I came up with that next idea by going to TED.

So I go to the TED Conference every year. Hadiyah, myself, Monique [Woodard], Nnena [Ukuku], we were all invited to TED in 2013, during the beginning of the Black Lives Matter movement. TED hosts these topic-themed dinners, and I went to a social justice dinner. Next to me is a woman named Laura Jana, who is a leader in the preschool space. She's going on and on about the value of preschool, and she's like, "You know, a lot of the things that you use today as a CEO, you likely learned in preschool." And I was like: *What are you talking about? That's so weird.* I started doing research on it, and it turns out that there's a lot of studies that say that you develop a lot of your social-emotional base in preschool, and socioemotional skills are some of the most important—likely the most important skills—for success in America. It's not academic skills. So I continued my research, and from there found that there weren't a lot of kids who got access to preschool, especially Black and Brown kids.

Then I came across this guy who went into a low-income community in Orlando, Florida, and created in-home preschools. His work really turned the community around over a timespan of thirty years. So I was like: *Okay, what if we created more in-home preschools? And what if we made it like an Airbnb for preschool?* That's sort of how the idea came to fruition.

The idea for Wonderschool was bubbling at the same time that Central.ly/Soldsie are in active development. How did Central.ly develop up until this point?

Bennett: I met my co-founder and CTO, Arrel Gray, at a networking event for people who wanted to expand their startups to China. I was going to some type of networking event every night, in the search for a technical co-founder. Arrel, a developer and entrepreneur, was looking for someone with business acumen. After we met, we just started working on things. I was working on an airline voucher marketplace at the time, and we eventually came up with the idea of Central.ly together. Then, we came up with the idea for Soldsie while we were in 500 Startups.

What was the process of transitioning Central.ly into Soldsie?

Bennett: It was really hard. It was really hard because we invested so much energy into Central.ly, but we realized that it wasn't going to be a venture-backable company in the long run. We simply couldn't get it to work in a highly scalable way. A lot of small businesses had websites at the time, and getting them to switch was a hard customer segment to crack. We wanted to build something bigger, so we decided to pivot the company in direct response to activity that our customers were already engaging in. Though this required a commitment to a new idea, a new vision, and a build totally from scratch, we did it. We launched Soldsie in 2012 before social commerce was widely understood and adopted, and it became one of the first tools to help people sell products on Facebook and Instagram. Soldsie helped merchants and enterprise clients monetize social media through consumer comments. Followers and visitors could simply write "sold" to buy items. Our back-end system allowed merchants to manage sales and collect payments. What really allowed it to take off was that we found all these customers who needed software, so we started building for them—and it literally just grew from there. We found people who needed something, and we built the solution. Then we turned it into a SaaS [Software as a Service] product, and it really worked. Within two years, we'd processed over $25 million in transactions.

Who was particularly helpful during this time?

Bennett: There's this guy named Jason Freedman, co-founder of 42Floors, who taught me how to fundraise. He really coached me on fundraising, which was so helpful. And then, of course, the 500 Startups community has all these mentors, and they were coaching us through everything as we were building the company.

What was the fundraising process like for you?

Bennett: Jason pretty much told me that we needed to grow. It was something so simple. He was like, "Startups are about growth." When I ran LiquidBooks, I wasn't trying to grow. I had no idea how fast we were growing. I didn't think about it at all, actually. It was just like: How much money do we need to make this month? Cool. We made money this month, so I can travel now. You know, I didn't think about whether it was growing month to month, or what the margins were. But Jason was like, "You need to track how fast you're growing on a monthly basis, month over month growth." It's such a simple concept, I just didn't know it at the time. Honestly, that's what all of my learning in Silicon Valley has been, in hindsight, such simple concepts that I just didn't know. But how are you supposed to know if you don't know?

So, once we got the lesson out of the way, Jason was like, "Grow faster." *Okay, I can grow faster*. And we did this by changing our approach. At first, we were trying to convince people to do something they didn't want to do. Then we changed our approach to understand what our customers were already doing and, instead, enhanced that process. When we made this shift, we started to grow faster, and were able to raise a round. No one would take us seriously before we took Jason's advice. Afterwards, we raised a little over a million dollars. It was pretty much as simple as that.

How did you manage Soldsie's growth with your continued exploration of the education space, or what would eventually turn into Wonderschool?

Bennett: Well, we were running the companies at the same time for a little while. So that was…it wasn't that hard but it was a little hard [*laughs*]. I hired the CEO for Soldsie, and he's running the company today. So that helped a lot. And with Wonderschool, we actually started our own school in Berkeley Hills. We rented a home, hired a teacher, and started a school to learn everything about starting an in-home preschool. We didn't build any technology at that time, but I use the learning from that first school today, every day, while I'm running the company. What it taught me was everything I know about what it's like to get a school up and running and operating. After about a year, we found a couple of people who wanted to start schools out of their own homes, and we supported them in doing that. We built technology to enable this, specifically a platform to help both educators and caregivers start, operate, and grow their own high-quality in-home preschools and childcare programs. Since then, we've just been scaling it. We actually ran that starter school up until this year, 2020. Today we have close to one thousand programs.

When did you decide to integrate technology into your approach for Wonderschool?

Bennett: In the very early days. I was doing more sales and a good amount of product work. And my co-founder was recruiting engineers and designers and everything. And that went really well, that was awesome. It was pretty straightforward because the Wonderschool story is a little bit unfair... I had so many connections at that point, you know? It was unfair in the sense that people were like, "Was it hard to raise a round? Was it hard to get XYZ?" Like: No, it actually was pretty straightforward with Wonderschool.

Soldsie, on the other hand, was clawing, like, ugh. And I didn't know what I was doing. Now I have a pretty good idea of what I'm doing. It's still confusing, but I have a much better idea of how to do things.

What lessons translated from Soldsie to Wonderschool?

Bennett: To build as much product as possible. To invest in product. That's what lasts. That's what sticks around. That's what scales. Also, to recruit people who are experts when they report to you. So, like, our Chief Revenue Officer, VP of Engineering. I ask them. They're coaching me all the time on how things work. I try to recruit experts because they can really change the trajectory of the company. Also, to invest in company culture. To consistently invest in culture early on. To focus on unit economics, track churn aggressively. Those are things that I didn't really focus on at Soldsie that I do now. And fundraising... You can fundraise when you're ready to fundraise. It's really hard to fundraise when you're not ready to fundraise. So don't try to fundraise when you're not ready to fundraise [*laughs*]. Even once you have money, you want to fundraise for your next round. But you might not be ready, and you just have to get ready.

What about in your position as a CEO, or how you approach leadership?

Bennett: Well, I don't think of myself as an expert on education. I think of myself as an expert on providing technology to the childcare community. I partner with a lot of experts: education experts, early childhood education experts, technology experts. I get them into the same room and facilitate conversations. But I'm by no means the expert, which is so interesting being the CEO. It's a really weird role to be in because you never feel like you know the most. It's those socioemotional skills again. You sort of just know how to get everyone in the room and get the best answer.

I have this belief that within the Black community the most revered jobs—doctor, lawyer, investment banker, dentist, less so with I-banker, but the other roles—require zero networking. You just need to do really well in school, do really well on your tests, and then, when you get a job, do really well in your job. And you can find a lot of success. So in that regard, networking makes no sense. I can totally see why it doesn't really matter. I'm sort of lucky that networking is somewhat intuitive to me.

> I don't think of myself as an expert on education. I think of myself as an expert on providing technology to the childcare community.

When I was doing my post-bacc for medical school, I had zero friends. All I did was work. All I did was study for a full year, and I got straight A's. It's another reminder that you don't need a network to do well in that type of profession. But when I was at UPenn, all I did was socialize. I was this party guy, I was always out with people, and I didn't do well, I didn't get that good of grades. But it turns out that those relationships are the reason why I ended up in Silicon Valley.

Those are the guys that convinced me to move to Silicon Valley, the places where I slept, and the friends who made intros for me were the people I partied with in college [*laughs*]. So, it's so crazy that it worked out. I found networking came natural. I remember I couldn't get a job when I first moved out to Silicon Valley. I applied to all these companies, and no one would hire me because I was this weird guy who worked in private equity, who started a tech company beforehand, who didn't know how to code. I didn't know how to do marketing. I didn't have any sort of tangible startup skill. So I couldn't get a job. And then I was about to get a job—and right when I was about to get one, I had already found a co-founder, and I was already planning to start up a company. That company was Central.ly. For me, I almost felt like I didn't have any other options, but I was also playing on my strengths.

For me, I almost felt like I didn't have any other options, but I was also playing on my strengths.

For the people that are super nervous about it or uncomfortable about it, I'm sure it's something that you can learn. But a lot of the people that I meet networking, that are doing it, like it. It just seemed natural to me and to them. No one was like: *I'm so nervous. I don't know if I should be here or if I should be doing this.*

How has it been navigating the impacts of COVID-19, within an industry completely turned upside down as a result?

Bennett: It's been pretty interesting times. We've done a couple of things. In January, we were gearing up to raise our next round, and when March hit, I remember looking at a friend of mine at an education networking event and being like: We're all fucked. It just hit me. I was like: Oh my God, every city in America is going to look like Wuhan, what are we going to do? So I start playing these scenarios out, and we're talking through it, and I'm like: Yeah, we're all networking here, hanging out, skiing. This might be the last time we do this for a while. I remember getting on a flight back to San Francisco, and now, I don't know when I'm going to get on another flight. Like, I don't know. So when I got to the office and started telling my colleagues this, there was that response, like, "It's just the flu" type of sentiment. And I remember thinking: You know, I'm going to go with the Wuhan stance. San Francisco's Wuhan is sort of what I'm thinking. And if that happens, we can't operate the company the way we've been operating it. We can't burn money the way we've been burning it. We can't; we're not going to be able to grow. So we did some cuts that were pretty deep, and that was hard to do, but it was required to keep the company alive. In hindsight, it was the right decision, for sure. I'm happy that many of the folks that were part of the layoffs have all found jobs since. I really wanted to do it early so that they had enough time to find other opportunities. Because I knew that we wouldn't be the only company to do it.

Then we started to notice that schools weren't going to reopen. When we saw that, we began to launch more alternative forms of education. One of them is called micro schools, which helps people start programs out of their homes for children over the age of five. Another is forest schools, which were outdoors before, but we started to promote them more in light of COVID-19 protocols. Those are doing really well too. Now we're growing really fast, the company is in a really good position. It's unfortunate that there's been so much pain for our country, but the company's in a really strong position and can provide a solution that many people need right now, which is great.

What's difficult about the journey of bridging traditional approaches to education with technological innovations?

Bennett: I don't even know how to reverse engineer it. A part of it is humility and recognizing you don't know things and that you don't have the time to learn it. I just don't have enough time to become an education expert. People get PhDs in education. That takes ten years. I might as well just partner with someone who knows how to do that.

And I know that for us to achieve our goals, it's going to require so many disciplines to work together, that I'm just not going to be able to go deep on anything. Part of it is recognizing that too. I also read a lot of leadership and management books. That's probably what I invest the most in: leadership and management and learning about leadership and management. One of my favorite leaders is Pat Riley, the coach of the Miami Heat. I read a lot about sports coaches and business leaders who work with teams. Then I always have a coach and a therapist, and I'm always part of a CEO group.

I'm always getting mentoring, so I can effectively lead the company and lead the team.

In hindsight, what might you have changed about your journey?

Bennett: Let's see, at Wonderschool, I think I should've invested in more product earlier on. I sort of had that learning at Soldsie, and at Wonderschool, I think I made the same mistake. Luckily, I've had enough time to fix it. Right now, we're investing a lot into product, our engineering team, and our design team. I also would have invested in HR earlier on, too, especially before we started scaling the company around this time last year.

Where was your attention instead?

Bennett: A lot more in sales. Now our ratio is three-to-eight for salespeople to engineers. And we're still hiring a lot more engineers. Before, it was the other way around.

What lesson or experience continues to propel you forward?

Bennett: I think the other thing is to not give up. There's this quote by Jason Fried, a co-founder of 37signals (now Basecamp) that says, "You shouldn't talk about what your exit strategy is, you should talk about what your commitment strategy is." I heard that and agree, it's totally right with tech companies. When you build a product, especially a SaaS company, it just compounds over time. The longer you're around, the bigger it gets; the bigger it gets, the more valuable it is to you. And, often, it's just like, just like waiting...like investing and waiting and not giving up. That's something I think a lot about and something that I'm really putting into Wonderschool, to keep building, to keep going. This is such a big opportunity. It isn't just, like, a year commitment, you know, this is what I'm going to be doing. We have work to do, and we have to make it work.

What about for non-technical founders?

Bennett: Well, I would actually tell them to learn how to code. When I was first starting out there weren't even boot camps like there are now. I took a class at the community college to learn Python, but now there's a boot camp on every block. There's so many places to learn to code, you know? And I have friends now who've gone through coding boot camps and then raised hundreds of millions of dollars from venture capitalists. And it takes only three to six months to learn. So, yeah, learn to code [*laughs*]. Outside of that though, it would really just be to keep working at it. I remember taking the MCAT practice exam while in my post-bacc, and I thought to myself: You know, if I keep working on this, I'm

Essentially, will you work hard enough for it to get the payoff? You might find out that you don't want to, and it's great when you find that out. Then you go on to something else.

going to do really well but it's going to take a lot of work. I don't really want to do all that work. I don't really want to be a doctor; I don't want to work that hard for this. And I quit again. So I was like: You know what, I'm going to find a job where I'm willing to work that hard. One that is meaningful enough for me. I think if you're someone who is a non-technical founder, and you want to start a company, you know, like, run that MCAT test prep. Essentially, will you work hard enough for it to get the payoff? You might find out that you don't want to, and it's great when you find that out. Then you go on to something else.

ANGELA BENTON

Founder and CEO, Streamlytics

Streamlytics uses first-party media consumption data to bring transparency to what people are streaming on today's most popular devices while helping consumers own their data in the process.

ngela Benton is a pioneer of diversity in the technology industry. As founder and CEO of Sreamlytics, she brings transparency to what people are streaming while helping consumers own their data in the process.

In 2011, she founded NewME (acquired in December 2018), the first accelerator for global minorities. Through her leadership, NewME has accelerated hundreds of entrepreneurs, helping nascent companies to raise over $47 million in venture capital funding.

To date, Benton has been recognized as one of Goldman Sachs' 100 Most Intriguing Entrepreneurs, *Fast Company's* Most Influential Women in Technology, *Business Insider's* 25 Most Influential African Americans in Technology, *Marie Claire's* 50 Women Who Rule, *Ebony's* Power 150, and many more. She's been featured in numerous national and international media outlets, including CNN, MSNBC, *Bloomberg, Inc., Forbes, Good Morning America,* and the *Wall Street Journal,* where she was a featured essayist, alongside Mark Zuckerberg, for the paper's 125th anniversary edition of "The Future of Entrepreneurship."

At the helm of Streamlytics, Angela continues to uncover untapped spaces in technology.

Twitter: @Abenton and @streamlytics
Website: www.streamlytics.co

Tell us about your background and where you're from. Where did you grow up?

Angela Benton: I was born in Chicago in '81. My dad has been an entrepreneur for quite some time and ran a wig store in Chicago for a while. At some point, he and my mom ended up working together, and that's how they met. I have two sisters and a brother. I'm the middle child.

We moved from Chicago when I was two, to a small town outside of Houston called Tomball, and it was *very* racist, to be blunt. This was the eighties, and it was a regular thing to see people in this small town riding on horses with KKK regalia. They were still burning crosses and stuff like that. As a child, it was scary living in that kind of environment. I have not really thought about it too much, but thinking now about my career, that might be why diversity is important for me. Growing up afraid your brother—in his rascal teenage years—might have something happen to him. You know what I mean? He would run into the house out of breath because he was running from the KKK. When I was eight and close with a White classmate, I got into a disagreement with her, and in response, she called me an N-word. That was crazy.

But there are also some great memories, too, like when Whitney Houston's early music came out. The only Black teacher in my school would play Whitney in the background as we did our schoolwork. As a young Black girl, it was great, and made me feel like I could be comfortable in my own skin as well.

I was in Tomball until about nine years old. My dad was a serial entrepreneur. Sometimes he had a job; sometimes he didn't. I think maybe one of his entrepreneurial endeavors wasn't going so well, so he went up to Northern Virginia because he heard it was better for people of color there. Eventually, me, my mom, and siblings moved up to Arlington, Virginia, to join him. From then on, I grew up in the DC metropolitan area.

You've publicly talked about how you started a family at a young age. Could you share how it has impacted your journey as an entrepreneur?

Benton: I think having a child at a young age shaped me incredibly. Lessons I learned as a teenage mom also lent themselves to being an entrepreneur because I just had to figure so much out. I got my first job at Montgomery Ward right before I turned fifteen, and was making minimum wage, which at the time was, like, $4.75. But they found out I wasn't old enough to work, and let go of me. Then I got pregnant, and I had to figure it out. Since I was fifteen, I needed a permit to work and could only work a limited set of hours.

My first legit job was at McDonald's. Because it opened so early in the morning, I could do a shift before school and another one after. I would wake up between 4:00 and 4:30 a.m., pregnant, to go open up. I'd work there for a few hours, go to school, and then go back to work. Thankfully, school always came easy for me. And since I was in advanced classes, I had some flexibility in my schedule and could get out of school early. This worked fine while I was pregnant, but it was harder to do once I had my daughter. I lived with my mom, but I didn't ask for a lot of support from my family, although my younger sister helped me a lot.

McDonald's didn't last. But what did end up lasting is that I found a job at Circuit City in the Customer Service Department. That was dope, but it was an electronics store, so I was around a lot of technology. I worked thirty-six hours a week while in high school. I worked twelve-hour days on Friday, Saturday, and Sunday.

I didn't go to school on Friday because I had enough credits. So that worked out.

They also had a daycare at my school, offered as a vocational training option. So I was able to bring my daughter to school, but I wasn't able to bring a baby on the school bus. And I didn't have a car. Mia, a high school friend, would sometimes pick me up in the morning, but then I had to take public transportation back. So I had this big-ass double stroller—don't ask me why my brother got me a double stroller, even though I was only having one baby [*laughs*]. Those things were huge. To do public transportation, I'd have my backpack, a baby in a front carrier, and then this double stroller basically on my back. I had to walk up a hill—I know I sound really old—but I had to walk up this hill to get back home. And I had to do that every day.

I think one of the benefits of being a mom, and especially a teenage mom, is that figuring it out becomes a way of life. It becomes your way of thinking; it becomes a part of who you are. It's the same skill set I've been using as an entrepreneur for the past decade.

Yeah, I had to figure it *all* out.

I think getting those lessons early as a teenage mom was super helpful for me. I think the figuring-it-out-ness, if that's a thing, lent me to being an entrepreneur. Like: *Okay, I have to do XYZ, or This is my goal. How am I going to do that? How am I going to use whatever resources that I have—or that I DON'T have—to actually get there?* I think one of the benefits of being a mom, and especially a teenage mom, is that figuring it out becomes a way of life. It becomes your way of thinking; it becomes a part of who you are. It's the same skill set I've been using as an entrepreneur for the past decade.

Let's go to the early days of Black Web 2.0. What led to its start?

Benton: I initially went to school to be a graphic designer. I wanted to do layouts for print magazines. I loved magazines. That was during Web 2.0, so everyone was talking about how print was literally going to be dead. I listened, and ended up teaching myself how to code. I did hella websites for free. It's crazy to me how, when I speak with younger people, and they want to be paid to learn. I did so much stuff for free [*laughs*]. That's how I developed my skills as an engineer.

> *I initially went to school to be a graphic designer. I wanted to do layouts for print magazines. I loved magazines. That was during Web 2.0, so everyone was talking about how print was literally going to be dead. I listened, and ended up teaching myself how to code.*

Then I went to Savannah College of Art and Design for an MFA, but they didn't have any web development classes. I really wanted to be more on the design side than the engineering side. Back then, you had to hand-code most stuff, which was fantastic.

I was already working at a big company, Interactive Corp (IAC), which owned Ask.com and LendingTree, while trying to get my master's. I realized that the assignments I was getting in school were easier than what I got at work. And what I was learning [at school] didn't apply to what we were actually doing in the workforce, so I stopped going to school.

But something was happening at IAC. While working there, the question running through my head was: *Were there any other Black people in engineering at this company?* Now, there were two other women in engineering, but no Black people in engineering. I was the only Black person—and woman—on the product development side.

I was coding something for the front end. And there was a distro [distribution] list where I had to send my code. That was before the days of GitHub, and you just checked in your code [*laughs*]. So I sent my code out and got this call from one White guy on the engineering side, questioning what I sent. HTML is really simple. So I'm like: *All this questioning is a bit crazy.* So there was a back and forth. Then I realized I was actually right. Other people came to me, saying: *I don't know what he's saying; you're right.* And: *I don't know why he's doing this.* And I'm like: *It's probably because I'm Black, and he hasn't dealt with anyone on the engineering side who's Black. So he's likely assuming that my code base is incorrect.*

From there I knew I really needed to create Black Web 2.0 to connect with other people like me in technology who were building stuff. I figured I couldn't possibly be the only one; there had to be other people going through similar stuff like me.

I forget where we hosted it, but I set up a little server, installed WordPress, and launched Black Web 2.0. At first, it was just me writing about things people were launching [that], from a design perspective, I thought were cool. But we ended up building a large community quickly, which was very satisfying because it confirmed that I wasn't the only one. That was before the web was filtered through recommendation engines. You could literally put something up on the web, and other people would just *find* it. Before social media, people would search for something, and they could land on your website.

I met Marcus Robinson, who is now the vice president of Innovation and Creativity at Interactive One. Marcus joined Black Web 2.0 about a month after I started. With his technical background, he did a lot more of the technical writing for me, and [he] both ran and developed our whole stack for all our properties. Marcus was cool; we loved working and talking about what Black folks were doing in technology. Since nothing like this existed at the time, we got amazing opportunities to interview people like Omar Wasow, who founded BlackPlanet. These were stories not being told *anywhere*, you know what I mean? A lot of times people would ask how we got such-and-such to do an interview. And I'm, like: *We just emailed and asked.*

TechCrunch was also new around that time. It was the go-to source for startup technology news. And entrepreneurs typically got featured when launching or raising money. But we never saw any articles on Black entrepreneurs. So is the problem that Black entrepreneurs weren't building products or raising money? Of course, we knew Black people were building stuff. [*TechCrunch*] just wasn't covering it.

What happened between Black Web 2.0 and the start of NewME?

Benton: Black Web 2.0 was a technology and media company. Our audience was a highly technical and highly professional community that no one was serving at that time, kind of like Blavity's audience but before Blavity. We made money by selling advertising. We did brand executions before it was called that. We also launched additional sites to grow a network across the Black diaspora. At one point, we had a column called Africa 2.0, so we were covering what was happening on the continent too.

But it was hard to make money in the media game at that time if you couldn't scale. We were niche, and we were the first—unfortunately. I don't know why I keep doing shit like this to myself [*laughs*]. Why the fuck do I keep creating stuff *first*?

No love for the first.

Benton: No love at all, and it's hard! We really had to convince people. We were generating some revenue through ads, but we ended up licensing our content to BET and other outlets with Black audiences like the *Root*. We launched another branded site under our network called *Politic365*. We were also doing podcasts—the first wave of podcasts at the time. We were also actively producing events as they were becoming more popular. So we were doing a lot of stuff to monetize. But it was still hard because we had a niche audience.

The idea of an accelerator—that if you have an idea, you could go raise money for it—was becoming more understood and talked about. And the place you had to be was Silicon Valley. That's where everything was happening. At that time, I was divorced. And the custody arrangement was that the kids would spend the summers with my ex-husband. So I had the summers free, and I was using the time to figure out what I was going to do. I was honestly deciding between going to Barcelona for the summer or launching NewME. I chose to start NewME.

So tell us about NewME. Walk us through the steps of starting it.

Benton: NewME stands for New Media Entrepreneurship. We started with the New Media Entrepreneurship Conference in 2010. It was meant to be small, limited to just one hundred people, and it brought entrepreneurs from around the country. We had Mignon Clyburn from the FCC come and speak. The event was structured around business growth and fundraising, but we also didn't want to leave the conference without actionable takeaways. A lot of times, you go to events, and it's a good conversation, but what's the action plan?

The takeaway from that action plan was that NewME should start an accelerator. So that was planted in the back of my head. Then I went to [South by Southwest] and connected with Wayne Sutton [co-founder of Tech Inclusion]. All of us knew each other because there weren't a lot of Black people doing stuff online. I was talking to [entrepreneur and investor] Jason Calacanis about this as well. I told him I had an idea for an accelerator and shared how I thought it was going to be a heavy lift. Jason was like: *No, just go on VRBO*—we were pre-Airbnb—*and rent a house.* Then I reconnected with Wayne to build out the accelerator. I'm like: *All right, well, let me start to put some legwork into this to see how much it would actually cost.*

What happened next?

Benton: I developed a framework for the accelerator, and a short pitch deck. We were able to reach out to people I knew at Google and other companies who were aware I'd had Black Web 2.0 before. I think we raised somewhere between $65,000 to $75,000 to fund a three-month accelerator. It might've been nine or twelve weeks, something like that. I was still doing Black Web 2.0 at the time. So we put up a post announcing the accelerator and got a lot of interest from founders.

Why do you think that support for NewME happened so quickly?

Benton: It was 1,000 percent due to the internal champions we had at companies. I think it's important to note that, throughout NewME, we really became integrated with Google and received a lot of support from them: funding, resources, and access to their product and mentors. But things were different when our internal champions left for other roles outside of Google.

There was a moment in time when all this worked because we had the support of Chris Genteel

There was a moment in time when all this worked because we had the support of Chris Genteel — who I believe is still at Google— and also LaFawn Davis [who has worked in diversity and inclusion at Paypal and Indeed]. They were our internal champions for sure.

—who I believe is still at Google—and also LaFawn Davis [who has worked in diversity and inclusion at Paypal and Indeed]. They were our internal champions for sure. And that's how we were able to get NewME off the ground.

NewME—and the first cohort's experience—was the subject of a CNN documentary, Black in America. How did the documentary happen?

Benton: The *Wall Street Journal* has these trade publications, and one of them is called *VentureWire*. Well, a writer wrote about us in *VentureWire*. A producer at CNN read that article while they were shooting *Black in America*. The producer was debating between featuring [ballet dancer] Misty Copeland or us that season. She ended up going with us. So that first summer in Silicon Valley we had cameras following us for the entire twelve weeks. It was a lot, but it also was a cool experience. The documentary was called *The New Promised Land: Silicon Valley*. It featured eight founders, but there were actually thirteen founders in that NewME cohort.

For CNN, the story was on eight founders because they didn't want to change the structure of the show since it had already been pitched to execs. After we accepted eight founders who were local in California, we decided to include several companies that we were really impressed with because we wanted to work with them, and it wouldn't incur too much additional overhead. They were already local, and we wouldn't have to house them.

There's a risk whenever you're creating something new, so trust must be present. How did risk and trust show up when creating NewME?

Benton: I think there's a layer of trust that exists with every single person that you come in contact with. Whether it works out for the long haul or not. I also think there is a level of trust that has to happen within yourself too. I can't say I fully trusted myself at that time because I didn't process it like that.

After the summer, I had to make a decision as a mother. We did NewME, and [the documentary] was going to air in November. It was like: *Oh shit. I did this thing, and it's poppin', and something's about to come out of it.* I didn't know what, but I had a gut feeling it had the potential to be a big thing.

> If I'm not in Silicon Valley, will it be just as big? I didn't feel it could happen in Charlotte. I was a single mom; I wouldn't have been able to commute cross-country. So I made the decision to move my kids to Silicon Valley

At the same time, I had children, and they needed to start school soon. But was I going to really benefit from all the work I did in Silicon Valley if I returned back to Charlotte?

If I'm not in Silicon Valley, will it be just as big? I didn't feel it could happen in Charlotte. I was a single mom; I wouldn't have been able to commute cross-country. So I made the decision to move my kids to Silicon Valley. Making the decision to move from Charlotte, where I had a cheap mortgage, was a big life change. And my ex-husband had to trust me about moving the kids away. So there was support and a layer of trust there.

With the NewME team and the portfolio [of] founders I worked with, for sure they had to trust me. We were a startup for startups. That's what I would say all the time: We were a startup ourselves, trying to figure it out. So there had to be a lot of trust from the founders, the team members—everyone.

My kids had to trust me. They're five, ten, and fourteen, and they're fantastic kids. When I asked them about moving to California, immediately they were like: *Okay!* My kids are like that about everything. They're always down to ride anywhere.

But really, there's a level of trust with every single person you come in contact with. Trust has to exist on so many different levels for anything that you're doing to actually work.

What about building the relationships and establishing trust such that people believe in your project enough to fund it?

Benton: Well, all the relationships I had were built from creating something new with Black Web 2.0 and being successful with it. So by the time I started NewME, I had four years' worth of relationships. We had the largest online community of Black professionals—of a certain age group—in digital media and technology. We had a lot of credibility. People knew of the work I had done. Because I was also a writer in the early days of Black Web 2.0, I was able to get my thoughts out there. People saw how I was thinking about things, which was another way I built trust. So when we did go in with a pitch deck, it was a quick, short deck. It was also very emotional because we were selling a vision.

What was the vision?

Benton: We were like: Hey, this doesn't exist in Silicon Valley right now, but we're here to change it. We're going to make history. That was literally written in the deck: We're going to make history. And people were like: Oh, shit. I think they liked the ballsy-ness of it, and people wanted to be involved. I never told anyone that CNN was involved. So the support we received in the beginning wasn't there because they thought they were going to be on CNN. They got involved because of the vision and the credibility.

What do you think was misunderstood about NewME in its early days?

Benton: [*Laughs*] The biggest thing that was misunderstood was that everybody who came to NewME was going to raise all this money from White venture capitalists in Silicon Valley. And if you're Black, this is where you come to do it. [There was this] idea that everybody's about to be successful. And that's just not the model of accelerators. That's not the model of venture capital. Everyone is not going to get the investment. Everyone is not going to win.

What we did at NewME was to build a network of investors and entrepreneurs, which came fairly easy because we had the media access, and we were the first to do something. We were really a conduit in the middle, connecting the two. We had to listen to what VCs wanted to invest in. We had to listen to what the market was saying at the time about certain investments. There was a point in time where people were doing web apps, and then, in the course of a year, it completely shifted to mobile. So we had to make that shift.

On the entrepreneur side, we listened to all the typical things that you do when evaluating a deal: the market size, the vertical that it's in, etc. What we did exceptionally well was looking at a founder's background above and beyond what was on paper. Our whole thing was: *If you can't get into Y Combinator, dope! Because you could probably get into NewME!* We were looking for people who were smart, and were hustlers, and were building stuff. We were looking for folks who had something that could go somewhere, but [they] weren't going to get into Y Combinator. And our other main job was to work with the founder to position their story in a way that was palpable for the investor. That framework allowed us to help so many people. We completely changed the way people thought about framing their business and the story they were telling. That methodology worked, and people were raising money left and right. Across all our accelerators, as well as events we hosted—like a pop-up accelerator tour—we helped entrepreneurs raise over $47 million.

> *That methodology worked, and people were raising money left and right. Across all our accelerators, as well as events we hosted—like a pop-up accelerator tour—we helped entrepreneurs raise over $47 million.*

In what ways has NewME shaped the technology and venture capital industry?

Benton: I was talking to somebody about this the other day, and I hate to say it out loud because it can sound egotistical, but we literally changed it because [a network of investors and Black founders] did not exist. What I have come to realize at my age is that you can impact things in multiple ways. You can impact things directly, which we did through NewME, and you can impact things indirectly, which we've done through things in the ecosystem. But now I'll meet founders who don't know who I am, or my work, but they've been impacted by somebody that I impacted directly. To be able to see that, it's like: Wow, this is a huge thing. So there's no real way to measure the impact that we made. And I don't even think it's necessary to measure it in quantitative terms.

But now I'll meet founders who don't know who I am, or my work, but they've been impacted by somebody that I impacted directly. To be able to see that, it's like: Wow, this is a huge thing. So there's no real way to measure the impact that we made. And I don't even think it's necessary to measure it in quantitative terms.

Simply put, there were not a lot of Black people in Silicon Valley. Like, legit. No Black people were raising money in Silicon Valley. There was nobody investing in Black founders in Silicon Valley. NewME changed all that.

NewME provided a landing pad in Silicon Valley for many Black and Brown entrepreneurs, and a lot of them have now gone into venture capital. NewME was that springboard for them.

Benton: Yeah, and a lot of people have not made that connection yet because life moves fast. We impacted founders directly. But now, when you look at Andreessen [Horowitz], Kapor [Center], or individual investors, those people [who came through NewME] are now investors at major firms deploying capital. McKeever "Mac" Conwell II at RareBreed Ventures, Chris Lyons at Andreessen Horowitz, just for an example. And there are other VCs all around the country.

Did you consider raising a fund?

Benton: My entire spin at NewME was about investing in others. Post-cancer, I was like: Fuck that. I'm not investing in anyone else; I'm investing in me. Even when I published my book *[Revival: How I Rebuilt a Life for Longevity After Cancer, Burnout, and Heartbreak]*, the entity I have for my personal company is Angela Benton, Inc. It's not egotistical; it's to remind myself of me. Because when you're investing so much in other people, you forget about yourself. And then you get sick or whatever ends up happening. I really just wanted to invest in myself, so after I sold NewME, I was the first investor in Streamlytics.

But, early on, when I did start talking to investors, I was surprised to find that my track record did not count. Within the context of [this book], I think there's a responsibility to discuss how our ecosystem is broken. And we should also hold our own Black VCs accountable and ask for more transparency in how and where they are investing.

I had forgotten about the brokenness of the industry until I started fundraising for Streamlytics. Even when fundraising from our own Black VCs, I went in thinking: *Okay, these people know my work. I don't have to explain my track record as an entrepreneur, and they will easily support what I do.* Because if this were set up like the rest of the industry, certain founders who had a track record like me would have an easier time fundraising. It's not like that in Black tech. At least not right now. We need to make sure the new investors that we're building [up] have a real risk tolerance for investing in Black founders.

I thought I was crazy until I started talking to White investors, and then White investors started validating me. That's what was crazy to me. I didn't end up taking money from White investors. All our investors *are* Black. The investors we are working with have been following my career for a long time. They were the ones who were like: *I don't know what you're working on, but I got a deck, I just want to be involved.* Our investors are dope: Base Ventures, Reign Ventures, and several Black angels.

How does Streamlytics work?

Benton: Streamlytics is measuring what people are streaming across different platforms. That's what we're doing today. The bigger vision though is transforming how personal data streams are used. The underlying technology for this is an algorithm that prices data, and the packaging of data, [which is then] enhanced with metadata, and sold to our B2B customers. The longer-term vision, and the reason why I'm passionate about this, is because the world is changing so rapidly with AI and other new technologies. And the scary thing is, none of us on this planet really own our own data. Nor do we have any say over what happens to our data. What is going to happen in the future—well, what is happening right now—is you're spinning off all these personal data streams. When you order an Uber, that's a data stream. When you watch something on Netflix, that's a data stream. When you order your groceries from Whole Foods, that's a data stream. We're spinning off all these data streams in our everyday life, but we don't actually own them. That becomes a problem when AI is now built on top of these data streams.

An example—it's a bit futuristic, but a good example—is a recent interview I watched with Elon Musk, where he discussed the *neural link*. He's five years away from being able to have this implant in your brain that can fix any diseases that you may have— like muscular dystrophy—and restore the functionality of walking or using your hand. That's the first step. Once we're able to help people with those diseases, then we can start to look at how neural links enhance cognitive abilities or other things.

Even though this is an extreme circumstance, and I definitely feel that we are far away from this, my whole thing is: *Who is going to own the data that's on the neural link?* Not us. So we're advocating for a federal data privacy law for specific guidelines to be in place for the use of our data. We're also trying to have a data standard that allows people to easily transfer their data back and forth from different platforms. And lastly, for communities that have been historically exploited, like the Black community, we're launching our consumer-facing apps in those communities first. Culture helps the Black community specifically own and monetize their data, primarily because there are trillions of dollars that are being made off data. And that can be a vehicle to transfer some of that wealth back into the communities powering a lot of that success.

What learnings or principles are you incorporating this time around?

Benton: I took all these experiences going through life-changing circumstances with me into Streamlytics. I was diagnosed with cancer in January 2016 at the age of thirty-four. It's had an incredible impact on me as a person. It reminds you of what is really important in life. You learn how you want to spend your time on this planet. And, honestly, I didn't feel like there was anything left for me to do with NewME.

But I wanted to sell it to someone who would maintain its integrity. We had gotten an offer from a large for-profit education company, but they were a university, and I felt the concept was going to change. When Candice [Matthews Brackeen] from Hillman Accelerator approached me, I had just completed our last accelerator and felt like it was the right fit. That was when I was going through chemo, and I learned a lot about myself, to be honest. I mean, there's no real way to sum it up other than to say that you learn a lot about yourself going through something like that.

After NewME, I didn't know what I wanted to work on next. So I started experimenting with producing different forms of content. I did a short docuseries when [I was] visiting one of the NewME companies in Malawi. I was just allowing myself to be creative, which most people cannot do because they have their ego in the way. But being right off cancer, I didn't have an ego. I was just happy to be alive.

After having been through this very serious experience, whatever I did next, I didn't want it to be so intense. Allowing myself to just simply create content and just experiment with different things ended up leading me to Streamlytics. During that time of just producing content, I started researching how people were spending their time online. I realized that this data didn't exist. I also realized there was data privacy tied to it. So I was receiving these little nudges on what I was going to do next.

What are some lessons you would like to share with the next generation of entrepreneurs, technologists, and investors?

Benton: I actually had a conversation yesterday with a Black investor who's been in this for a long time. My biggest piece of advice is what I was talking to him about: Play your own game. When you're looking at VC, entrepreneurship, or anything, it's easy to look at a framework and say: Okay, Marc Andreessen did it this way, or Ben Horowitz did it this way. Clubhouse is doing this; Facebook is doing this. That's what I should be doing. What we tend to ignore are the things that we do really well ourselves that other people can't replicate. I would say lean into that more. That's going to be your value proposition.

People want to take money from people that they like. But in order to be likable, you have to be authentic. There are a lot of people, even with my current company Streamlytics, that I didn't take money from because they weren't authentic. Some of them were Black investors, as well. But something felt off about it. I mean, you *can* get by with inauthentic mannerisms or behaviors, copying what you see in the ecosystem. I think, at the end of the day, being yourself—even if that means you have to walk away from certain things—is okay. Being okay walking away from stuff is the most empowering freaking thing that you can do. That's your swag, especially as an investor. And when you start talking to limited partners, you're going to need that swag. It's a real shift in mindset.

Play your own game. When you're looking at VC, entrepreneurship, or anything, it's easy to look at a framework and say: Okay, Marc Andreessen did it this way, or Ben Horowitz did it this way. Clubhouse is doing this; Facebook is doing this. That's what I should be doing. What we tend to ignore are the things that we do really well ourselves that other people can't replicate. I would say lean into that more. That's going to be your value proposition.

We're in a very interesting time where some of us who started at the same time are the same age, and maturing. So there's this group that can now impart things that we didn't know—things that no one told us when we were coming up—onto the next generation. I think leaning into that authenticity and not being afraid to walk away from stuff are both key.

CHARLES HUDSON

Founder and Managing Partner, Precursor Ventures

Precursor Ventures is a classic seed-stage venture capital firm investing in long-term relationships with founders they believe in.

C harles Hudson is the Managing Partner and Founder of Precursor Ventures, an early-stage venture capital firm focused on investing in the first institutional round of investment for the most promising software and hardware companies. Precursor Ventures invests in long-term relationships with founders they believe in.

Prior to founding Precursor Ventures, Charles was a Partner at Uncork Capital (formerly known as SoftTech VC). In this role, he focused on identifying investment opportunities in mobile infrastructure, mobile applications, and marketplaces. In addition to his investment activities, he supported SoftTech portfolio companies in business and corporate development matters. He was also the CoFounder and CEO of Bionic Panda Games, an Android-focused, mobile games startup based in San Francisco.

Prior to joining SoftTech VC and co-founding Bionic Panda Games, Charles Hudson was the VP of Business Development for Serious Business until the company was acquired by Zynga in February 2010. Prior to Serious Business, he was the Sr. Director for Business Development at Gaia Interactive, an online hangout and virtual world for teens. Prior to Gaia, Charles worked in New Business Development at Google and focused on new partnership opportunities for early-stage products in the advertising, mobile, and ecommerce markets. Prior to joining Google, he was a Product Manager for IronPort Systems, a leading provider of anti-spam hardware appliances (acquired by Cisco Systems for $830 million in 2007). Before IronPort Systems, Charles worked at In-Q-Tel, the venture capital fund backed by the Central Intelligence Agency, where he invested in early-stage hardware and software companies.

Charles graduated from Stanford University with a BA in economics and Spanish, and holds an MBA from the Stanford Graduate School of Business.

Twitter: @chudson
Website: https://precursorvc.com/

———— *

Tell us about your background and upbringing, up to your first professional job.

Charles Hudson: I grew up in a small Michigan city outside of Detroit called Southfield, which is literally on the other side of Eight Mile in Detroit. It's one of the first suburbs you bump into as you leave the city. I grew up there with almost my entire family—grandparents, aunts, uncles, cousins—living within thirty miles [of our house], so I grew up spending a lot of time with my family. I'd say it was a pretty typical childhood for a kid who was born in the late seventies. You go out and play with your neighborhood friends, you ride your bikes after school, and you come home in time for dinner—things that seem foreign today [*chuckles*].

I went to a public elementary school. At the time, Southfield was a city changing in many ways. It had originally been a predominantly White suburb, but it was becoming more integrated, and not everybody in the city was happy about that. So there was definitely some tension.

When I was in fifth grade, the principal of my elementary school went to my mom and told her: *I've been a principal in the school district for a while. Your son should look at this private school on the outskirts, in the farther north suburbs of the city, because I think he would really thrive there. I think he'll get a great education.*

After her prodding and nudging, my mom took me to take the entrance exam for this school called Cranbrook [Kingswood Upper

School]. I ended up going there, and it totally changed my world. I went from your typical suburban neighborhood public school to a school where the kids who were in my class had parents who were super senior executives or owners of big companies like Penske. The daughter of Ford's then-CEO was in my senior class. I had never been exposed to wealth like that, or to people who came from that world. That was not the world that I came from.

I went there from middle school to high school. And I really enjoyed it. It was a very nerd-friendly school [*laughs*]. There was a lot of emphasis on reading and writing, a lot of emphasis on critical thinking. It was like the ideal training ground for someone who wanted to have a liberal education. I graduated from there and decided to go to Stanford.

It was a big deal to move from Michigan to California, [where] I didn't have a lot of family. I have one cousin who lives out here. I'd only been to California one time before when my cousin graduated from Marine boot camp in San Diego. So I showed up not knowing anything at all about what Northern California was like, and it was a big culture shock for me. Michigan, at the time, was mostly a Black and White place, with also a pretty strong presence of people from the Middle East. That was kind of it. We didn't have a large contingent of Asian American folks, didn't have a large contingent of Latino folks. So Northern California was very eye-opening just in terms of its racial makeup.

Detroit is a grittier, grindy kind of place—hardworking, nose to the grindstone. Northern California is a little more positive and optimistic. It was a real adjustment for me to get used to the

California lifestyle. I did not figure it out for a while. And the weather was a big change.

At Stanford, I studied economics and Spanish, thinking I wanted to get a PhD in economics and maybe go into international development work in Latin America. But the more upper-division economics classes I took, the more I began to realize I was probably not cut out to be an econ PhD. There were people in my junior- and senior-year classes for whom the material just was supernatural. For me, it just wasn't. But I liked markets, and I liked ideas, and I liked the notion that you could apply frameworks to solve problems. That's what I always liked about economics. And Spanish, I just enjoyed the language, and enjoyed the literature, and reading about the history and the people.

Then, the summer before my senior year, I interned for an Internet company called Excite, which is sadly no longer around. It was one of those serendipity things; I actually found out about the job from a flyer in the Stanford coffee shop.

So coming out of undergrad, I was really confused as to what I wanted to do. Like a lot of people, I had those traditional banking and consulting jobs, the kind of things which are par for the course at Stanford. Then, the summer before my senior year, I interned for an Internet company called Excite, which is sadly no longer around. It was one of those serendipity things; I actually found out about the job from a flyer in the Stanford coffee shop.

This was in 1999, the very go-go times of the Internet, and Excite was a pretty wild and crazy place to work as an intern. That was my first real exposure to the Internet, and I loved it. When it was time to make a decision about what to do after college for my first job, I realized the Internet [was] for me. Even then, it felt like a once-in-a-lifetime opportunity. I felt like banking and consulting, and all the other jobs I was looking at, would probably be around in the future, but the chance to get in on the Internet right away probably wouldn't.

Even though I didn't have a background in computer science—I didn't take even one computer science programming class when I was at Stanford—I decided I was going to do something technology-oriented.

What was your first job following university?

Hudson: As luck would have it, I ended up moving into a venture capital group called In-Q-Tel that invested money for the Central Intelligence Agency. In true weird serendipity, when I was an intern at Excite, I had a succession of different managers—the company was growing fast, people were getting moved around. One person took me under her wing and looked out for me. It just so happened that her husband was running In-Q-Tel at the time. He was in venture capital, and she's the one who encouraged me to meet with him and talk about what the firm was doing. I didn't really know much about venture capital. It wasn't as much in the zeitgeist when I was in school. But I went and had breakfast with her husband, and he offered me the chance to join In-Q-Tel as an analyst.

The firm was mostly based out of DC at the time. I was told that we were on the verge of opening an office on Sand Hill Road.

I think it probably took two years to get that office open. So for the first two years, we worked out of a Regus [co-working] office in Foster City, overlooking the freeway. It was me and two or three other guys in an office trying to help the CIA through a bunch of technical challenges, where they thought there might be commercial solutions to help address some of the problems that we're facing.

What happened during your journey at In-Q-Tel to becoming a general partner at Precursor?

Hudson: Sure. I was twenty-two years old when I joined In-Q-Tel. It was my first real full-time job. And I think working with the government involves a certain amount of formality that for me was foreign. I ended up spending a lot of time getting to know my colleagues and getting to understand as much as I could about how the agency works. I got a ton of latitude and support at In-Q-Tel. The management team really invested in me and empowered me. And I felt like anywhere else I went, I was not likely to have as great of an experience.

I ended up staying at In-Q-Tel for three and a half years. In the end, I felt In-Q-Tel wasn't structured at the time for me to go much further than an associate-type role. I [also] felt like any other job I took in venture would be similar to In-Q-Tel in terms of not really giving me the chance to go to the partner level. At that point, I was twenty-five years old, and the only full-time experience I had was venture, and I didn't plan to stay in venture. So I went to business school at Stanford to figure out what to do.

While [in business school], I realized I wanted to try being an entrepreneur. I really liked the idea of entrepreneurship.

I asked a bunch of my mentors: *If you're not technical, and you have aspirations of being a tech entrepreneur, what's the best job to take?* All of them said: *The best job you could have is to find a role as a product manager. Even though you're not writing code, you're talking to engineers, you're spending time with them, you're helping them think through features, you're talking to customers. It's a very interesting role; you have a lot of responsibility and influence but not a lot of hard power.*

It sounded great. *Are there firms that would take somebody like me as an intern coming out of business school?* I got some really great advice from people, like finding two-hundred- to three-hundred-person companies that can afford to invest in you and give you an opportunity to grow. Where you're not the only product manager and everything is dependent on you.

So I ended up joining a company called IronPort Systems that made anti-spam hardware and software products. It was an amazing experience. It took me all of about seven months to realize I was not destined to be a great product manager. The job just didn't speak to me. At that particular company, the product management role was more technical than I was capable of handling, but I also didn't realize how inward-oriented the job is. I had this dream that a lot of the job would be going to visit customers, hearing about their pain-points and their problems. But a lot of the job was understanding our product, its capabilities, and learning how to write really good feature descriptions and product requirements documents. Learning more about how you scope what's possible to be built given the engineering resources you have.

I walked away after a couple of months, feeling a ton of respect for people who can be really good at product management. The people on our team were exceptional at the job, and I realized there was a huge gap between what I knew and where they were. The ceiling for me as a product manager was maybe a solid B; [that] was as good as I was going to get.

Someone who'd been an intern of mine in undergrad had joined Google, and I told him I was thinking about [trying] something different.

He told me, "I think you might want to come join Google. We have this group called New Business Development that's run by a woman named Megan Smith. They're doing some really interesting stuff. It could be really a great place to be a generalist, and it could be a great role for you."

I ended up going to Google, and stayed there for about two years. I realized that business development was just a much better fit for my personality, the things I enjoy doing, like talking to people, trying to build partnerships. I really enjoyed it. Then Google got to the place where it was so large that the things

I enjoyed most about my time there (which were more on the entrepreneurial side) were becoming harder to do. Google was becoming a bigger company, a very good company, but just bigger. It's crazy to think Google had fewer than five thousand people when I joined. By the time I left, it had about 25,000 people. It grew very, very, very quickly.

So I decided to leave, and really, *really* wanted to be at a startup. I hadn't, at that point in my career, really been part of a super small company, and I had gotten interested in the world of virtual goods. Just to contextualize this, it was 2008, before we had the iPhone App Store, and before the Facebook platform had games on it.

I was really interested in the next generation of games, so I joined a company in San Jose called Gaia Interactive, which was building a sort of virtual hangout for teens. They had raised money from some great firms like Benchmark and Redpoint, and had grown really quickly. They also had a great management team, and I thought I was going to be the first business development person there. I really thought there was just a ton of opportunity for me to grow there. For the first time, I was in a small company where we were figuring things out as we went. And I realized that was what I really enjoyed. That was the right environment for me.

After about a year and a half, I wanted something different. We were growing, but every time I looked up, more and more people I knew were building apps and services on top of the Facebook platform. There was a ton of growth happening there. I got introduced to a company that was based in San Francisco called Serious Business that was building games on top of the Facebook platform. They were a bunch of young guys who'd come up with one game that was doing really well, and they were looking to grow the team. There were probably four or five people on the team when I first met them, and at that point in my career, what I wanted most was to be part of an extremely small team.

I enjoyed that experience. We had such a fun time, really great people, and the business continued to grow. Eventually, we got to a place where we had to make a decision about whether or not we were going to continue on as an independent company or combine with somebody else. That was around 2010, when companies like Zynga, Playdum, Playfish, and a handful of others were becoming big and meaningful players on Facebook. It was becoming clear that there was going to be a few really large players, and then everybody else. So Zynga ended up acquiring [Serious Business], and I ended up not moving along with them as part of the acquisition.

I decided to start my own tech startup. That was 2010. I had done some other businesses on the side before. I'd had a conference business, I had a media business, but I had never tried to start something that was—at its heart—a software business. I called someone who'd been the head of engineering at Serious Business— he had also decided not to go to Zynga—and we ended up spending time thinking about a bunch of ideas. I had this teeny, tiny office in Mountain View that we used as a place to work.

The first thing we built was a product that was like LinkedIn on top of Facebook. We'll just say: That product was not successful. After trying to run away from games, we realized there was one really interesting opportunity in games we wanted to pursue: building games exclusively for Android. We could build a unique set of skills, abilities, tech, and talent that would come in real handy because very few other people were focused on building for Android. And so we raised about $2 million and got about a dozen employees at that company, Bionic Panda Games.

In retrospect, we were early for the platform, and we probably would have been better served if we had gone slower. I think we had gotten ourselves into a place where we had more head count and more burn rate than the market opportunity around a purely Android-focused game company would support. We ended up in the really interesting position of having to figure out what we had to do; we ended up selling the assets of that company to another player.

As any entrepreneur who's had a company that doesn't work out knows, the last bit of time when it's not working is really frustrating. It's difficult from an emotional standpoint. So after that company was done, I was ready to put the entrepreneurial/ startup/founder era of my career away. I was willing to walk away from that and focus full-time on being an investor.

When I started the company, I'd also thought about going back into venture capital [but] wasn't ready to jump into venture with both feet. I was ready to jump into venture with one foot and make my way back into it. I felt like I'd had enough experiences that I could be more useful to entrepreneurs, provide better advice, and have better insights. So I ended up splitting time: I was the CEO of a venture-backed company. I was also a venture partner in a firm then called SoftTech, now called Uncork.

I have to say it was incredibly difficult trying to run and build the startup and also be a contributing member of a VC firm. It was tough. I did it for a few years, then, after we sold the company, I felt really burned out. Trying to do two things for that long was hard. As any entrepreneur who's had a company that doesn't work out knows, the last bit of time when it's not working is really frustrating. It's difficult from an emotional standpoint. So after that company was done, I was ready to put the entrepreneurial/ startup/founder era of my career away. I was willing to walk away from that and focus full-time on being an investor.

When I joined SoftTech, the plan was to raise a $35 million fund, which turned into a $55 million fund. In the years I was at SoftTech, we went from a small fund that had $15 million under management to a fund that now has half a billion dollars under management. It was a really cool experience to see what happens when a seed fund gets momentum. It was cool to see we had companies that people understood. We made progress. All these things really started to get momentum.

What I realized, four or five years into my time at SoftTech, was that we were in a really tough place for me personally, and that, as our fund got larger, our minimum check size got larger, and the stage at which we would invest in companies went up. I really felt like the thing that made me happiest was the ability to invest in companies at the earliest, earliest stage. I didn't enjoy investing in companies that had traction as much as I enjoyed finding them pre-traction. So after a lot of wrestling and thinking about it, I decided to start my own fund. And that's how I left to start Precursor.

What, if any, challenges did you experience bringing in your full identity while navigating graduate school, Google, and Silicon Valley?

Hudson: When I was younger, I think I was less aware—maybe naive is a better word. I didn't think about institutional racism or discrimination when I was in my early twenties. Because I went to school here in the Bay Area, and had been in tech, I think I had embraced this idea that tech was pretty fair, which is weird because I basically almost never saw Black people in any of those spaces. But I don't think I had really thought about why. I was just kind of like: Tech talks about fairness. Tech talks about equality. A lot of the people I know seem like nice, good people. There must be a reason why there aren't that many Black people in technology or why I don't see them that often.

But, you know, when I worked at Google, the new business development group rolled up to legal, which, at the time, was run by David Drummond, and my little corner of Google felt pretty diverse. There were Black people on the corporate development team; there were Black people in the legal team. Google was one of the early companies to have an Employee Resource Group, the Black Googler Network. We had some pretty visible people between David, Stacy [Brown-]Philpot, Maria Rivera. We had people that you could, like, *see*.

But I never really processed: *I can see them, but they are a tiny fraction of everything that's going on here.* I will say, that was also the era when tech was like: *We are not discriminatory; we focus on ideas. The best ideas win, and the people who get money or access to opportunities aren't because of relationships or networks. That's the East Coast biased way to do it. We're different here.*

At what point did you start to make a connection to institutional racism? Well, I'm making the assumption that you did, eventually, arrive [laughs].

Hudson: [*laughs*] Yeah, I did arrive. I wish it had happened earlier, but I think it happens for everyone when it's supposed to. I went to a predominantly White, wealthy day/boarding school for high school, so I was used to being in those kinds of environments. I wasn't when I showed up as an eighth-grader, but, by the time I graduated, I was used to being around wealthy, connected White people in their environments, where I was oftentimes the only Black person.

I think sometimes you get used to something and stop reflecting on it... You know, Stanford was probably 7–10 percent Black when I went there. So it didn't *feel* that different from high school. Most of my first jobs didn't feel that different from high school... I was so used to being the only Black person in the room that

I think sometimes you get used to something and stop reflecting on it... You know, Stanford was probably 7–10 percent Black when I went there. So it didn't feel that different from high school. Most of my first jobs didn't feel that different from high school... I was so used to being the only Black person in the room that it never occurred to me to ask: Why is this the case? It was just normal for me. I go into rooms and am probably going to be the only Black person, and I figured out how to navigate that.

it never occurred to me to ask: *Why is this the case?* It was just normal for me. I go into rooms and am probably going to be the only Black person, and I figured out how to navigate that.

I would say what really changed for me is I got to know Mitch and Freada Kapor in 2008 through Freada's then-chief of staff. I started hanging out with them more, and they were talking about all these issues. I started listening to some of the things Freada was doing at Level Playing Field Institute and to some of the work they were doing with the Smash Scholars program—just getting plugged into a set of people whose voices and perspectives were different. It's important to remember that, in 2008, there was *barely* a conversation in tech at the highest levels about gender equity. Racial equity wasn't even on people's radar yet at the leadership level.

What I realized was that everybody I was surrounded by in tech pretty much thought the system was pretty fair, and worked. For some of them, the fact that I was able to navigate it was evidence that it was fair. I hadn't had much exposure to people who could see that, even though 99 percent of the people in this ecosystem and around us think it's fair, that doesn't mean they're right. I had never really considered that maybe the dominant narrative of the work and social environment in which I was a participant was just wrong, and that there were things happening [that] people either couldn't see because they didn't have the vocabulary, or they chose not to see.

At first, I didn't know what to do with that. For a few years, I was like: *Well, I agree that this is an issue, but I don't know if it's MY issue. I don't know if I want to take up this cause or make this my thing. I don't know that I'm the right advocate. I'm very much a beneficiary of privilege in terms of my educational background and my access to some of these networks, rooms, and I just don't know if this is my thing. I don't disagree that these [things] are happening, and that the system is not fair; I just don't know what my role is in fixing it.* What I realized is, sometimes when you work for other people, it can constrain your view, your voice. Even if they're not doing anything specifically to silence you, it ends up being a self-imposed thing.

Particularly towards the end of my tenure at SoftTech, I realized I was meeting every Black entrepreneur who was raising money. I don't think it was because I was the best investor for those founders. I think it was because everyone was like: *It's a Black founder. We're going to send them to Charles!* That was kind of messed up both for that founder and for me.

But when you're in other people's platforms, whether it's a public company or a small partnership, I do think it causes you to think: *Is it my place to bring this part of my personality or voice to work?* I remember meeting Black entrepreneurs as an investor and thinking: *If I say yes to this deal and sponsor this company, and it doesn't work out, will the industry, my colleagues, or my peers draw the erroneous conclusion that investing in Black entrepreneurs is wrong just because one deal didn't work?* It might be the only one they see. I was like: *This is bad!*

Now, this was not something I was receiving as active feedback from my colleagues at my firm. This was a narrative I had internalized. *This is really messed up. This is not healthy. This is no way to live. I need to get to a place where I can explore these things without dragging my colleagues and peers into conversations, or fights, or discussions that are not really theirs.*

I give Mitch and Freada a lot of credit because they were very patient in allowing me to go on this journey. It would have been very easy to just say: *Hey, you're a Black person in a position of power and authority. It's not your choice to not work on this. You HAVE to do it.* They very much could have taken that point of view; I probably would have been resistant to it, but they could have done that. Instead, they created room for me to get there on my own.

Getting people to understand some of the structural barriers that exist in tech and venture is something I feel really strongly about in the work that we do at Precursor, [as well as] creating a firm that I'm proud of and that reflects my values based on who we hire, who we promote, and who we invest in.

If I'm honest, it probably took me five years to go from a general awareness that this is not *right* to a place where I found a role for myself in trying to address these issues.

If I'm honest, it probably took me five years to go from a general awareness that this is not right to a place where I found a role for myself in trying to address these issues.

It's helpful to hear your journey and thoughts. I think there are a lot of young professionals who are navigating spaces for the first time and trying to figure out whether they have a responsibility in their role.

Hudson: I think it's harder now because, when I went on the journey, there wasn't as much social media. There wasn't as much of an opportunity for people to criticize where you were on your journey or to call you out. I think I would have had a much harder time doing the work I had to do in an environment where I was visible but not doing it, if that makes sense. I'm very sympathetic, particularly to people who are earlier in their career, who work at a big tech company and wonder if they [should] advocate for this: Am I putting my career prospects at risk? I think it becomes easier when you feel more secure, like, no one's going to fire me from my own firm unless my investors decide not to continue funding us [*laughs*]. I don't have to worry about what management's perspective is on these things. And I try to make sure the people on our team feel empowered to speak out if they see something that bothers them that's a social issue. They don't have to run it by me. I think this idea that you should be able to be yourself at work, as much as possible, is healthy.

What were some of the challenges that you went through in launching a fund and raising money for a startup? And, given your experience, how different would it be for you to create this fund today?

Hudson: Oh, boy [*laughs*]. This is going to make me sound really old, which I am, but when I started at In-Q-Tel in 2000, we got business plans in the mail. People would FedEx us their business plans, it would show up on my desk, and I would read a paper printout. [People] would call me or email me later to make sure I received it. In 2000, there was no blog, podcast, Medium.com, or Substack culture around information sharing. VCs had almost total power asymmetry relative to founders when it came to knowledge and sophistication about how the venture business works. Maybe a repeat founder had slightly better odds because they've been through it once before, but venture was dark arts.

There's still a power differential between founders, entrepreneurs, and VCs, but I think there's less of an information asymmetry.

I look at how different the world is now, twenty years later. If you're an entrepreneur who wants to understand funded mechanics, term sheets, all these things, there's an *abundance* of information out there. There's still a power differential between founders, entrepreneurs, and VCs, but I think there's less of an information asymmetry.

I think the world of starting a venture fund is still very much dark arts, like venture was in 2000, for a couple reasons. One, I honestly think it takes about $1 million to start a venture fund from scratch—a small venture fund—because it takes about two years to raise a fund for most people, so you're going to have to support yourself financially for two years. And, assuming you live in a reasonable part of the country, that's going to be expensive.

Second, until you close your fund, there are some non-reimbursable travel and fundraising expenses you're going to have to absorb, which are not fun. Depending on your relationships with legal and other service providers, you might have to pay as you go for those. You might not be able to do this otherwise. Then you've got to put up 1 percent minimum of your own fund, and you're probably going to have to do that for two successive funds before you get to a place where you're able to feel good about this. So if I add that up, it's probably, like, a million bucks.

And for people who have been subject to targeted policies designed to reduce wealth in our community, there are not a lot of people who have that kind of money lying around. So the financial costs associated with getting off the ground as a venture fund is a legitimate hurdle for many people Black, Brown, and otherwise—but particularly *us*.

Then, if you're in tech, you can't open Twitter without bumping into some VCs spouting off some pearl of wisdom. VCs are relatively easy to find because, for the most part, they want entrepreneurs who are in their focus areas to find them. Generally speaking, limited partners are much more private, much more difficult to access and find. I spun out of SoftTech, so I knew LPs, I had met them. Some of them had invested in our previous SoftTech funds. I knew where to look, and I had people I knew I could ask for help as guides. But I think if you're coming at this as someone who's only been an angel investor, or [someone who] doesn't have those connections, it's really unclear to me how you build the list of LPs to go after.

Then there are all these other things that are difficult. A lot of limited partners want to see a previous track record of investments in order to evaluate [your ability to source and structure deals]. But if you haven't been an angel investor, either because you haven't had the financial resources, or [because] people in your network aren't starting companies, you're not going to have a track record. That's pretty tough. And last, but not least, a lot of the diligence that I see done by limited partners is community-based. I guess I feel this way because I'm on the receiving end of these calls now. And by community-based, I mean if you're an investor in a bunch of seed funds, and a new person comes to you with an idea for a seed fund, you likely call the seed managers you know and say: *Hey, do you know person A, B, and C are starting a fund? What do you think?* If you're outside of that reference network, you're not going to get a lot of help.

I always tell people there's this hierarchy of risk-seeking behavior or risk tolerance. Entrepreneurs have a very high tolerance for risk; the payoff for success is great. VCs have less risk tolerance than founders and substantially more risk tolerance than limited partners. So it's a real challenge, which is why most VCs come from other VC firms. And who are at most VC firms? People from Stanford and Harvard who worked at a pretty short list of tech companies.

So unless you start to change who gets the chance to start VC firms, the only way you're going to really change the makeup of what the next generation of firms looks like is to change who's at existing firms, which I think is, like, unlikely to happen—and that's a longer story about how VC firms hire and promote. But there are so many barriers for people who are not already in the venture ecosystem to start. It's daunting.

Is there a particular mentor or advisor you call when you don't know what to do? Why is that advice you respect?

Hudson: It's a really good question. I have two sets of people I call. My old boss from In-Q-Tel, Stephen Mendel, is someone I go back to a lot, mostly because he's known me for my entire professional career. And I think he knows me well enough to be honest about when I'm doing things that are true to who I am, and when I'm not. He has a good compass on that.

I also have a few people in my life who make decisions _very_ differently than I do, who are far more conservative. Sometimes I go to them just to figure out whether or not I'm thinking about the full range of possibilities in front of me. For me, it's important because I know my tendency is to bet on myself, and that can be a reckless decision. So sometimes, I do want to hear from people whose natural inclination is _not_ to do that—how they think about an opportunity that I'm considering.

Can you share a risk you took that didn't work out well?

Hudson: Oh my gosh [_laughs_]. So many things, unfortunately, have not worked out. I basically took the proceeds from selling Serious Business to Zynga, and plowed that all into trying to build that Android game company. That decidedly did not work. We were just way too early and also way too impatient. Had we just stuck with Android and built the products that we knew worked, maybe the company would have had a different outcome.

I think it would have been easy to go back into venture after business school. But instead, I took a product management job that I don't think I was particularly great at. I wouldn't say that worked. And I would honestly say my first attempt at fundraising for Precursor really didn't work at all for the first year. Thankfully, we eventually got it together, but for the first year, I definitely had days where I thought I had made a colossal financial and professional mistake by starting this firm because it does not appear to be popular with the LP crowd. And I am not getting a lot of people telling me that this is a great idea.

What motivates you to keep betting on yourself and to risk taking another leap to follow your passion?

Hudson: That's an interesting question. I just always felt like: If not me, then who? Or: Why not me? It didn't dawn on me that my risk tolerance was that different until I started telling some of my friends who are visible senior executives at big tech companies who happen to be Black: You should go do a startup! You should go join a venture firm! And a lot of them just don't want to do that. I think some of them liked the positions they were in, liked the influence that they had.

I realized I'm kind of a restless person. All the things I thought were risky—and this might sound silly—but I thought they would all work. Like, Precursor was pretty irrational. The first three venture funds you raise are the hardest. If you can get through three, you've got a good shot at staying in business.

We had just finished closing our fourth fund [at SoftTech] when I started talking about maybe doing something different. It would have been way easier to just stay at SoftTech, rather than take everything I had and put it into starting another venture fund. The feedback from the market was that there were already too many venture funds. And, at SoftTech, I was the most senior, non-founding partner, so I felt like I had a pretty good read on the place. I liked working with my colleagues. I liked the founders that I backed. It wasn't a bad place. I just felt like the idea of Precursor was so obvious I couldn't *not* do it.

In the same way, I quit Google to go to a no-name startup. My parents were like: *What are you doing?* It was just very clear to me that I wasn't supposed to be at Google anymore. It was time for me to go do a startup, and I [had to] go do it.

Maybe it's self-confidence. I don't know for sure, but I've always been comfortable doing things I think are risky if I think that they'll work. Precursor is by far the biggest professional risk I've taken, but it's also where I've had the highest conviction: to solve the need for checks for people who don't fit what today's seed funds want. It was obvious to me because I was saying no to those people every day at work.

Had I known how hard it would be, I might have thought about it a little bit more. But I left [SoftTech] definitely feeling Precursor was a good idea, even though I got a lot—*a lot*—of feedback that it was not a good idea, that I shouldn't do it, that it was dumb. Well, I'm doing it now, and we're going to make this work.

MELISSA HANNA

Co-Founder and CEO, Mahmee

Mahmee is a HIPAA-secure care management platform that makes it easy for payers, providers, and patients to coordinate comprehensive prenatal and postpartum healthcare from anywhere.

Melissa Hanna, JD, MBA, is co-founder and CEO of Mahmee, a comprehensive prenatal and postpartum care coordination platform. Backed by Serena Williams and Mark Cuban, Mahmee increases positive health outcomes for moms and babies. By using its proprietary HIPAA-secure technology, Mahmee's staff of certified and trained maternity support professionals are able to deliver proactive, ongoing education and guidance to new families everywhere at a fraction of the cost of traditional care. An activist–entrepreneur, Melissa received her masters of business administration from the Peter F. Drucker School of Management at Claremont Graduate University, and her juris doctor from Southwestern Law School, where she now teaches as an adjunct professor of corporate and technology law. She has worked in operations and strategy at startups in healthcare, education, digital media, and consumer goods. Prior to launching Mahmee, Melissa served as Assistant Director of the Eugene Lang Entrepreneurship Center at Columbia Business School. Melissa's modus operandi has always been to forge cross-industry collaborations and partnerships to solve big challenges, and she believes that equitable access to healthcare for women and children is a challenge we can all solve by working creatively together. She's been featured in *Entrepreneur*, *Business Insider*, Cheddar TV, *Black Enterprise*, *USA Today*, and many more. Melissa was recently named to *Inc.* magazine's 2019 Female Founders 100 list.

Website: www.mahmee.com

What were you like during your early years leading up to college?

Melissa Hanna: I've always been a self-starter, a project-starter kind of person. I always had ideas for stuff when I was young. And [when I was] growing up, my family was always very supportive of me taking on new projects and trying to build and create stuff on my own. I was raised by my grandparents, aunts, uncles and my parents—we were an extended family, and they were always very supportive of me trying new things. My family is mixed. I'm first generation American on my dad's side, second generation on my mom's side. My mom's side are Holocaust survivors from Austria who immigrated to New York during World War II. My dad's side is Bahamian.

I always had a lot of extended family around me. I'd travel back and forth between Los Angeles and Nassau, Bahamas, frequently as a child. So I really have a mixed cultural upbringing, and a mixed religious upbringing as well. I was repeatedly encouraged to pursue new things and create solutions to problems that I saw in the world.

In junior high and high school, I would get ideas when I felt like there was an opportunity to innovate, to do something different than what was originally offered in my school experience or my social experiences. Some things were more serious and others more superficial. In junior high, I thought the student dress code policy was really skewed disadvantageously toward women and girls and the styles that we wore. There were a lot of dress code restrictions, and it was pretty easy to get in trouble for not dressing appropriately.

This was a public school without a uniform, so you were allowed to wear whatever you wanted, but not really when it came down to it. The result was a very oppressive policy. If [the administrators] determined that you [had] violated a restriction, you had to change into old gym clothes that were left in the locker room, and would have to wear those all day. It was really a very punitive system. I told my family about it, and I thought it was really wrong that women and girls were so unfairly impacted and other policies, like anti-sagging, were very targeted and disproportionately affected young Black men. All around, it was a very unjust and discriminatory policy.

So I authored a new policy for the school, framed as a petition, and my parents' response was: *Why don't you see if you can make a change on this?* I asked how I would do that. *You're going to want to build a coalition. You're going to want to get other students to sign on and do this with you. Ask your friends if they want to help petition for this.* I eventually took the petition to the dean's office at school and demanded a meeting with the dean [*laughs*]. I did stuff like that, very socially active, social justice things.

> There was both the need to keep me occupied so I didn't get bored, and probably the understanding that I wasn't going to stop, anyway, so people just sanctioned a lot of what I did, and would just say: Go ahead; try that; see what happens.

Then, in high school, I expanded my interests beyond social justice but continued to advocate for things that were missing from the experience. There wasn't a marching band at the high school I attended, even though we had a football team. I thought we should have a marching band like other schools do, and my family was like: *Why don't you make one?* I played flute and saxophone, so I recruited a bunch of friends to be in a marching band. Then I became the band leader and would call for practice after school [*laughs*]. There were maybe ten to fifteen [of us]. It was not a marching band [*laughs*].

So, I would do stuff like that. I'd have an idea for something, and had a lot of support from teachers, my parents, and my family. *Why don't you try that?* I think some of this had to do with the fact [that] I was always a very precocious child. I was identified as gifted from a young age. There was both the need to keep me occupied so I didn't get bored, and probably the understanding that I wasn't going to stop, anyway, so people just sanctioned a lot of what I did, and would just say: *Go ahead; try that; see what happens.*

Were you influenced by a family of entrepreneurs, or by observing businesses being built around you?

Hanna: Yes, but that was never part of my understanding of doing things, of taking on initiatives and creating solutions. It was never from a business or financial standpoint. It wasn't like: How are you going to make money doing this? No one ever asked me that. No one ever said: You're going to need to make it on your own one day. It was always more like: If you pursue real solutions to real problems, you'll be successful. You'll find a way to do something important in society.

There's privilege baked into that. I grew up in an upper-middle-class family. I did see the highs and lows of wealth when my parents got divorced, and I was living in two single-parent households. They had changes to their businesses over the years. They lost businesses, they sold businesses, they renewed businesses. But we never had [real] money from the businesses. It was just something that you did, that you worked. In some cases, some years, my parents worked in their own businesses. In other cases, or other years, my parents worked for other people. And none of that was really tied to my understanding of what I was supposed to do in the world.

When I was younger, I actually wanted to be a forensic pathologist. I never wanted to be an entrepreneur. I was really interested in math and science. I was really fascinated with criminology, and I watched a lot of *Law & Order* as a kid, which I probably shouldn't have [*laughs*]. But my grandparents would let me watch it after school—they watched me because my parents worked day and night. My grandpa would have it on while I was doing homework, and it prompted this idea that I wanted to work in the morgue or a hospital or the police station. To me, it was like a puzzle that was interesting to solve. And I think that was definitely fostered in my upbringing: If you see a problem like a puzzle, you want to solve it, you want to come up with a solution.

When I started my first business in high school, it didn't occur to me to actually make money doing the business. So that tells you just how extreme that was in my upbringing. A lot of my friends wanted help booking gigs for their bands, and I had bands I was in myself. I was like: *Okay, I could figure out how to do this.* So I started learning about how to book gigs. I read books about the music industry, and since I grew up in LA, it was all around me.

I started trying to book bands for shows, but in the beginning, it was mostly unsuccessful. I failed a lot. Then I started getting some success, and I never thought to ask anyone for a cut of the money from the show. I was like: *Oh, this is cool. I did a thing. I accomplished something.* And that felt good. I'm very driven by accomplishment, so that was rewarding in and of itself. And afterward, I'd have this childlike wonder: *Oh, man, I can't believe I did that. That's so crazy.*

I still have that to this day. I think that's something that a lot of my employees and colleagues in the company see in me. On a very regular basis, something will happen at the company, and I'm like: *I can't believe we did that! We just got that contract! We just released that feature!* And everyone else is like: *Yeah, we've been working on [that] for months. Of course we did it.* But for me, when it finally happens, it has a different tone to it, or feeling, for me. That's something that's definitely from my younger years.

What was your initial career goal? When and how did you make the pivot into entrepreneurship?

Hanna: In college, I stopped focusing on math and science pretty early on, actually, because I had a lot of negative experiences in those courses throughout high school. When I started freshman year it was fifty-fifty, men to women. By junior and senior year, I was the only girl left in several of my college-level courses. I was taking all AP classes, and I got hazed a lot. I got teased and harassed and mocked by the men in the classes, and the teachers were pretty ambivalent. When I got to college and had the choice to pick my classes, I was like: I don't have to take that [treatment] anymore. I don't have to deal with that. I pretty quickly steered into social sciences, and I found a deep love for sociology. I took psychology, sociology, and anthropology courses to understand the differences in social studies. I really fell into sociology and understanding groups of people.

I did not have an idea of what I was going to do with it as a career path, and that definitely made my parents nervous. I remember having a very heated discussion with my dad about it. He wasn't mad, but he was concerned. *Where are you going with this? What is this going to mean for you?* I didn't have a good answer: *I'm really happy studying this. I'm good at it, and I know I can find ways to apply it over time.* I was pretty confident about that, and my parents let me continue. Halfway through college, I had thrown myself into it, and there were not that many classes left to take. By junior year, my academic advisor helped me brainstorm how I would fill up my remaining time. So I added on a secondary study in public policy, and that actually opened up a new line of thinking on how I could apply the sociology studies. It showed me that there was a whole world out there of people focused on social impact; and that I could use this understanding of how different groups of people operate and behave in society to create policies that could make life better for people.

> It showed me that there was a whole world out there of people focused on social impact; and that I could use this understanding of how different groups of people operate and behave in society to create policies that could make life better for people.

That's really when my public policy and social impact passions blossomed into a potential career path. I started studying health care law and education law and social policies related to healthcare, education, and labor to understand the fabric of democratic policies in the United States. I thought about studying this long term. I thought about going to Washington, DC, after school, and interning there, but I decided against that. I thought that DC might be too cutthroat for my personality.

I'm a very internally competitive person, but I've never been very externally competitive. I'm always more interested in beating my own record than in taking on other people. I mean, I *will* if put up to the challenge, but when I do, it brings out a very, very competitive side of me. So I don't indulge in that often. If I have to come up with a way to beat another entity, another person, or now, with a business, another company, I'm either thinking: *How do we either squash that company* or *how do we partner with that company?* Either beat them at their own game or figure out how to do it together.

I really like partnership. I would much rather come up with ways to work together with people. My first instinct, always, has been: *Well, how can we work together on this?* So that tells you a lot about Mahmee's personality as a business in the market. I think we are becoming very well known for being a partner-oriented company. There are people out there that may think we're their competitors, but if someone asked me: *What do you think about that other business or that other organization as a founder,* I'm not likely to express the same level of competition. My first response would be: *Oh, you should partner with them.*

> My first instinct, always, has been: Well, how can we work together on this?

Moving to Mahmee, can you walk us through your decision to become a founder? When did you decide: I'm going to take on this problem right now. I'm the best person to do it. And I can't walk away without solving it.

Hanna: Well, that didn't happen right away. That grew over months and years to a place where I feel that now, but it's shifted overtime. There's a feeling of: I'm really committed to a solution to this problem; therefore, my commitment extends to anyone else who can solve it better than I can. That's one side. And then this other feeling of: No one else is doing it right! I gotta keep trying.

Early on, I thought: *This is a really big problem to solve. I hope someone solves it. Maybe I'll try, but if someone does it better than me, better than my team—great. More power to them. Someone's gotta do it.* But I just kept looking around, waiting: *Who's going to do this? Who's going to really tackle the maternal health care industry? Because it's messed up!* And, over time, that shifted to: *I can't keep looking around and waiting for someone else. I have ideas now. I have people who want to work on this with me. I have investors who are willing to fund this. I've got to try! I've got to give it a really good try.* And that's where it's come to today.

But the other feeling never goes away. And, to me, that's very connected to this partnership idea; if someone else came along and was really killing the game, and I thought: *Your solution is a better approach. You've got a better solution than we do to the same problem,* I'd be very motivated to figure out how we bring what we have over to the other team. More often, though, what's happening now is, people are coming to me with that.

And again, it's this feeling of childlike wonder: *You want to take what you have and bring it over to our team? Why? You're the one doing it; you're making it happen.* And I think it's important not to lose that. I do get mocked a little bit sometimes. My team members are like: *Come on Melissa, stop playing so humble.* But I'm not being humble; I'm shocked we're still at it, that we're still doing it [*laughs*]!

If we could go back about five and a half years, what happened once you finally made the decision that you were the one who had to solve this problem?

Hanna: Before Mahmee was incorporated as its own company, I was working alongside my mom and my stepdad, who owned the family business that they ran, a private practice, in breastfeeding support and postpartum care. But building Mahmee was actually not a part of my professional roadmap. I never intended to work in the field of maternal and child healthcare. Not only did I not intend it, I swore I would never work in this industry. Reason being is that my mother, and now co-founder, Linda Hanna, is one of the pioneers of the industry; so I didn't want to live in her shadow. I didn't know what I was going to do with my life, but I was pretty sure about that part. She had designed some of the most successful maternal health and breastfeeding programs across southern California. They were so successful in their early days that they grew and got replicated in health systems across the US.

But ten years ago, she had really hit a point in her career where she'd just sworn off the industry, and said: *I've done all I can here and we're still not reaching every mom. We're still not connecting to providers the way we said we were going to through these programs— in the hospitals and out the door, in the allied health community, the folks who visit you at home, those who teach you breathing classes, and infant feeding classes, and all of the birth workers and professionals that are advocates along the way. Advocates that are not your OB-GYN or pediatrician.* I'd hear her rant about this to the point where she actually ended up leaving her job at the hospital. I asked her what she was going to do next, and she said, "I'm going to go out on the road and visit a bunch of people in their homes, and I'm going to go back to the basics." So she got an RV, a twenty-five-foot-long Winnebago, and she actually drove around Los Angeles, with the inside outfitted as a really cute doctor's office, to do in-home lactation and postpartum recovery work as an OB-nurse by training. Her company is called My Nursing Coach.

About five years in, she came to me and said, "Have you heard of HIPAA? It's a law that's going to affect all of us. We're going digital, but we have to go securely digital, and actually find better ways to communicate securely. We can't use SMS texting anymore. And we have to use digital charts, but they have to be secure and encrypted. And, I don't know, but I'm freaking out, all of the home health service providers are freaking out about going digital because we're all using paper charts right now." I said, *Mom, this is a tech problem. We can solve this. I'll look online, I'll find you an app, and it will be done, okay?* And I went online to try to find the app, and I couldn't find anything. I found half-baked things, like a piece of something, but not the full solution.

So the earliest days of research and development and product testing were done without a company, during this exploration stage helping my mom while still in graduate school pursuing a JD/MBA. In-between law school and business school exams, sometimes in the same week, I was going home to help solve this digital problem for home health in maternal healthcare. Which brings me to the first piece of advice I give to founders: Don't incorporate too soon. People will say: *When is the right time to incorporate?* When someone has a check with your name on it, and you don't have a bank account to put it into. That's when you need to make a company official.

That's not when I did it. I did it too soon, and I feel, in some ways, that created drag on the company because you want to be able to move quickly, and you need these milestones to occur [in order] to superpower you forward, to accelerate your different points. I was working on this idea of software for providers to connect with patients—based on my mother's own needs in this space, as a provider trying to connect with her postpartum patients. As that developed it got to a point where I thought: *Oh, this could be a thing, and it could be venture backable, and it's software that other people might want to use. My mother not only needed to connect with her patients but to other providers as well. Because we know that maternal healthcare doesn't happen in a vacuum or in a silo, I shouldn't build it inside my mother's company. I should separate it out and make it its own entity. This was really about changing the fabric of this industry. No one actually does this alone, so why don't we hand off patients properly through the ecosystem?*

And though it still really wasn't the right time to incorporate, I did it because I got invited to a pitch competition where you had to have an official company to participate. A lot of them don't do this now, but back in the day—five, six years ago—there was a lot of bad advice out there for founders. Anyway, I did that, and now I have an entity as of 2014, but I didn't even have the name for

> *Don't incorporate too soon. People will say: When is the right time to incorporate? When someone has a check with your name on it, and you don't have a bank account to put it into. That's when you need to make a company official.*

the company yet. We had a corporation called MCH Ventures. We didn't even have the name *Mahmee* yet. We didn't know what to call the company. That came later.

The first version of the product started developing about six months after the company was incorporated. That is another hint that it was too soon. We didn't even have a thing yet. So what did it look like then? It was a WordPress site that I built myself.

> To hold people close to you, find people who can really challenge you to change the way you think.

I added a bunch of plugins to it, so it had interactivity: You could pay for stuff, you could read things, you could watch videos, you could send a message to the site and get help on breastfeeding topics. I built what I envisioned to be the first version of the Mahmee app but using tools that were easy for me to use.

This came about by attending events in Los Angeles. I went to a few different networking events, like monthly founder meetups and co-founder things—*Come meet someone to make a company with! Share ideas!* I went to investor meetups—*Meet investors in LA!* Very few real wins came out of that. I didn't meet a ton of people through these things. Well, I met a lot of people but not a lot of people I ended up working with. Some I worked with in the early days but aren't around anymore. It was hit or miss, basically.

But these events were a great way to get a lot of feedback, very quickly. And I remember two things that happened early on. One event was almost like open mic night, where you could go up in front of the room and pitch your idea. Following my pitch, a guy came up to me.

"I think you've got a great idea."

"Oh, thanks."

"I think there's one mistake, though."

"What is it?"

"Well, you said it could be a million-dollar company, a million-dollar idea."

"Yeah, I did."

"I think it could be a *hundred*-million-dollar idea."

And I said: "*What?*"

He said, "Yeah! Don't sell yourself short. What you described was, like, a big opportunity. There are a lot of moms out there that need help."

And that was the first time someone had spoken to me that way. I give founders advice now: to hold people close to you, find people who can really challenge you to change the way you think. I felt really uncomfortable when the guy said that: *A hundred million dollars? That's crazy. I don't know how I'm going to make this into a hundred-million-dollar company.* But no, based on this market, based on this idea, if you did this right, it would not be worth a million dollars but a hundred million dollars. And then I thought about it: *That's actually very logical. There's no emotion in that; that's just fact. So why am I telling myself my idea is only worth a million dollars?*

Another formative experience happened with a different man and at a different event. Somebody introduced me to him as an investor. So we're talking, and I'm telling him the whole idea.

He said, "So what have you built so far?"

"Oh, I haven't built anything yet."

I told him I had a pitch deck, all these mockups and drawings, but I don't know how to code, so I hadn't built anything yet.

"Well, you should figure out what it would take for you to build the first version. It doesn't have to be fancy; it doesn't have to look good; it doesn't have to have a bunch of features. But until you build something, you're always going to be behind this one big hurdle. What could you do right now to try and make a version of what you're talking about?"

"I don't know. I don't know how to code, but I know how to make WordPress sites."

"Could you make this in WordPress?"

Maybe I could. I hadn't thought about that previously. I was stuck on what I didn't have: *Well, I don't know any developers. I don't have any friends who can code. I don't know how to code. Therefore, I cannot make an app.*

Fast forward to today. There's obviously a lot of different ways to make technology without having a very high level of technical skill. There's a lot of tools you can use out there. [But] back when I started building Mahmee, those tools didn't really exist yet. So WordPress was the most efficient way for me to do this. But it wasn't until someone again challenged my own self-perceived limitation that I actually moved on it: *Well, why haven't you done this yet? Why don't you just try? Go do it using what you know how to build.*

> WordPress was the most efficient way for me to do this. But it wasn't until someone again challenged my own self-perceived limitation that I actually moved on it.: *Well, why haven't you done this yet? Why don't you just try? Go do it using what you know how to build.*

That's when I built the first version of Mahmee. Once I had a version that got the point across, then I could show it to people. *Oh, I get what you're trying to make now. I can see it.* That really started building momentum.

Did you have active users at this point?

Hanna: We had about one hundred users. Not overnight, but we got to that point after a few months. My mom was a customer too. And that was one of the goals that I'd been told early on: See if you could get to one hundred people. I was taking in all of this information, all of this advice people gave me. Some of it made sense, some of it didn't. One hundred people. That seems like a lot, but, okay, let me try.

I entered into a different pitch competition, sort of like an informal accelerator program where you could present to a group of investors and receive some coaching along the way. I made it to the final round of the top three founders. And then I found out about the terms of winning, specifically how much of your company they would take in return for the investment. I did the math on it. *I don't think this is a good deal.*

I called the organizers and told them I was dropping out of the running. *You can give it to one of the other two companies because I don't really think that this is a good deal for my company.* I talked to a lawyer, too, and asked his advice. [The people running the competition] didn't like it. I should mention that I was in law school at the time, but I didn't know enough to be a lawyer—I was just starting law school [*laughs*]—but I knew enough to say:

This doesn't sound perfect. Let me call someone. They were not happy with me dropping out of the running because they really liked our company.

One lady called after, on her own, to follow up with me. "Hey, I heard you dropped out of the running. We really liked your company. We were probably going to pick it."

I [said] I didn't really like the deal and didn't want to give them so much of my company. We just started! [*laughs*] I knew enough to say: "Once the equity is gone, it's gone. I don't really want to take that risk."

She said, "Well, I still want to invest."

"How do you want to do it?"

"Well, why don't you tell me what you think is reasonable? You didn't like the other terms; can you come up with new terms?"

I started doing research and reading books, like Brad Feld's *Venture Deals*, and blog sites of different investors. I learned about convertible notes where you could take on investments as a form of debt that you technically have to pay back. But instead of paying them back, once you have more investment later on, and you know the true value of the company, then you convert the debt to equity. I did a convertible note with this investor, and she wanted to put in $20,000. I was petrified because I had never taken money before. That was the first money in. And, for a while, that was the only money in. For several months. I spoke with that woman, probably every other week, or every few weeks, we would check in, or I'd call her and ask for advice.

Was she an established investor or an entrepreneur herself?

Hanna: She was an angel investor who had gone through a course for women on how to become an investor. She was an active philanthropist otherwise. That's a common theme. A lot of women are philanthropists, and give away their money, while men invest it. She wanted to learn how to invest, so she went through a program called Pipeline Angels, which teaches women how to be investors. That established an early relationship with the Pipeline Angels network, and from there I got connected to more investors who, over time, have invested in the company.

> For the investors, it's about picking the right founder. For the founder, it's about picking the right investor.

But, back in the day, it was just her [that first investor's] money, and she was the only one I would talk to about what was going on with the company. It's not that she had a ton of opinions or strategy or guidance for me. It was more like a sounding board. *I think this is a really important idea, and I want you to have a champion. I want you to have somebody to cheer you on.* That goes back to the same theme of finding people that will be early believers, early champions, without condition. If you have people around you that believe in you, that support you and keep you focused on what you're trying to achieve, then you're going to get there. Or, if you don't get *there*, you're going to get somewhere. And, in that regard, it's really all about relationships.

For the investors, it's about picking the right founder. For the founder, it's about picking the right investor. I had some people early on that really believed in what we were doing, but on condition. *I'm down if you do it THIS way.* And I don't talk to those people anymore because, as things evolved over time, some of the decisions I had to make took us in different directions away from what I originally thought we were going to build. And they weren't down with that. They weren't down for the ride to say, *I'll support you, I believe in you,* when the difficult decisions you have to make as the CEO might change the course of the company over time. They were like: *Oh, you're going to do that over there? I don't care about that.* People come and go over the years. Employees come and go over the years. Advisors come and go, and that's just how it is. I don't think of any one relationship as being permanent to the existence of the company. Of course, I hope that everyone will stay along for the ride. I'm very proud of the earliest people who've been involved in the company, both employees and investors. And I cherish those relationships because they were there when we had nothing. They were there when it was the hardest to build the company. People coming in now get a lot of the good times [*laughs*]. The hard times were had before.

Things evolve, though. The company is not me. It can't be explicitly tied to my personal feelings or my identity. It's on a mission to do something in the world. I'm just accruing the teammates on the ship taking this journey, and some people are going to hop on and hop off at different points. It's up to me to manage those relationships so that people stay along for the ride, but also not take it personally if they leave. I have people that worked with the company really early on—my good friends—that don't work at the company anymore. They've moved on to other things in their own careers. I miss them, but Mahmee wasn't for them in their long-term career path.

Who were some of those early teammates who helped get Mahmee moving? And what did it feel like once things really took off, what you call the money-in-the-bank day?

Hanna: The mistakes that I made early on correspond with another point of advice for founders: Work with people who are going to directly impact the task at hand. Once you start thinking about an idea and building out a company, if you're doing your job right as a founder, you're going to be thinking three steps ahead. You're going to think about what you have to do today, what you have to do tomorrow, and what's going to happen way beyond today and tomorrow. That's the third step ahead, but it's murky and undefined. Oh, one day we might have to deal with this issue.

The mistake founders make is trying to solve that issue out there in the future. You don't have enough information to solve that problem yet! You've got to solve what's happening today and what's going to be happening tomorrow—the tasks at hand. As you're finding co-founders and early team members and employees—folks to work with you—every single person who joins must be able to contribute to the task at hand. It is not helpful in the early days

The mistake founders make is trying to solve that issue out there in the future. You don't have enough information to solve that problem yet! You've got to solve what's happening today and what's going to be happening tomorrow—the tasks at hand.

of the company—even as you're growing, once you have some venture capital money—to have people who are trying to solve that third step out in the future. All it's going to do is stress you out when you need to figure out how to make money now to pay people tomorrow, or when you need to make your customer happy, so they stay with you and continue using your product or service. It can also cause a lot of internal confusion when some of the team is planning for the future and others are worried and need support in doing something *today*. You want to have a very tightly focused team that is working on the tasks at hand as they evolve. As today and tomorrow occur. They need to be focused on building a product that solves those immediate needs. The team members who had the most difficult time working in the company were working on things unrelated to the task at hand. So they started getting bored too. *I'm trying to work on this feature, I'm trying to work on this strategy, or on this marketing campaign that is so far in the future that I don't even know if it's ever going to happen.* That can be demoralizing for people.

It's most exciting for your co-founders and your early team members to be working with you directly on the stuff that's going to bear fruit early on. It creates a feedback cycle of momentum. *Oh, we did that! Cool, we shipped that feature. We shipped that product. We sold that customer.* That's the long answer to the question: Who do you need early on, who are those early people? The people that

> *It's most exciting for your co-founders and your early team members to be working with you directly on the stuff that's going to bear fruit early on. It creates a feedback cycle of momentum.*

were most valuable, it didn't matter what they did—marketing, sales, pricing, financial modeling—they were the ones who could do the thing I needed help doing. There were points where, just for a few weeks or a few months, I had someone who would work with me on marketing. Why? I was working on a marketing campaign. After that, sometimes those people would bounce because they weren't as useful around here anymore. *Okay, that's fine. I'll call you again when I need some more help with marketing.* Or someone who is good at sales and pricing or financial modeling. *Okay, let's do that together right now because I need to figure out pricing for this product.* But if we have no customers, and no one is asking me for the price of the product, why do I need to work with someone right now to try to figure out the pricing, when it's going to change as soon as someone else comes along who doesn't want to pay that price? So, you really want to take in information actively. *What problems do we need to solve today, and who can help me do that?* In an early-stage business, you should expect [that] there's going to be a lot of flux in who's working with you at any given point in time.

And, as far as the money-in-the-bank moment?

Hanna: Advice that I also give to founders that I haven't always taken myself—so at the risk of sounding hypocritical—is to celebrate wins of whatever size as they occur. It's not just the money-in-the-bank day. It may be the day that a customer agrees to do a free pilot. There may be no money coming in the bank that day, but you have a customer now that really believes in what you're doing and wants to try it out for themselves. It may be the day that a new team member joins. It's important to celebrate the wins that signal things are moving forward. However those happen.

However, money-in-the-bank day is its own very special day that makes it very real that you can now start tackling some of the challenges that you might have been blocked on without having the financial resources to achieve those things. If you're doing it right, it's a thrill every time. And what I mean by that is, the first time that we got $20,000 was very exciting.

It's important to celebrate the wins that signal things are moving forward. However those happen.

After we got that, the next check that came in was another $20,000 check. *Two people giving us a $20,000 check?* The next time was an $80,000 check. *What? That's so crazy.* And then a $100,000 check came.

You always want to be pushing that boundary and not settle for the same thing over and over again in relation to investors or customers. After you've achieved a certain milestone, consider: *What can we do now to show that that amount of funding produced this kind of result? What will help enable us to produce an even greater result next time?* You want to demonstrate exponential growth over time to yourself, to your team, and to your investors.

I'm not saying to never settle. Rather, it's about having an internal compass that makes you naturally competitive with your own record of progress. We've done that at Mahmee. Every time we have a money-in-the-bank moment when we raise, it's not always about more money. Sometimes it's about the way the money happened. I recently had a money-in-the-bank moment where we received funding after I spoke with an investor about our strategy.

The investor was really excited and said, "Can I give you guys $500,000 for the company? When can I put some money in?"

Wait, I didn't even ask you. I didn't even say we needed money, and this person just offered $500,000? No one had ever just offered that kind of money to me before. We've since raised millions of dollars, but it was a new moment for that money to come without even asking for it. Just because of the way I spoke about my vision for the business, the way I spoke about my team, about what we had coming up next through our strategy, it resonated with this investor, and it was one of the proudest moments I've had recently. For me, that also signaled I had turned a corner in my ability to pitch the business and talk about it in a way that people would say: *Where do I sign up? How do I get involved?*

Another moment was the *all-in* moment. Following my stepfather's death from lung cancer, it became clear to me that my mother needed support in running operations for her maternal healthcare business. My stepfather was gone very quickly and we were very close, so his loss impacted all of us. But my mother had lost her life partner and her business partner. He was the backbone of her business, her co-founder, and they were seeing thousands of patients across Los Angeles using the Mahmee software—along with other people who were using the Mahmee software.

I was in the middle of the 500 Startups program in Menlo Park, and got the call of his passing. I was lucky to be able to get back and be there. It was a tough day. It was a Saturday morning, and I said to my mom: *What should I do? How can I be here for you?* She wanted me to go back to Menlo Park—I had my big break, and it was happening. I didn't want to leave that Monday, but I did. But it soon became apparent that she needed my help—with payroll, with maintenance, with other things that my stepfather typically did.

It became apparent pretty quickly that I wasn't going to be able to live out my dream of building this software platform that powers companies like my parents' if my parents, and, at this point my mother, couldn't keep the business open. I went to our investors, who were pretty new—some of them had only just written a check days before my stepdad had passed—and I said: *We have a really big problem. The only way that I'm able to build this company is [due to] the privilege of having a family that is supporting me.* Sidenote: The one thing that ties all high-growth, venture-backed founders together is privilege, the ability to do it. It takes a lot. And privilege shows up in different ways. For me, it was an incredibly supportive family that was willing to let me move back home to build a company. That was willing to support me going back to Menlo Park for 500 Startups in the middle of my family grieving my stepfather's death. And yet, I was about to lose all of that privilege. Because if my family business went under, then my startup was about to go under.

Sidenote: The one thing that ties all high-growth, venture-backed founders together is privilege, the ability to do it. It takes a lot. And privilege shows up in different ways.

I said to the investors: *How much do you believe in the vision for Mahmee?* They said, "We're all in." It gives me chills to this day because to hear someone say, *We are all in, I am all in, I believe in you, and I believe in the problem that you are committed to solving,* is so powerful, and it's something I come back to quite often when days are rough. And days are rough all the time. The frequency doesn't change, the problem changes. But having people say, *We are all in, we believe in you,* is so powerful. It's also sometimes the prelude to bad news, as it was in this case. *If you really believe in me, you need to believe in what I'm about to tell you I have to do next. I have to buy my mother's company, and I have to merge it into our company. And I know you all said you wanted to invest in and build a tech company, and just be pure tech and pure SaaS [Software as a Service]. But this is a services business, and I know that doesn't sound sexy or exciting, but if we do not do this, your investment is gone anyway. The only chance that we have at this point is to support my mother and to support the team that she's built and the ecosystem that she's built around her business. Which is truly what's powering the potential for our business now.* Thankfully, they supported me, and we were able to make that happen.

> I said to the investors: How much do you believe in the vision for Mahmee? They said, "We're all in." It gives me chills to this day because to hear someone say, "We are all in, I am all in, I believe in you, and I believe in the problem that you are committed to solving," is so powerful, and it's something I come back to quite often when days are rough.

At the time, it was a painful and almost shameful decision to make. It felt like epic failure that this was happening to me, and I was out of control. There was no way to be sure it would pay off, but I knew that the opposite, the other choice, was not going to work. So now, I was splitting my time between running a software business and whatever is needed to support that—finding the

I was doing everything that needed to be done on that small family business to keep that going, while also trying to build what had to be pitched at that time as a billion-dollar opportunity. It felt like such a cognitive dissonance.

rest of our tech team and working with our CTO to really build that product out—and working with my mom on a daily basis just to make sure that her staff was covered, trucks were working, patients were being seen, calendaring, answering phones, etc. I was doing everything that needed to be done on that small family business to keep that going, while also trying to build what had to be pitched at that time as a billion-dollar opportunity. It felt like such a cognitive dissonance.

That's the tension that founders feel. It's very real and it looks different for everyone, but it feels the same inside: *Am I even doing the right thing anymore? Is this even a viable path to building the company I originally told people I was going to build?* That's where that shame comes in: *Well maybe it's not, and how horribly embarrassing [it] will be to go back and say that we ended up with something else. We took an off-ramp. I thought we were going the right way, and we ended up with this now.*

Where did you go from here, and how did you regain your confidence or shed the shame?

Hanna: About one and a half years later, we got into a program that was focused on healthcare companies, and I went to go pitch a bunch of insurance companies, health systems, and hospitals to become our customers. At this point, we had software in the market. We were making money, we were providing and powering services through the platform, but I really knew that this was not going to work until it got into the healthcare enterprise, until we were able to pitch it and get it to the biggest players so that everyone would be able to access it—all of the providers and the patients within that network. That was always the end goal.

We finally got to a place where we could get into those rooms, and it took one and a half years of us trying, for anyone to take my call and let me into a room of C-Suite executives. When we got in, I was feeling so ashamed, and I didn't want to tell people what was really powering the business and making most of the money, which was the services side. Services make a lot of money versus software when it's in its earliest stages. And no one likes to really talk about that. I didn't know how common it was for software companies to be supported by services in their early days, so I felt somewhat ashamed at the time. But I went in, and I spoke with the C-Suite of some of the biggest names in the US healthcare system, and said:
We've got software that, if connected **The road rises up to meet you.** *to your industry it would be a game changer. It can do this and this and this: messaging, video calls, support groups, and all these features. All you have to do is write the Mahmee platform into your electronic health records system, and your tool is set.* I got a lot of excitement as the first comment. And then the "but" came. The "but" was: "That sounds great. We love the idea of software, but we don't have enough people here to power this program. We don't have the staff to take care of every mom in the building, that's why we don't."

That was the behind-closed-doors conversation, one of operational capacity to actually power the platform. What came out of this was a request for a services business! The road rises up to meet you. Luckily, I had just bought a services business eighteen months prior, and knew how to run it better than anyone. I had figured out all the kinks and flaws in what makes it challenging to run a network of lactation consultants around the worst city to drive in [in] the US [*laughs*]. Lucky that I ended up being *that* person. When I later got in the room with Serena Williams and all the other people that invested in later rounds, I was able to say, *I know what the market needs. I thought I knew what the market needed, but then I went out there and validated it, and here's what the market really needs. And lucky for you, you're sitting across from the person who can actually do it.* And that's what got the cash in.

Tell me about your pitching process. How have you navigated the vulnerability that comes with being so transparent, or being told no?

Hanna: At this point I've done somewhere between 250 and 275 pitches to investors. I've done many, many more pitches beyond that because I also still participate in pitch competitions and accelerator programs and special events where I get invited to tell people about the company. You will be pitching for your entire life as the founder of a company. Every day someone will ask you: Oh, tell me about what you do. Tell me about what your business does. And so you will pitch it.

But as far as investor meetings, the bulk of those happened between the beginning of the company in 2014 and the $3 million seed fundraise that we did in June of 2019. Between 2014 and 2019, I pitched about two hundred investors. Then, between 2019 and [the end of 2020], I pitched about fifty or seventy-five investors, so you

That journey between what you know to be true about your business idea and the way to say it that makes it immediately understandable and accessible to everyone else around you, to tell it to a five-year-old, is something that takes years to truly master.

can see the acceleration. Basically, it's been a few dozen people that I've pitched just in the past year. The reason why is because people know about the company now, and I don't have to go out and source new investors; they come to me, and I decide: *Do I want to pitch them?*

That's a really big tide change for the company. And sometimes I [think]: *You know what? I don't want to pitch you. I don't think I want your money. I don't think you understand what we're doing around here. Or maybe you do, but I don't think that you're going to be the most value-add investor for us.* So there are times where I refuse to pitch people now, which is insane because, for the first five years of the company, I would just pitch whoever would let me pitch them.

The journey of building a pitch is a very painful process. A lot of what you might think is valuable about your business idea is tested: *Why does this business idea matter? What's it really getting at? What's the real problem it's trying to solve?* Or *What's the need in the market?* You might know that, but that doesn't mean that you know how to explain it to someone else in a way that gets them to say: *Where do I sign up?* That journey between what you know to be true about your business idea and the way to say it that makes it immediately understandable and accessible to everyone else around you, to tell it to a five-year-old, is something that takes years to truly master.

I'm still on that journey. The more complex the problem is that you're trying to solve, the longer it's going to take to get there. The [simpler] your problem is, the faster you're going to get there. And an inevitable part of the founder's journey is developing a great pitch of what they're trying to do in the world. The tips for that? Be prepared to create many, many pitch decks. You will constantly be iterating on your pitch deck. You will iterate on your pitch deck even between investor meetings. I'd have meetings in the morning, then I'd work through my lunch break to change a few words, a slide or picture before pitching to someone else that afternoon. I was always making changes to find different ways to better communicate my point, to help it resonate more.

You should practice it with your friends and family. You should make everyone sit in the living room with you—or, now, during COVID, do it on Zoom. Have people just sit back, pretend they don't know what you're trying to do, just listen, and then tell you if it makes sense. You're going to have to run that show many times over with people till they're bored and don't want to help you anymore because they've heard [it] so many times [*laughs*].

It's important to not take it personally when people don't get the pitch or don't like the pitch. But also, don't take all the feedback. There is no way that everyone's opinion is correct. There is no way. You're the one with the idea. You must know something about this. Not everyone has a better opinion than you do about your business. There will be some people who do have a better opinion of how to solve the problem, or a better idea of how to make your pitch. Part of the journey is figuring out what advice to take and what feedback is helpful.

But if you know from the beginning that not everyone is correct, that's a big step and gives you an advantage over earlier-stage founders without a lot of experience Every investor I talked to, I thought they were right. If they said: *Oh, you should change this, you should do that,* I would do all the changes they recommended.

It got to a point where I was confused about what I was trying to say to people. *This doesn't even seem like my original business idea. What happened?* I realized I took all the advice that I was given instead of being discerning. I went back and thought: *Did that person really know what they were talking about? Did that person really understand what I'm trying to do in the world? Does that person really care about this issue?*

As I started to scrutinize all the feedback I had received, I was able to sort and filter what had been shared with me. Then I went back to my pitch deck and recreated it to reflect the advice that I felt was good advice, without taking away from my original idea of what I wanted to build.

After all, this was my problem to solve.

FREDERICK HUTSON

Co-Founder and CEO, Pigeonly

Pigeonly provides a simple, affordable way to stay in touch with your inmate from any phone, tablet or computer. With subscribers in over eighty-eight countries, Pigeonly has become the largest independent provider of inmate services.

Frederick Hutson is the CEO and co-founder of Pigeonly, a platform that makes it easy for people to search for, find, and communicate with an incarcerated loved one. A born entrepreneur, Hutson launched and sold his first business at the age of nineteen, while on active duty in the Air Force. He soon left the military (with an honorable discharge) to launch his second business, which he also sold for a profit.

Though his entrepreneurial spirit often led him to new opportunities, his desire to attain the American dream on his terms took him down the wrong path and, at twenty-three, he was sent to federal prison for the illegal distribution of three thousand kilos of marijuana. It was this life-changing experience that motivated him to build a solution that would positively affect the lives of people no one else was paying attention to: inmates and their families. The idea of Pigeonly was born.

Although the company is still young, Pigeonly has become one of the largest independent inmate services providers in the country. With users in eighty-eight countries, Pigeonly saves families over $2 million dollars per year in communication costs. Hutson leads a growing team from Pigeonly's Las Vegas headquarters, and has raised over $10 million in funding from notable investors, including Erik Moore (Base Ventures) and Mitch Kapor (Kapor Capital).

Twitter: @IamFastFreddy

Website: https://frederickhutson.com/ | https://pigeonly.com/

What experiences helped shape how you think about business or entrepreneurship?

Frederick Hutson: I was born in Brooklyn, New York, but raised in St. Petersburg, Florida. And all through middle school and high school, I was always looking for different ways to make money—

yard services or window cleaning or any job I could find—to buy shoes or CDs or whatever the case may be. My parents divorced before I was born, and I was raised by a single mother, so I was exposed to seeing her always making ends meet, taking care of my four siblings and me. It was something that always stuck with me from a very early age. She was always doing entrepreneurial things—catering jobs, cooking and baking, or working as a seamstress—to take care of us. I saw that early on, so [entrepreneurship] was normal to see.

Fast forward to when I got to high school. There were only two images of success that I was exposed to growing up: one was my uncle, who was in the Air Force, and the other was my older cousin, who was selling drugs. With that in mind I decided to go to the Air Force because I had no big desire to go to college. Seeing the level of success my uncle reached, from my perspective, it was a good option. And I was always good at troubleshooting and solving problems, so I thought the Air Force would be a better fit.

You weren't new to the business of entrepreneurship when you launched Pigeonly. What were your first steps as an entrepreneur?

Hutson: So, my first business was a window tinting business, which I started at [age] nineteen, and sold for $150K within only six to eight months of growing the company. Then I took the funds from that business and bought a cell phone activation store that was already in operation. I bought it and took it over, but it didn't work out well, so I ended up just getting my money out of it. During that time, though, I also bought the shipping store, and would eventually run a marijuana operation through it.

Once [when I was in], in the Air Force, I ended up being an electrician on an F-16 aircraft. From there I ended up at my first duty station in Las Vegas. I think this experience really taught me how to work with other people. Being in the military required me to work with people from all over the country, from all different backgrounds. And they become your colleagues; their job depends on you, on your discipline.

Shortly after being stationed in Las Vegas, I bumped into close family, friends, and relatives who were also part of that drug culture, and they were moving weed from Nevada to different places in Florida, like St. Pete, Tampa, Miami, etc. To make a long story short, I saw the logistical challenges they were having in getting things from one point to another, particularly as volume increased. My natural tendency is to always look for a solution to a problem, so I came up with a solution to move a lot of marijuana from Mexico to Tucson, Arizona; from Arizona to Vegas; and from Vegas to multiple cities throughout Florida. By that point, I already had an honorable discharge

Once I went through sentencing, landing five years, I was exposed to the prison environment for the first time. You start seeing the inefficiencies and other problems when it comes to communication. You could see that there could be a much better way to stay in touch with your support network of friends and family on the outside, but no one had ever really built anything that would work well for this specific demographic.

from the military, and it was full swing, moving marijuana from Mexico to Florida. It got so efficient, and the volume so large, that it ended up catching the federal government's attention, and I was indicted when I was twenty-three.

Once I went through sentencing, landing five years, I was exposed to the prison environment for the first time. You start seeing the inefficiencies and other problems when it comes to communication. You could see that there could be a much better way to stay in touch with your support network of friends and family on the outside, but no one had ever really built anything that would work well for this specific demographic.

This was right around the time when the iPhone and [Apple] App Store were getting popular. I just thought to myself: *Why, why, why not build something so we can make it easy? If someone wants to send photos, they can just grab the photos from their phone, click a couple of buttons, and then have the photos printed.* That was really the genesis of the idea. And then, from there, once I was released, I got with my co-founder, Alfonzo Brooks, who I [knew] from the Air Force.

At that point, our only ambition was to make a platform and process that would allow people to upload and send photos. That was as far as we were trying to take it. We didn't envision achieving what we have now, but that was the starting point.

How did you meet your co-founder in the Air Force? Was it a natural fit?

Hutson: It was a very natural fit. We were both from similar areas in Florida and had become friends in the Air Force. Then, while I was in prison, he had tried his hand at a couple of entrepreneurial things: cleaning franchises and tax franchises. I would talk to him about future plans, about what I wanted to do when I got out. So he was somebody that I was in pretty regular communication with.

Once I got started, I went to him: *Hey, why don't we do this together?* He was at the point where he was looking for his next move, and I was definitely looking at what my next step was going to be. We felt that even though we were both not technical, we had skill sets that complemented each other. So it was a very natural thing in the beginning.

The next challenge was that we had to get tech help because, at the end of the day, we were building a technology company. I did research and posted a job listing on Freelancer.com for someone to help me build. We had a few responses come in, and I selected one person. And that was the beginning of our tech build.

How did you go about finding tech support as a non-technical founder? Was it difficult to translate your vision?

Hutson: I didn't go out and look for someone technical to build it, actually. What I looked for was someone who was technical enough. I wanted someone who could communicate and convert my vision into technical specs that could be handed to any developer. A lot of times, people look for the person to build the thing. I took a different approach and, because I wasn't technical myself, I was concerned that if I went to someone technical to build it, I assumed (and I think it was a pretty safe assumption) there was going to be a lot that would be lost in translation simply due to me not being technical or me not understanding how things come to be, as far as building a tech product. Which, when you're outsourcing it, you're paying by the hour. So bad [communication] or miscommunication, unclear expectations, and things like that can add up very quickly. What I looked for with that first freelance hire was "looking for someone to do functional and technical specs." And when I selected the person I went with, I was looking for someone I could speak plain, non-technical language to, and then that person could massage what I'm saying into something I could hand to any developer (that is, a decent developer) who could then follow those specs. Then I'd end up with what I expected.

Where'd you go from there?

Hutson: At that time, I didn't know what I didn't know, so I was just going bit by bit, learning as I went. It actually started very simply as talking and sharing my ideas, and what I wanted to do, with as many people as possible. A big mistake people make is that they're afraid to talk and share their ideas with people in the early days. They may fear that their idea is not good enough, or that someone might steal it, or whatever the case may be. But that process of talking about what you're building, and talking about what you're working on, allows you to potentially get that co-founder, get that technical talent, or someone who wants to join your team because they believe in what you're solving, and they want to be a part of the solution that you're building. That's how it worked out for me. That's how we got our first developer; that's how we got our UX [User Experience] designer, who did all the design workflows. It was all about talking and sharing that this was what we were working on. And the people that it resonated with wanted to be a part of it. And they wanted to be a part of it with their sweat equity versus payment. And that's how we built up our very early team.

What was the general reception of investors? What was it like to define and communicate the reasons you built this solution?

Hutson: In the early days, I struggled with how much of my personal story should be involved in my presentation and my pitch. What I had to come to terms with is that anyone who wasn't willing to invest in me knowing my story, or knowing my background, or knowing how I came upon this idea, or why I was addressing this problem, is probably somebody that I don't want to do business with anyway. And it wasn't a matter of seeing how far I could get without my story being front and center; it was really about leveraging my story—front and center—as my credibility, why I was the right person to solve that problem.

So once I got comfortable with that, it really, really shifted the dynamics in a lot of investor meetings, where, as much as they were trying to evaluate us as a potential investment, I was trying to evaluate them as a suitable investor. I was trying to rule out people as quickly as I could because fundraising is a very time-consuming process, and the longer an entrepreneur is fundraising, the less time they're spending on actually building a business, and you start losing momentum. So I was trying to get through that fundraising process as quickly as I possibly could, and the fastest way is by ruling out investors that, for better or worse, are going to waste your time. They may not *feel* like

What I had to come to terms with is that anyone who wasn't willing to invest in me knowing my story, or knowing my background, or knowing how I came upon this idea, or why I was addressing this problem, is probably somebody that I don't want to do business with anyway.

they're wasting your time, but you'll have someone from a firm whose job is only to reach out and take meetings with founders, to fish around and see what they're building, so they see what's out there and get a first move on it. You may *think* that it's real interest, but at the end of the day, it's on you to determine if this is really interest or a fishing expedition that's not going to turn into anything tangible. You can take meetings all day long, but you won't really be building your business, and it won't necessarily result in you raising funding.

Once I got past that part, I was pitching something that investors in Silicon Valley hadn't heard of or been exposed to. Even though they've heard just about every pitch about every business under the sun, this was something that was new to them. And before I could get into my solution, I had to spend a lot of time educating them [about] why this is a problem. *Inmates don't have access to the Internet; they don't have access to cell phones. A phone call can cost as much as fifteen dollars for fifteen minutes, and here's why our solution makes sense.* I had to take that time to educate across all of those variables because, before I can tell you that we make phones cheaper, that's not as compelling as if I can show you that: *Hey, no one should be paying one dollar a minute for a phone call, not when phone calls legitimately cost fractions of a penny.*

> Just because you can't relate to it doesn't mean it's not a problem large enough, or it's not a problem that can't be a big, impactful business if successfully solved.

So when you're able to articulate that, *then* the solution is that much more impactful, and [it] resonates because they understand the whole problem, even though they may not have personally related to it. I think that was the biggest thing; a lot of investors that I talked to early on did not personally relate to it. They didn't know anyone personally that had been in the prison system. But just because you can't relate to it doesn't mean it's not a problem large enough, or it's not a problem that can't be a big, impactful business if successfully solved.

Of those first investors, who stands out as a mentor and source of support during your seed raise?

Hutson: One of our early investors was Erik Moore from Base Ventures, and he was a huge, huge help in more ways than one. He provided that early support that really made a difference because investors tend to follow the crowd, and once you have one investor who says: I like this; this makes sense. I'm going to put my money here, at the bare minimum, other investors are going to pay attention. That doesn't mean they're automatically going to write you a check as well, but they're going to pay attention when their colleague is investing. With Erik being a first mover, that perked up the ears of other people. Then we also had Mitch Kapor, which perked up more people, which was really helpful in our first round.

Additionally, during that time, being able to get feedback—candid feedback—from someone willing to invest in you as an individual can [help] you improve your presentation and work on the right business metrics. Getting candid feedback without fear of losing your investment or losing the opportunity to work together was invaluable. That's the kind of support that we got super early on from Erik.

How much did you raise during your seed round? What did you do with it?

Hutson: Our seed round was $1 million. That was across six investors. And to give a sense of the amount of pitching you're doing, I probably pitched maybe sixty to seventy people to narrow it down to the six people who said yes and cut the check. Up until that point, everything had been bootstrapped. We were outsourcing technology development and didn't really have an in-house team. For a lot of things, it was just my co-founder and me juggling a lot of what needed to happen. And once you close that round, you're like: Oh wow, I can actually hire people now! And we can build a team. That's where the bulk of expenses were in the beginning.

When you go so many months or years always being resource-constrained, the first thing you want to do is to fill every seat in the office because you think, if you throw as many people at it as you possibly can, that's going to equal speed. But it doesn't necessarily mean that you're going to move that much faster. And I also quickly learned through that first round that, as large as a million dollars sounds, it goes *extremely* fast when you have a headcount of thirty-plus people.

What I found was that we were more impactful and more successful as a team when we had a very highly focused and highly skilled small team, versus a big team that might've had more mediocre people. So that's one of the early lessons that we learned is just making sure, when we were building a team, that we were really focused on getting the best talent, and not necessarily thinking that if you throw ten people at something—versus five—that'll allow you to do it twice as fast. It doesn't always equate that way.

How did you source and connect with the team members referenced?

Hutson: We had one thing that worked well for us. We had a lot of press and media coverage in our early days. And what was interesting is that we never paid for press or sought it. It was just one of those things where it was always very organic, and we would get a lot of inbound. So once our story got out, the problem we were solving resonated with people. I was surprised at how much the story resonated, and we would get a lot of people that wanted to work with us as a result. So, when hiring, we would filter through inbound, use technical recruiters for the engineering side, and we also asked within our network. And the thing about hiring is that, with powering through your network, a lot of times—at least during that time—you'll probably have less luck. When someone has a good engineer, they're not necessarily going to pass that on because a strong engineer is hard to find, unless the company is winding down, and the CEO is trying to help his talent have a soft landing. That's one thing. But, at the time,

"[Getting people to work for you] came from telling a story about who you are, what you're doing, why it is impactful and why people should care. That's what resonated. People wanted to do something they felt good about."

there weren't a lot of companies being wound down, and there was a lot of money flowing. Many companies were getting funded, so it was very competitive to get talent. So the way you would get talent is when people wanted to be a part of your mission and wanted to work for you. So it came from telling that story about who you are, and what you're doing, why it is impactful, and why people should care. That's what resonated. People wanted to do something they felt good about. That was a big part of it.

Then the recruiting services [are] pretty straightforward. In the early days, it was driven by talking about our mission and seeing the people who wanted to be a part of our solution. That said, I also noticed we had a lot of folks who would talk just good enough to get in the door but were not able to deliver, and ultimately were not a good fit, either from a tech perspective of actually going to do whatever the job was, or from being a culture fit. What I learned through that time is that it's expensive to hire somebody, and it gets more expensive when you have somebody on the team that is not a good fit, and you're slow about letting them go. I learned to take my time with hiring, and as soon as you realize that someone is not a good fit, cut your losses as quickly as you possibly can.

In what ways did your vision expand as your resources, team, and advisor network began to grow?

Hutson: When we started, we had one simple thing: uploading photos to an incarcerated loved one. Today, we have seven consumer-facing products that fit into three categories. The first category is our phone product that allows people to save money on expensive prison phone calls. The second is our financial services product that allows people an easy path to put money on an inmate's commissary book or phone account. And then, finally, our postal mail services, which is similar to where we started. That allows folks to send printed greeting cards, photos, letters, postcards, etc., directly from any cell phone, tablet, or computer to their incarcerated loved one.

Over the past eighteen months, the postal mail services category has led to the development of technology that helps institutions prevent contraband from coming into the mail, particularly synthetic drugs, whether opioids, suboxone strips [used to treat opioid addiction], K2 [synthetic marijuana], or any type of synthetic drug. We didn't intend to address this, but we realized that institutions were having a very difficult time preventing contraband because synthetic drugs can be infused into paper and ink [used in sent letters]. And there isn't a reliable way to detect which letter is laced, and which isn't, from one [to another]. There was also no way to authenticate where mail was coming from—like telling the difference between mail that's coming from the Pigeonly secure facility or mail that's coming from somewhere else—so we don't know whether or not its contraband. As a result, staff screening mail coming into the facility [were] getting sick from getting exposed to foreign substances, and they didn't know what they were exposed to. It would take weeks for the labs to come back with results. On top of that, the increased drug use within the facility was leading to overdoses, deaths, and violence-related incidents.

With everything we do, we always ask the question: Does this fall in line with our mission? At the core of our mission is making sure that family members and loved ones can stay in touch with their loved ones on the inside, and making sure people on the inside can stay in touch with their loved ones on the outside.

So we've expanded our offering to offer software that allows us to determine the difference between something that is contraband-free versus something that isn't. And that fits squarely with our overall starting mission. With everything we do, we always ask the question: *Does this fall in line with our mission?* At the core of our mission is making sure that family members and loved ones can stay in touch with their loved ones on the inside, and making sure people on the inside can stay in touch with their loved ones on the outside.

And that's important because, when it comes to successful reentry, when it comes to recidivism, communication and education are the two most important factors that impact an inmate's ability to reintegrate successfully with the outside world. The more institutions are struggling with contraband, the more restrictive they get on communication. Now, the only way they can communicate might be through more expensive, predatory means. So for us to keep communication open and accessible, we had to create a solution that allows mom to still handwrite or type a letter and be able to send it at the cost of a postage stamp and nothing more if that's what she wants to do.

So these developments fell squarely in line with our mission, and they took us down a whole new path of building a B2G [Business to Government] company when our entire business up to then was building a B2C [Business to Consumer] company. That involved working in Washington, DC, and spending a lot of time between different congressional members' offices to build support, even to the point of securing co-sponsors, and eventually introducing legislation. It's been a very intense process that has taught me a lot about the process of selling to the government, and the strategy involved, and how much that differs from selling primarily to consumers.

How has it been navigating this shift in landscape—from business to government? First, as a founder raising within an industry accustomed to pattern matching, where investors evaluate opportunities based on prior experience, and then as your model pivoted to a new customer segment?

Hutson: I think I had the perspective of changing the dynamic. When I first started fundraising, it almost felt like I was asking for money, and that was never comfortable for me. When I realized what was happening, that it's not me asking for money, but rather me giving an investor the opportunity to be a part of something that I'm building, something that is going to make an impact, it changed the dynamic a lot for me. It made my ability to present the opportunity a lot stronger because it shifted from: Are you going to write me a check, or are [you] not going to write me a check? Am I good enough? Do you like me enough? to Here's what I'm doing; here's where I'm going with or without you. This is how you can be a part of it. Here's what's going to be in it for you, and here's the impact we're going to make if you're a part of it. It just changed the dynamics a great deal.

> When I first started fundraising, it almost felt like I was asking for money, and that was never comfortable for me. When I realized what was happening, that it's not me asking for money, but rather me giving an investor the opportunity to be a part of something that I'm building, something that is going to make an impact, it changed the dynamic a lot for me.

That was helpful for me to navigate going into rooms where I was the only Black person, talking to folks. I'm not typically what they would invest in, nor am I in their comfort zone of the patterns that they tend to follow when investing, so it helped me navigate that. And there were plenty of times when someone would say: *You know, I just can't wrap my head around investing in someone who's been in prison*, and that's fine. It was just about getting to *that* as fast as possible, so I didn't spend one minute of extra time on someone who couldn't get past that mental block. I tried to evaluate the person I was talking to as quickly as I could, to get down to: *Okay, is this going to be a waste of time or a fruitful interaction?*

While fruitful interactions don't always lead to a check, sometimes they will lead to another introduction. I got into the habit of, when people say no, I'll ask why they turned it down. Sometimes the feedback is bullshit, but a lot of times they'll give valuable feedback on why they can't invest: maybe the traction or growth rate is not strong enough, or the market size is not big enough, etc. But all those little tidbits of information allow you to go back and make tweaks and adjustments to your plan so that the next time you present, it's going to be that much stronger. So there's a lot to learn from the nos just as much as you get benefits from the yesses.

What constructive feedback did you receive during this time? Was there any advice that you were reluctant to take?

Hutson: Some of the professional feedback in the early days was about focusing on my target market. [Back then], we were thinking that, yeah, inmates need access to photos, but so do military people deployed in remote locations. All that might be true, but it's so much better to be focused on a single demographic, a single problem, then leverage our domain expertise and try to be the best at that. Feedback early on helped us focus so that we could try to do that one thing very, very, very well.

Another thing was understanding the market and the market size. That was something that I struggled with in the beginning because, when I thought of the market, I was thinking of the inmate population. But then, after getting feedback, and going through this with multiple investors, I actually realized that the market size is the multiplier of the people who are *connecting* to an inmate. So you may have ten inmates, but if there were two people connected to each one of them, then your market side is actually twenty versus ten. So that was helpful [in] learning how to articulate what the true market size was to have a clear picture of what our market looks like: it's the friends and families, the five to seven people that each inmate knows. So we're talking about twenty to thirty million people. It took time to go through that pitch with so many people, to finally get to the point where you can clearly articulate all those nuanced points that make a big difference in someone's ability to weigh the opportunity.

As far as advice I was reluctant to take, but then ultimately did, I think that was probably learning that it's okay to release a product that's not perfect because it allows you to get feedback, then iterate and make adjustments a lot faster than [if you're] spending all your time—and all your engineer's time—building something in a vacuum before the market even gets a chance to tell you whether they like it or not.

Things don't have to be perfect. Product doesn't have to be perfect. And it's better to get feedback from your customer base sooner than later.

In the beginning, I always wanted everything to be exactly right, exactly how I saw it in my head, super polished and perfect, but it slowed our growth. My desire to push out a perfect product became the bottleneck, which severely impacted our ability to gain traction, keep traction, and generate revenue and profits. Things don't have to be perfect. Product doesn't have to be perfect. And it's better to get feedback from your customer base sooner than later.

The failure part is important because there are so few opportunities for us to take risks and land—maybe not where we intended but with progress towards our vision, nonetheless. When have you failed, and what did you learn from that experience?

Hutson: We don't have enough time [*chuckles*]. There's plenty, but I think first, trying to build the product in a vacuum, and second, trying to be all things to all people. Those are, like, two extremes, but we were trying to do both of those at the same time, as crazy as it is.

Like I mentioned before, when you build something in a vacuum, you're not getting valuable feedback from people telling you exactly what they want, or how much they're willing to pay, [and other] key pieces of information you can only get from the market you're starving yourself from. And when you're trying to be all things to all people, you have a product that's too big or too complex and complicated because you're trying to make all different segments of the market happy before you've figured out how to make even one core segment happy. That's another extreme on the opposite end of the spectrum that's equally deadly. We burned through a lot of money and burned through a lot of time [doing both things at once].

Also, when you have six or seven engineers constantly building, building, building, and never releasing, and what's built is edited and changed because you want to add another feature while trying to be all things to all people, that never-ending cycle will burn your team out and will definitely lower the morale. Just like anybody else, your technical team needs to be able to see what they've created out in the wild, being used in the way [they] intended. Changing [it] before it even sees the light of day, every time an idea pops into your head— *Oh, this would be nice! Oh, yeah, we should add this too!*—keeps you stuck in product mode, and you're not transitioning into a business.

I learned there's a key distinction between those two things. You can have a product, and you can have a business. They're definitely not the same, and that was the problem I had from the leadership perspective. I was stuck in product mode and not in building-a-business mode with the product.

I learned there's a key distinction between those two things. You can have a product, and you can have a business. They're definitely not the same, and that was the problem I had from the leadership perspective. I was stuck in product mode and not in building-a-business mode *with* the product.

While Pigeonly launched as the innovator in this space, what does your competitive landscape look like now, and what has been your response?

Hutson: When we started in 2012, we were a big tree in a very small forest. There wasn't anyone talking about criminal justice in this way, neither from a policy perspective nor a criminal justice technology perspective. Those conversations are being had all the time now, but I think the expansion of the ecosystem helps us all. Seeing more people—or at least seeing technology— tackle different issues within a criminal justice system is a good thing. This is such a large, outdated system that it needs as many brilliant minds as possible to carve out a section they believe they can build a solution for and fix. And they definitely should. I have seen a number of companies that are tackling different aspects of it.

I think that also puts pressure on the incumbents in the industry that have [earned] millions and billions of dollars with very predatory business practices. It puts pressure on them to change their image, their motives, and their business processes. I've seen that happen over the years, where some of the big prison phone providers are now trying to clean their image up and lower their rates. So I definitely think it's a good thing, and I'm looking forward to the continued innovation that the space is going to have.

What's been most surprising to you through this journey?

Hutson: Hmm...I think how effective you can be with a very clear and concise plan, and then being able to lead your team on that plan, versus just very broad strokes. We've accomplished a lot more by being very focused, with my leadership skills having improved and developed over the years. And being hyperfocused has allowed us to do a lot more with less, whether it be less resources, less time, less people, etc., as opposed to when we were just throwing money at every problem.

There's a level of time when you're building a company where you can push the ball forward with just sheer will and determination. But as you start growing as an organization, that becomes less effective. It turns into more of a nuanced balance of focusing on hiring the best people you possibly can, getting the right people in the right positions, and making sure you're building the team, which allows you to operate so much better. How impactful that is to everything else at such a higher

A company is not a one-man show. If you want to build something powerful, if you want to build something impactful, focus a lot more on the team that you're building. That's your ticket for where you want to go.

level is probably even more surprising to me. I've learned over the past few years why a company is a company. A company is not a one-man show. If you want to build something powerful, if you want to build something impactful, focus a lot more on the team that you're building. That's your ticket for where you want to go.

What's next for Pigeonly?

Hutson: I'm excited about what we're doing on the government side [through] legislation that we're pushing to protect access to mail for everyone, and how that impacts the consumer side. Over the past year, we've become actively involved with our congressional delegation and other senators and congressmen who share our commitment to inmate rights and the best possible communication with loved ones, as well as local elected officials in Washington, DC, who are focused on prison contraband and safety issues. There's been a lot of interest in these issues, and we've been able to make great progress in a short period of time at the intersection of these two public policy objectives. For example, both the Senate and

House version of the fiscal year 2021 appropriation bills include direction to the Federal Bureau of Prisons to adopt our solution, and we are on the verge of introducing closely-related authorizing legislation in the House of Representatives. One of our strongest advocates has been our own member of Congress, Rep. Steve Horsford [(D-NV)], who was just reelected to his fourth term in Congress. He's a successful Black small business owner, and [he] has brought that perspective to Congress and to the work we've done together. So I'm excited about what's on the horizon in that regard, [as well as] the maturity and growth that we've had as an organization.

JAMES JONES, JR., ESQ.

Founder and CEO, Ownors

Ownors is the #1 AI-powered platform for virtual one-on-one mentorship and managed micro-advances for creatives.

J ames Jones, Jr. is the Founder and CEO of Ownors, an AI-powered analytics marketplace matching top entertainment industry executives with creatives for one-on-one live sessions and managed micro-advances.

He has been featured in *Forbes*, *Fortune*, *Essence*, *Black Enterprise*, *TechCrunch*, and many other publications. Jones was named Winston-Salem State University's Student of the Year in 2002, a Thomson Reuters Super Lawyer in 2017, and *Black Enterprise* Tech Entrepreneur of the Year in 2019.

Using only $1,500 from savings, he co-founded his first startup with his wife: a legaltech marketplace connecting consumers with court attorneys. As the company's CEO, he raised over $7 million and led the company's growth from zero to being valued at $23 million with over fifty employees across the United States. He is also a former business and entertainment attorney, representing professional athletes, artists, and more.

He has a BA in communications from Winston-Salem State University, a JD from the University of Florida, and a Scaling Ventures certificate from Harvard Business School.

Website: https://ownors.com
Twitter: @ownors
Facebook/Instagram: @ownorsinc

What were you like growing up?

James Jones: The best way to describe me was observant, an inquisitive student of life that was unafraid of a challenge and always wanted to try new things. If you were to ask a lot of my friends and family, they would say that I was a very quiet kid. We spent a lot of time on the road. My father was in the music business. He was also an engineer, but mostly "a traveling minister and musician selling his music" is the best way to describe him. My mom took care of me and my siblings. But as a family, we would travel up and down the east coast from Washington, DC, down to Florida, and back. We stopped at churches along the way. He would preach, teach, and also sell music. He would also teach ministers and different church congregations how to play music. The earliest thing that I can remember from my childhood was spending a lot of time on the road listening to his music, the music that he created.

I also watched my father build things. He built computers, speakers, even cars from scratch. That was the engineering side of him.

My parents also exposed me to the court system. During the summertime, when school was out, we would stop by the courthouses in Tampa and just observe lawyers in action, judges in action. We would observe defendants that were facing charges. I was extremely observant and analytical and, in hindsight, I think my parents did that because they wanted to make sure that we understood the consequences of getting into legal trouble. This experience gave me an up-close and personal view of the American justice system.

On one occasion, I remember a guy was brought into the courtroom in handcuffs. He was accused of assault and battery on another patron at a local bar in Tampa. I remember the defendant, a Black man in his twenties or thirties, wasn't represented by counsel, and

As he was being taken out of the courthouse in handcuffs, I remember seeing his face as he looked back at us, and he shook his head as if to say: You know the system doesn't work for us. That really stood out to me. That experience served as a career launching pad for me.

he was facing a really aggressive prosecutor that was essentially just leveling these charges against him. I don't think the defendant said one word. The judge ended up finding him guilty of assault, battery, and some other charges that I cannot recall. As he was being taken out of the courthouse in handcuffs, I remember seeing his face as he looked back at us, and he shook his head as if to say: *You know the system doesn't work for us.* That really stood out to me. That experience served as a career launching pad for me. It really propelled me to pursue a career in law.

So fast forward, and I'm in college. I went to Winston-Salem State University. I played college football my freshman year, though I wasn't really motivated to play. Unfortunately, my grades suffered while [I was] playing football. I remember getting my first semester grades and thinking to myself: *Wow, I need to explain to my mom why my grades don't look so great.* And, more importantly, I need to shape up or else I'm going to be kicked out of school. So I essentially did a course correction. I decided to choose another major. When I first arrived on campus, I wanted to study something that would help athletes recover from sports-related injuries. The problem with this was that there simply was not enough time to devote to hard sciences like biology, physics, etc. as an athlete. It was difficult to balance that type of study and also dominate on the football field. So I started thinking about what other majors and fields of study would make the most sense. I wasn't strong at communicating and wanted to become a better writer and orator, so I eventually settled on a communications major with a focus on journalism, and minor in Spanish.

In shifting courses, I decided to give up sports and take academics very seriously. As an athlete, I knew the path that I was on wasn't a good path. As much talk as there is about being "student athletes," it's really "athlete student." Especially when you are playing one of the major sports like football and basketball. So with this course correction, I spent a lot of time in a computer lab and ended up getting a job on campus fixing computers. I found out that I was actually really good at it. I'd usually work the third shift where I oversaw a two-room lab. One room was about thirty computers and the other room was about another thirty to forty-five computers. And students would come into the lab all the time talking about the latest music coming out, but they were frustrated that they couldn't get access to it. The closest record store was in the mall—about thirty minutes away in a car, or an hour and a half by bus. And by the time they'd make it to the store, the album they wanted was sold out. Every single time.

This is around the time that peer-to-peer music file-sharing was gaining in popularity, but was largely undiscovered and untapped on my college campus. I started asking people what types of music files that they wanted access to. They'd say, "I want this song, I want that song. I wish I had this album. I want to create a playlist with these songs." Since I worked the third shift some weekdays and every weekend, the computer lab was mostly empty. So after I fixed all of the computers, I started mining for music files in the empty lab and adding them to blank CDs. I simply did the math. I'm making ten dollars an hour working eight-hour days, so that's about eighty dollars a day, gross pay. Now I'm charging people five dollars for personalized CDs that I can burn for them in the middle of the night while they're sleeping, while they're resting, and I can use forty-five unused computers to do so. So that's just what I did. I'd create unique and personalized playlists like *Felicia's Smooth Grooves* and *Jamal's Rap Classics*. I'd sell them for five dollars a CD. I was making more money off of the CDs than I was working this job. It turned out to be a great value for lots of students. They were able to get access to the music they wanted fast. They didn't have to waste time calling the record store over and over without receiving an answer. And they didn't have to waste time fighting traffic, or even worse, dealing with the letdown of finding out that the music they wanted to buy was sold out after they arrived at the store.

That was the early beginnings of entrepreneurship for me, where I started just finding value creating solutions to problems that students were facing. I was also a hustler in a sense. I was the editor-in-chief of my campus newspaper, and I worked as a journalist at two major newspapers in Greensboro and Winston-Salem, North Carolina. So I had the attention of a lot of people in the community and on campus, which meant access to a lot of potential customers.

I ended up graduating with a 4.0 GPA, and won a Student of the Year Award, which was really a testament to my decision to abandon athletics. And that decision, and all of the different things that I became involved with as a result of the decision, was what enabled me to start thinking about entrepreneurship. After graduation, I ended up taking a job as a journalist and decided to go to law school. I did internships at law firms in-between college and law school, and I was always fascinated by the lawyers who were solo practitioners. One lawyer that I interned for once told me, "You know, James, you can get an MBA, and that just means that you can go the business route, but you can't go the law route. But if you get a JD, you can go the legal route *and* you can also go the business route too." That's actually why I decided to pursue a law degree. Eventually I did do Harvard Business School but at least initially, early on in my career, I took the JD route. And I think the path was pretty set at that point.

There's one other thing worth mentioning. I think we underestimate how much your childhood shapes and molds your life. The exposure to the courtroom, and that experience, was pivotal to my career. Additionally, we didn't have much. We were in an extremely bad financial situation for years. We didn't have a home, and we had to do a lot of things that most people would be shocked by. It was terrible, but it's a part of my background. It's a part of my history. But looking back, you see how beneficial that adversity was. You think about how you focus on reading rather than watching TV. You didn't have a TV because you couldn't afford a TV, so you found other ways to entertain yourself. We spent a lot of time in the library, so when you're going through it you're like: *Oh, my friends are watching this show, they're watching that movie.* And you can't contribute to the conversation because you spent your weekend reading, right? But in hindsight, all of those things were so important and so critical in terms of growth and being where I am today.

How did the idea for Court Buddy come about?

Jones: It was sort of an accidental business. What I mean by that is, you know, I was going about my daily, day-to-day, practicing of law, and since I was a litigator, that meant that I went to court a lot. In my frequent trips to court, I'd run into a lot of people that were self-represented and about to appear in front of a judge. To put this into context, I was in south Florida, the Miami area at the time. And every time I go to court, I've got about a dozen or so people like, "Look, I'm about to go in front of a judge, you're going in front of the same judge. Can you help me? Are you a lawyer, sir?" And I would say: Look, I really can't help you at this late stage, but maybe I can look over your paperwork. I can maybe give you some potential arguments you can make because I've been in front of this judge a lot of times, and I know how this judge thinks. So they would pretty much show me their life story and give me all their paperwork to review. As I'm looking through it, I'm like: Wow, you're about to get a final judgement entered against you where you're going to lose your home.

And you know, these self-represented litigants would just look at me and say, "Well, how am I going to go to your office and meet right now? I'm about to go in front of the judge right now." That's when the wheels started turning for me. Is there something that's going to limit me, or is there a rule or regulation that limits me from just taking these clients right here, right before I go in front of the judge, and representing them?

Or: You're about to lose custody of your kids. Or, you know: You're about to get judgement against a loan that you didn't pay. And it's not like they couldn't have fought this, it's just that, they waited too long, and now the other side hired a lawyer and has stacked the deck against them. They'd be pretty saddened by this news and would say, "Look, well, is there anything I can do? Can I just pay you a flat fee, you know, of $300 to go in front of the judge right now and represent me?"

No, no you can't, I'm sorry. You need to meet me at my office, and I'd need to charge you a retainer. And I bill $350 an hour, and that's the way the process goes. And you know, these self-represented litigants would just look at me and say, "Well, how am I going to go to your office and meet right now? I'm about to go in front of the judge right now." That's when the wheels started turning for me. *Is there something that's going to limit me, or is there a rule or regulation that limits me from just taking these clients right here, right before I go in front of the judge, and representing them?*

Then I started thinking to myself: *I wonder if there are a group of lawyers who would be interested in taking these one-time court appearances.* Because, on the other hand, we had a group of lawyers that were always complaining about not having enough clients. And I'm thinking to myself: *How is that possible? I just met thirty people at the courthouse that were looking for representation and were willing to pay.* These were middle-class folks that weren't looking for pro bono support, and were making twenty-five to forty-plus dollars an hour. They had a mortgage, rent to pay, and take vacations. They were hard-working individuals that just needed a break. But they didn't have legal representation.

So, I would talk to my wife about this. At the time, she was working at an ad agency, and we decided to start building, to start testing. She was able to put together a team of engineers based off of her connections at the ad agency, and we'd talk to her contacts and developers in the IT department about how to leverage technology to bring court attorneys together and match them with consumers that needed court appearances. We wanted to do it where people paid court attorneys a flat rate for their service, and just see what happens. So we built an MVP [Minimum Viable Product] with developers that we hired. And essentially Court Buddy was born.

How did you fund your MVP?

Jones: We self-financed. We used a very modest amount of our savings, around $1,500. We also kept our full-time jobs. As first-time founders, we had no idea about how financing worked, about how to even ask friends and family for money. We just said: Look, here's a problem. Let's test a possible solution to this problem, and let's see what happens right here in Miami. And I mean, right now it sort of seems like it may have been overnight, but within a few weeks or months, we started getting a lot of inbound from people outside of Miami. We kept it exclusively to Miami initially, but inbound began to flood from Orlando and Jacksonville, then from out of state. Things took off from there.

> *As first-time founders, we had no idea about how financing worked, about how to even ask friends and family for money. We just said: Look, here's a problem. Let's test a possible solution to this problem, and let's see what happens right here in Miami.*

Where or how did this inbound originate?

Jones: So, I was still practicing law. Since we were bootstrapping, we really didn't have a choice. I was still going to court, and I was still able to talk to people and say: You know, I can't represent you personally because I have a lot of other cases that I have, but you can go to Court Buddy and get matched with an attorney that can go to court for you. My wife, who still had her job at the ad agency, started talking to potential customers to collect feedback. The best way to describe it is an on-the-spot survey from potential customers.

We'd come back home from our respective workflows, and she'd say, "Look, you know, today we had people asking, 'Hey, are there clemency lawyers on the platform? Are there property lawyers, are there foreclosure lawyers?'" And then we started thinking: *Okay, well, if we're getting that type of demand, or those types of inquiries, we may be on to something—and that's just in one location.* Then we started doing research. We found out there were hundreds of millions of people facing some type of court-related issue every single year, whether it's voluntary or involuntary. At the same time, there's some 300,000 solo lawyers across the US that are struggling to get clients. Those lawyers don't work at the medium and big law firms. We started doing the math, and it was a massive, multi-billion-dollar market opportunity. Once we did that research and really thought about competitors and how we could be different, we just went from there.

When did you decide it was time to seek venture capital? Once decided, where did you go for support?

Jones: The decision was sort of made for us. And what I mean by that is, we were pretty active in the Miami community. We did a lot of pitch competitions; we won the *Miami Herald* Business Plan Challenge. And because of these small wins, we started getting more exposure to the investor world. I think it was 2015, a few months after we launched and had won the *Miami Herald* Business Plan Challenge, that we were also named finalists for eMerge Americas' startup showcase. eMerge was and is south Florida's premier tech conference. We had a booth set up, and people would come by and say, "Hey, you know, I'm an angel investor, how much are you looking for?" And we're like: Uh, what do we say? Do we say fifty thousand? Do we say five thousand? We just didn't know at the time.

But the fact that we were able to get investors interested at the angel investor level at least, revealed to us that maybe we should think deeper about this fundraising process. It would certainly be a relief to have other investors, other people's money if you will, invested in this venture, and not just our own money going towards building Court Buddy.

So we, again, did research, and one of our earliest pitches was with a Miami-based fund. I think they were more like an angel group than a VC fund. But we pitched them and found out in a side conversation that less than, like, two percent of startups get funding. And I was like: *Wow, that's a pretty dismal number, right?* We were just kind of running blind and really didn't know how big of an uphill battle we were waging in terms of obtaining funding. We didn't get funding from that angel group, but did end up eventually receiving an investment through a connection made at a conference. Representatives from the American Entrepreneurship Award, AEA, approached our booth and suggested that we apply. They were looking for great founders to provide interest-free financing through a competition. It was run by and sponsored by President Obama's My Brother's Keeper initiative and *Shark Tank*'s Daymond John. So we ended up applying, and we won. Again, these small wins ended up adding up to an introduction to 500 Startups. 500 Startups wasn't really on our radar, though we had heard about it. We were also finalists in *Black Enterprise*'s startup pitch competition in Atlanta. It was these small, incremental steps that helped us tremendously because we had zero clue about how to fundraise. We had zero clue about how to go about the investment process. We were just really, really fortunate to have people along the way, and to get those small wins under our belt to get us to the point where we could actually properly fundraise.

> *We had zero clue about how to go about the investment process. We were just really, really fortunate to have people along the way, and to get those small wins under our belt to get us to the point where we could actually properly fundraise.*

With angels interested and Court Buddy gaining notoriety through pitch competitions, who became the first investor?

Jones: Outside of winning an award from the American Entrepreneurship Award, which was interest-free funding for $12,500, 500 Startups was the first check in. With the 500 Startups investment, we also had to participate in the 500 Startups accelerator beginning in January 2017. After about thirty to forty-five days into their accelerator, we received the $150K investment from 500 Startups. Well, in actuality, we netted about $120K of that investment due to an accelerator tuition fee that all startups are required to pay out of the investment. The investment was made in exchange for a 6 percent stake in Court Buddy.

It wasn't the job of the investor to understand our numbers. It was our job.

When we first applied to 500 Startups, we didn't know how to fundraise or how the process worked. We just applied, made it to the interview, and were denied. They said it was because we didn't know our numbers: "You don't know your KPIs, but once you button that up, we encourage you to apply again." So we made sure that we focused on the numbers—number of users, CAC [Customer Acquisition Cost], customer LTV [Lifetime Value], etc., which actually helped us to better understand our business. It wasn't the job of the investor to understand our numbers. It was our job. The second time we applied, we actually had a warm introduction from one of the advisors from the American Entrepreneur Award, who had also taken a company through 500 Startups. This time, in

2017, we got further along in the process. We ended up having to decide whether we'd meet with the final investment committee in person or a conference call online—since at the time we were still living in Miami. We made the decision to do it in person because of what was at stake. And that was an experience.

To make a long story short, we ended up missing our flight from Miami to Los Angeles because we had to drop off our daughter with my in-laws. All the remaining flights were canceled because it was December, and the winds were just horrible, with a crazy winter storm rolling through California. We eventually got a flight into Los Angeles, and ended up renting a car to drive up to San Francisco from LA. And those rains are probably the worst rains I've ever driven in. Ever. We were like: *It's not supposed to rain in Southern California. So, why is it raining? And why is it the worst rain ever, right now?* So we're driving up to San Francisco at, like, six in the morning. The meeting with 500 Startups' investment committee was scheduled for 10:00 a.m. We arrive at the hotel, check in, and maybe get about an hour and a half of sleep. Then the car didn't start once we got up and were ready to go downtown [*laughs*].

We get it going, and finally get there. Then the elevator didn't work in the building, so we had to walk up six flights of stairs. Then we get to the floor that 500 Startups is on, and the door is locked from the outside. So we're knocking trying to get in. And luckily, and I mean, this had to have been the universe saying, "Look, we're going to make this work after all you've been through," [*laughs*] because there happened to be a janitor in the middle of the stairwell that had a key to the door. He opened the door, and we walked in as if nothing had ever happened. We just walked in fresh. We did the interview, and we got the financing. We got selected to join 500 Startups Batch 20.

So, you've got 500 Startups in your pocket, and now you're scaling. How did you filter the panoply of advice as more investors and advisors joined your journey?

Jones: That's a great question. I think one of the things that we've learned as founders, repeat founders, is that you know your business better than anyone else. Investors can help since they see a lot of businesses, they see a lot of startups, so they bring different perspectives from a 3,000-foot, bird's-eye view. But you're in the trenches, you're the operator. So who better to know your market, to know your business, than you?

I think that's one of the benefits of being a repeat founder or a serial entrepreneur. You have the benefits of an arsenal of learning opportunities and successes under your belt that propels your next venture to perhaps be even more successful.

We had to learn early on what to focus on and what metrics mattered for us. 500 Startups really helped with this. Should we focus on the supply side: the lawyers? Should we focus on the demand side: the consumers? Should we really be buttoning up the CAC to LTV ratio? How should we articulate the market opportunity to investors? Will they understand how big of a market this [is], what's the serviceable market and not just the total addressable market? So we had to really dive into those details.

Once we just sat back and said: *Look, we know our strengths, we know our weaknesses, we know the business. Who can we hire? Who makes sense to bring on board in terms of fit from an investor perspective or an advisory perspective?* You know, I think those are lessons that we probably, definitely, know about now, more so than when we were in the trenches and still trying to figure things out. I think that's one of the benefits of being a repeat founder or a serial entrepreneur. You have the benefits of an arsenal of learning opportunities and successes under your belt that propels your next venture to perhaps be even more successful.

How has this process changed for you—from raising seed versus Series A, and then Court Buddy versus your second venture, Ownors?

Jones: There's a couple of reports, ProjectDiane and Harlem Capital, and a handful of others, that show that about 1 percent of VC dollars go to Black founders. That's obviously unfortunate. I've lived in DC, I've lived in Virginia, Tampa, Miami, and in a lot of predominantly Black areas. I've also lived in a lot of really diverse areas across the country. I mention this because I don't think that there is a certain type of mold or description of an entrepreneur. Entrepreneurs can be any color, any ethnicity, any gender, and be as successful, if not more

Entrepreneurs can be any color, any ethnicity, any gender, and be as successful, if not more successful than the subset of "entrepreneurs" that Silicon Valley, TechCrunch, and venture capitalists seem to focus on and glorify.

successful than the subset of "entrepreneurs" that Silicon Valley, *TechCrunch*, and venture capitalists seem to focus on and glorify.

In terms of the fundraising process, we ended up closing a $1 million seed round in September 2017, which was about three months after we completed the 500 Startups accelerator. We spoke to roughly 200 investors. And we heard every single excuse you can imagine: "Oh, you're too early." "Oh, our check size is X amount." "Oh, come back to us when you have about $200K left in your round. Great progress though!" "Oh, you now have $200K left in your round? Well, our minimum check size is actually $500K, so we won't be able to invest in this round. Sorry." I mean, we heard all these different excuses and it was hard to make sense of it. *Is this really a legitimate excuse for not investing? Are you stringing us along? Or are you just, trying to find a reason to say no?*

I even remember one meeting with a VC, and he said to me, "Wow, you're a man of large size. You have to learn how to deescalate the room." I'm like: *What does that have to do with the merits of my business?*

So, as I mentioned before, we spoke to roughly 200 investors and got 193 nos. Think about that from a psychological standpoint. That's a lot of rejection, right? *But you have to weather all of that and keep pushing forward.*

And now with my second venture, Ownors, it's easier for me [to] understand the fundraising process because I have battle scars. Additionally, I'm no longer an unknown in the investor world. Investors know me and are willing to take meetings with me. And, therefore, securing investment has been much easier with Ownors. Fundraising is still difficult and challenging, but certainly much easier as a repeat founder than when I was raising for Court Buddy, and no one knew me.

What gave you the mental fortitude to keep going?

Jones: It's resiliency and being relentless. That's part of my DNA. I mean, it's a part of our DNA, right? You know, I grew up in a pretty poor family. We fell on very hard times for years. Part of it was just because of the nature of my father being a traveling minister, musician, and salesperson. And then my mom and dad divorced. And my mom, who hadn't held a job because she was raising my siblings and I, was suddenly forced to find a job and be the only source of household income. My dad avoided paying child support, which made it even tougher for us financially. Through those experiences, you learn that tough times are temporary. The best thing you can do in those moments is sharpen your mind. You can pick up books, you can read, you can dream about the life you want, and you can get smarter. A lot of things can be taken from you: money, material possessions, property. But no one can take your mind away from you.

> It's resiliency and being relentless. That's part of my DNA. I mean, it's a part of our DNA, right?

Within the context of fundraising, you take that resiliency that you developed at an early age, and you start telling yourself: *That's one person's opinion, that's one person's perspective. Whatever their reason was for saying no, it has really no bearing on me or what we're doing. And if we keep at this long enough, then we know that the sun is going to shine through at some point. The sun is going to peek through the clouds.*

So it's that mental framing and really having supreme confidence in myself that propelled me forward. Despite being raised in a single-parent household, I graduated from law school. Despite the odds, I'm a high school and college graduate. I earned a Scaling Ventures certificate from Harvard. I never would have ever imagined I'd have anything with my name and Harvard Business School on the same document. I've now founded and co-founded several multi-million-dollar companies. Some may attribute success from the first company to a fluke or being lucky. But when you can do it again, then you know that it's not a fluke or luck. It's skill, intelligence, focus, resilience, and being relentless. It's an unwavering commitment to the process, which leads to the desired results. So you just keep pushing, and keep getting better, and gaining more self-confidence.

So going back to Court Buddy, resilience and being relentless was critical. With 193 nos and seven yeses, we closed the round. Series A was no different. We still had a lot of nos [*laughs*]. We really had to convince investors that this [was] a company that was going to take off.

How large was the Court Buddy network at this point, during Series A, when some investors were still not convinced?

Jones: Tens of thousands at this point. I remember the first investor meeting that we had when we were still in Miami, the angel group that I referenced earlier. We were in due diligence, and they were like, "I don't understand how this can ever sell." Yet we had just shown them data that showed we had sales within the first week of launching. Like: Was that something you just happened to overlook in the due diligence documents? I mention that because I think sometimes investors are trained to say no to some things, or they're kind of trying to find a "got you" reason to say, "No, we can't invest in your business."

I remember talking with a group of founders one time, and I said, "Look, for some people there's this concept that you learn in law school called *rebuttable presumption*. If you're Black and Brown, there's a presumption that you do not know what you're doing, but you can rebut that presumption by actually proving that you know what you're doing. If you're a White founder, there's a presumption that you *do* know what you're doing, but you can rebut that presumption by not knowing what you're doing. So, at first blush, it seems like that's a level playing field for Whites and non-Whites, but it's really not. If someone looks at you, and they say, "You don't know what you're doing," then you're starting off in a pretty bad position. It's an uphill battle from there. If someone looks at you and says, "You know what, we presume that you *do* know what you're doing," you're starting off in a pretty good position to win. I think that's the dilemma, that's a part of the problem.

So for our Series A, it was the same stuff. "How does this scale? Why should we invest?" "You need to get to X amount in GMV." "We don't invest in husband-and-wife companies." "You need a lead investor." It was the same gauntlet. A lot of nos and a few yeses.

When did you and your wife, Kristina Jones, know that it was time to switch gears? How did you all know it was time to step away from Court Buddy?

Jones: So like I said before, Court Buddy was an accident of a business. We saw a need in Miami, and we wanted to solve a problem. We saw an opportunity to solve a problem, and we did that. Kristina unfortunately lost her father when she was ten, and she's always had this desire to write a children's book because of her experience trying to deal with and navigate coping with the loss of her father. And, well, she kind of got dragged into Court Buddy. She was in the advertising space and wanted to help her husband who was this young and ambitious lawyer, so she became the co-founder of Court Buddy. But she always wanted to get back to helping grieving families and writing a children's book. So, for her, there came a point where we looked at the company, and we said: Look, this company can scale without us. We don't need to be at the helm. We don't need to be managing the day-to-day affairs of this company. We'd done a really good job of hiring.

> *For her, there came a point where we looked at the company, and we said: Look, this company can scale without us. We don't need to be at the helm. We don't need to be managing the day-to-day affairs of this company.*

At our peak, we were at fifty employees across the country. So we were pretty confident in the leadership and the team we had built. And we decided to sell our stake in Court Buddy so we could work on the projects that we really wanted to work on.

For me, inspired in part by my father's music, engineering, and teaching background, I was always curious about how I could leverage technology to help out creatives. Whether it's writers, musicians, authors, actors, actresses, etc. The wheels were already turning, and we decided that this was the time. We'd raised a Series A, the company has millions of dollars in the bank, we've taken care of our team, so let's think about our next move. So in 2019, we stepped down. We went to Thailand for about a month and started gaining a deeper understanding of our spirituality, why we continued to have a burning desire to create value for others, our emotions, our financial status, and the interconnectedness between it all. Thailand also allowed us to regroup, refocus, and become more reflective. It was a chance to think about our purpose and what we wanted to do next.

So I said: *Let's think about what we want to do next.* She wanted to write a children's book and also create a platform to allow for grieving families, specifically children, to connect with counselors around the world. It's called Guardian Lane. And I wanted to get more into mentoring and creating a platform that allowed creatives to get mentorship, feedback, and advice from industry executives—whether it's A&Rs [Artists and Repertoire Representatives] or VPs of marketing at entertainment companies. And also to help creatives with obtaining advances without having to sign with a label, so that they could market and promote their songs, their ideas, their craft. So that's what I've been really working hard on, and that's what she's been really working hard on too.

It's meaningful that you recognized and seized an opportunity but didn't allow that to take over your or your Kristina's passions. You all made room for both. What other lessons or experiences from Court Buddy have translated into your journey with Ownors?

Jones: We're very fortunate to be in a position financially where we can pick and choose the investors we want. It was the opposite when we were building Court Buddy. We didn't know enough about the fundraising process, about investors, and ulterior motives to really understand who could be an ally or who would really have our backs—or who really wouldn't. So for Ownors, it's really now a matter of being really strategic. We have a great group of investors, such as executives from entertainment companies, TV studios, VC's, and family offices. We've had commitments from investors that we've known from our Court Buddy days who invested in Court Buddy, and then invested in Ownors. So the fundraising journey this time was less difficult. It's never easy.

This goes back to your mentality. It goes back to sharpening your mind and the mindset you must have to be wildly successful. Through reading, through studying other successful people, through understanding that success leaves footprints, and with financial freedom, you can now make different choices.

And you know, you mentioned a new journey. I think if you can find someone that can do a process over and over again and be successful, that tells you that it's not a fluke, right? Sometimes you may have beginner's or first-time founder's luck, whatever you want to call it. But the question becomes: Can you do it again, though?

This goes back to your mentality. It goes back to sharpening your mind and the mindset you must have to be wildly successful. Through reading, through studying other successful people, through understanding that success leaves footprints, and with financial freedom, you can now make different choices. And that's not to take anything away from other founders who may be in a less fortunate position. But I think from our vantage point, it's a little bit easier now to say, look, we can pick and choose who we want to work with and how we want to go about doing things.

One of the things we are doing differently is picking and choosing who we want as investors and understanding the real value add that they bring to the table. And we are really making sure that we have the right people on our board. We are making sure that we have the right advisors around us. We have people that are really thinking about the founder, and building and scaling the company, and less about some ulterior motives, trying to find flaws in you, or something up their sleeve that we don't know about.

Did you find it difficult to balance the profit-driven motives of venture capital with building a social- or mission-driven company?

Jones: I think that my life's purpose is to leave an impact driven by mission and purpose. To leave a positive impact on people's lives and to help them create success for themselves. I think as a founder you have to understand that, at some point, if something does not align with your vision, with your mission, with what you believe, with your morals, values, and principles, that it's okay to say: You know what, I can go in a different direction. Now, of course you have to have supreme confidence in yourself that you can do it all over again from ground zero.

But in terms of the tension with VC, there's always going to be tension with VC. VCs are reporting to LPs and the LPs are expecting venture returns. The LPs are telling the fund managers at VC firms that if you're taking some portion of our endowment funds or our pensions, or if it's a family office, and the family office is investing several million dollars into the VC firm's fund, then we're expecting you to outperform the stock market returns or the returns of other asset classes like real estate. So there's always going to be tension with a founder or entrepreneur that's thinking about their customers, that's thinking

> I think as a founder you have to understand that, at some point, if something does not align with your vision, with your mission, with what you believe, with your morals, values, and principles, that it's okay to say: You know what, I can go in a different direction.

about, *How can I make an impact that truly moves the needle for my customers while also maximiz[ing] shareholder value*, versus a VC that's thinking about, *How can I move the needle for my LPs and return the entire fund with the expectation that there may be some other companies in the portfolio that may not perform well, or may fail altogether.* So, there's always this tension, and I think there's always going to be a struggle to balance those tensions.

A part of it is on the founder to understand what comes with taking VC dollars and to understand the expectations. So founders have to make the decision to take VC money soundly and wisely. But it is also important for VCs to take a more reflective approach and say, "Look, it shouldn't always be about outsized returns." "What about the impact that we're making on the world?" I mean, we're in the fourth quarter of a hotly contested presidential election, and there's all sorts of information and misinformation being disseminated. And we just saw a couple of tech founders, Jack Dorsey and Mark Zuckerberg, testify in front of Congress about determining what to allow on social media platforms, and how to determine what is and is not newsworthy. Those are ethical and moral issues that both the founders and their investors should be deeply thinking about addressing. But investors are going to keep pushing—they want profit, they want to pad their wealth. Ethics and morals take a back seat. And there's nothing inherently wrong with pushing for profit because profits are a byproduct of a successful company. Who doesn't want to be a part of a successful, profitable company? But there should also be alignment between the founder or founders and the VC, and an understanding of what VC dollars does to your company. What does this VC believe in?

Profit at all costs? Or are they driven to invest based on a company's mission and values? So long as there's alignment, then founders and VCs can coexist.

Though your second time around, the atmosphere is quite different, how has the COVID-19 pandemic impacted building a startup?

Jones: Despite its broader health and economic impacts, it's actually been pretty wonderful. The reason is that a lot of people that normally would have been really busy have been really accessible by email, videoconference, or phone [due to local stay-at-home orders]. I've been able to send surveys to artists, I've been able to talk to influential executives within the entertainment industry. I've been able to get a lot of really quick and valuable feedback. Even before our core product was built, when it was just an idea, we relied heavily on feedback we received from artists and executives. We did a lot of market testing without spending marketing dollars, just to see what the response would be to using our product. So in that regard, it hasn't been as difficult as it may seem.

Some of the questions that I had initially [were]: *What would the business model look like? Could creatives afford this? Will industry execs be willing to pay for our platform or pay to use our platform?* Just like anything else, we did some testing and sent out a survey to artists. We figured out the pricing sweet spot. We did some price testing even in a COVID market. And it worked out really, really well.

And, you know, we had a couple team members get sick and actually test positive for COVID-19. It didn't affect the entire team because we're all working remotely. But it's obviously a challenge when a team member has to quarantine in a separate room or just be more isolated or away from their loved ones. It's also difficult to get any work done when you're sick. That's obviously a challenge from a business standpoint, but we worked through it. And it just goes back to the early days where you say: *You know what, if I can face this adversity, whatever it is, head-on, not having food in my stomach, not having a roof over my head, trying to figure out where the next dollar is going to come from, if I can face that adversity at the age of six, seven, eight, nine, and ten years old, then I will be able to withstand any other adversity that comes my way throughout my life.*

And so it's unfortunate that some team members got sick, but getting sick happens. Delays happen when you're building a product. But we still forged a path, and we were able to build out our core product in the midst of a pandemic. We were able to raise from several investors, and we're on a great trajectory to become the category leader for mentoring plus micro-advances for creatives worldwide.

JUANITA LOTT

Investment Partner, Portfolia Investment

Portfolia designs investment funds for women, backing the innovative companies they want to see in the world, for returns and impact.

Juanita Lott is an experienced technology executive, entrepreneur, Board Member, and Advisory Board Member with specific expertise in enterprise software and human resource management.

She is currently an investment partner with Portfolia Investments, where she focuses on enterprise software and women- and minority-led early-stage ventures (Portfolia was named one of *Fast Company*'s ten most innovative companies in 2020). She serves on the boards of Accion Opportunity Fund, the country's leading nonprofit small business lender, and as Chair of the Governance Committee on the National Board of CollegeSpring. CollegeSpring equips schools and their educators with test prep and college curriculum to prepare underserved students to succeed on the SAT/ACT exams, enter college, receive better financial aid, and achieve higher graduation rates.

Juanita founded and served on the Board of Directors of Bridgestream Software, a market leader in role management, and was one of the early African American women to found and lead an enterprise software company. As founder and CEO, she led the company in its development of role management software, enabling businesses to provide secure access to the business applications that support employees, customers, and suppliers. Gartner, Inc. recognized Bridgestream as a leader in role-based security, and Juanita was described as a pioneer in role-based technology by the Burton Group. (Bridgestream was acquired by Oracle).

Juanita has also served as an advisor to entrepreneurs and company executives, offering product and market positioning advice to early-stage businesses. She served on the Advisory Boards of Talent Sonar (merged with TalVista), a talent management software company that used a values-based hiring approach to enable its customers to make data-driven hiring decisions, and Rally On, an employee wellness platform that utilized innovative gaming methodology to improve employee health and wellness.

Juanita received her bachelor's degree in liberal arts from University of California, Davis, and her master's degree from Mills College. She attended Stanford University's Director's

College in 2016 and the Deloitte Director's Academy in 2018, and she is a member of the National Association of Corporate Directors (NACD).

Website: http://linkedin.com/in/juanita-lott-9495454

Where are you from, where did you grow up, and what was life like leading up to the start of Bridgestream?

Juanita Lott: Okay, and I'm going to keep it brief because there are a lot of roads that you don't want me to go down [*laughs*]. I grew up in the Bay Area in Oakland, California, so I'm a local. My parents were working class. My mother was the traditional, stay-at-home mom. My father worked for the Port of Oakland. Three kids, five-person family in a two-ish bedroom home in East Oakland.

At the time, families were really bullish about education. And there was never a question that you're going to go to college. If it had been up to my father, I would have been a doctor. But I knew early on, since I struggled in biology and with carving things up, that was not going to be my path. I was fortunate enough to go to UC Berkeley as an undergrad—and I was not a STEM candidate. I was

> *I come from the working class. There were two entrepreneurs in my family. Both my aunt and my mother started beauty salons at some point in their career, and I consider that one of the early experiences: We figure out how to build something to take care of our families, and it's just the way we live, right?*

Liberal Arts. And if I look at what that provided, that informed Bridgestream down the road.

I think UC Berkeley had a lot to do with getting me ready for an industry where you have to think on your own—an industry where you have to know you're right if everybody else around you is telling you otherwise—and have a thirst for knowledge beyond what you know today, right? I think one of the best things I did was to get a very good, broad education. In my senior year, I transferred to UC Davis because I married my husband—who is still around—and he was at the law school up there. So that was my initial foundation. I come from the working class. There were two entrepreneurs in my family. Both my aunt and my mother started beauty salons at some point in their career, and I consider that one of the early experiences: *We figure out how to build something to take care of our families*, and it's just the way we live, right?

So how did I get into Bridgestream? When I got out of college, I really did not know what I wanted to do. But the wonderful thing, luckily for me, was that I found myself in a staff job at Stanford University. I had never been down that far south in the Bay Area. I was an Oakland kid, and found myself with a new degree, dropped right in the middle of Stanford University, at a time when it was totally about innovation. Silicon Valley was booming. There wasn't a person on campus that wasn't building something, starting something. That

I found my way into a tech company, and worked in tech for about ten years before I started Bridgestream. My entry into tech was through Human Resources.

was around the eighties. I will never forget sitting and listening to [Intel president] Andy Grove when he was on campus talking about things. That was a big deal.

That was the point in time when Silicon Valley was figuring itself out. It was exciting. And so very soon after that, I found my way into a tech company, and worked in tech for about ten years before I started Bridgestream. My entry into tech was through Human Resources. I went into a software company that was maybe a year or so past its startup stage, with a team of a few hundred people. I was lucky enough to get in, and over the years, I became the chief human resources officer. I was one of the top seven or eight executives in the company, and they went through an IPO (initial public offering) and grew from one hundred to six thousand people, and from a few hundred million dollars in revenue to over $1 billion. So I ended up sitting in a room with some of the most creative software executives at the time, and given my tendency to really be the sponge in the room, learned a tremendous amount. Not just about the technology that we were building but the marketing of it and the issues they were dealing with in terms of the evolution of technology and what kind of growth we needed [in order] to be global. We ended up becoming—second to Oracle—one of the top database companies in the industry at the time.

But the wonderful thing about that is, after the seven or so years I spent there, I decided I was ready to do something else, and I started talking to everybody I've worked with—all my senior execs, all the members of the board that I worked with on a regular basis, and everyone who I had learned from and got to know in the industry. And the wonderful thing about that is, at the time there were a couple of African American senior executives in the industry who had done some pretty significant things. It was a small community, so we kind of all knew each other, but they were tremendously accessible. They would sit down with you and talk you through what you were thinking about doing and how it was going to work.

I got a lot of support from the network. *Yeah, you could do that. It's possible.* But my question was: Can *I* do it? I knew the business from sitting in the chair that was not the developer's chair. But what I *did* understand, which was particularly useful to me, is how enterprise businesses run at a very, very detailed level. So I went into Bridgestream with an understanding of my customers, what they needed, how it needed to work, and that the technology could now enable it. I had a lot of things lining up for me at the time that made Bridgestream a great idea. So I launched the company.

The lightbulb moment for Bridgestream was really tied to the fact that there were changes in the way technology was being developed that was going to be a big sea change for the industry. We knew what a lot of Fortune 1000 and Fortune 5000 companies wanted to do for enterprise software, as it was likely going to be part of this next evolution of technology.

At the point when you launched the company, you had experience under your belt—

Lott: But no money [*laughs*].

So how did you fund the launch? In what ways did your personal life impact your ability to start the company?

Lott: I married my husband out of college. I had one child, a son. And my husband was working, so there was that little bit of a safety net in knowing you could step out of that regular paycheck but still have a roof over your head. So my risk was mitigated from that perspective. It could change our quality of life, but we could survive it.

For the most part, if you're building a software company [today], you really do have to go the venture capital or angel route. But, at the time, there weren't a lot of sources for investment that were open to us, right? There weren't the incubators you have today. There were very few venture funds focused in this area; I think there might have been one or two. Instead, [you went] to the network of people you knew who had resources, which is what we ended up doing.

We raised a friends-and-family round through two guys; without them we would have never gotten the company started. One was Mike Fields. Mike was one of the first VPs of sales at Oracle. He lived in the Bay Area and had done fairly well with Oracle. He was one of those guys who really believed in helping young entrepreneurs. The second person

He came over to my office one day, and it was a very warm kind of introduction but with no expectations. It was just the Black network trying to find its way, right? It's how we are; we will find a way to know who you are, know you're out there, and connect. It was a social connection. When I was ready to start the business, I called him.

is Frank Green, one of the original Fairchild semiconductor engineers, and he had started a small fund. If you were an African American in Silicon Valley looking to invest in other African Americans, these were the two guys [you went to].

Mike was introduced to me through a work colleague. *Hey, do you know this guy? You really should know him; he's really cool. You need to meet him.* He came over to my office one day, and it was a very warm kind of introduction but with no expectations. It was just the Black network trying to find its way, right? It's how we are; we will find a way to know who you are, know you're out there, and connect. It was a social connection. When I was ready to start the business, I called him. Mike connected me to Frank, who also connected me to a number of people. And so we started building the network that way.

Mike did a couple of things. One, he bought an old bank building in downtown Oakland and set it up as an incubator and brought in around five founders—small businesses like mine—and allowed us to do what we were doing. I think there were two women and three guys, and each of us had an area within the building and were given the ability to be there rent-free and work on our businesses. He was an advisor, obviously, and was a big help, connecting us in the industry with other people.

The space was rent-free, but was there an expectation of equity?

Lott: Oh, yes, of course. The way we structured it, which was the way that worked for both of us, was that we would give him warrants at a certain dollar amount that would be reflected on our balance sheet. At the end of the day, if we were successful, he was building equity in the business. If we failed, we failed, and there was no cash issue. There was no buying him down or buying him out at the time. That was one of the best arrangements that really helped us get off the ground and get the company started. And we had a roof over our head. That's where we started.

There were also several people I worked with who had a great network of contacts, like Dave Duffield out of PeopleSoft [now called Workday]. He was investing and, quite frankly, wrote an angel check without really knowing who I was. It just shows how the network works. The network isn't about vetting your product, at least at the angel stage. The network is someone who is well-respected saying to someone who has money and is interested in investing: *If I were you, I'd write a check here.*

That's the difference from a network that typically works for the White male founder. The connections are made, and checks are written without any validation or vetting *whatsoever*. And I know that to be a fact because I saw those checks arriving and thought: *He knows very little about me and what I'm doing*, but I was happy to take the angel funding because of a recommendation.

How do you build up that reputation?

Lott: That reputation came out of those years I worked as the chief human resources officer for the software company, period. When I was at that level [CHRO], I was sitting with those guys who—at the time—were doing well just as members of the team. And they were the guys who knew Silicon Valley. They were the Silicon Valley elite, major venture capitalists who got to know me in a different way. [Once it was time to build Bridgestream], they knew I knew Silicon Valley. And I didn't hesitate to call and ask for a meeting with anybody, right? If you were able to get in front of them, and they knew you from another perspective, it worked.

Once you get into the network, you realize how influential those connections are, and you also appreciate how disadvantaged women and minorities are when they're starting a business. We are led to believe there's some kind of fair assessment of [a startup's] ability to grow, and that [venture capitalists] do this deep dive and really understand the industry we're talking about. But none of that is true, especially when you're talking about angel investing, which is investing in the person that's sitting in front of you.

We got to our first $750K, almost $1 million on angels, right? People like the ones I just mentioned and other execs who would say to people who had worked with me five years before: *Did you know she's doing X, Y, Z? Why don't you write her a check?* Those checks were written without any real valuation. We set up our cap table and had a valuation assumption—untested—that was not worth a lot at that stage since we had no product, no sales, no market clarity. We were lucky that way.

But I do think that's why I concern myself with early-stage founders who want to start, but are coming right out of school. That's definitely harder because, unless you bring a network with you, and have access to that angel capital, you're not going to get to step two.

Could you talk about the early days of Bridgestream, especially the process of building without having a technical degree? Once you got to the point of making the product, could you describe the team you assembled? How did you find them?

Lott: So again, I already understood how software businesses worked. I was the person who, over the years, had hired several thousand technical people of all levels, up to and including EVP of Research and Development and CEO. I knew who was in the industry. I knew what they were doing. I knew which ones were interested in staying where they were, and which ones were not—or were looking to do something else. And I had a sense for people who had the right skill set for what we were trying to do, and for the people who really had an appetite for entrepreneurship, for founding something—that's not everyone; that's a certain type of person.

When I started getting really serious about this, I started floating the idea to a couple of people I had worked with. *You know, you've done some things here, you're probably going to want to do something new soon. Have you thought about just going into a startup? Would you do that?* I talked my VP of technology into coming on board for stock because, at that point, I did not have enough cash to pay what they were currently making or what they would normally make. How do you talk a very talented engineer, who could work at any number of places, into joining you? They have to believe that what you're doing might turn into something bigger. You have to sell them on the vision. And quite frankly, there were a lot of folks who would rather do a startup than be in a big company; it was the nature of the industry at the time. So it wasn't a hard sell.

In terms of my contribution, I was the one who described how the product needed to work, what it needed to do, etc. I had worked enough with the industry to understand what the product needed to do and how it would function if it were going to take advantage of the new tools that were available. I couldn't code it, but I could tell you precisely how it needed to operate. So my product lead and I together were the right combination of skill sets. And we started with some high-level architectural discussions around what it needed to look like, and continued to talk to anybody in the industry who I thought could help us figure that out, whether it was technology-based, or market, or opening doors for capital, because I was always looking to raise more money. In those days, you needed a pretty good-sized engineering team to build anything enterprise-class—an expensive undertaking. Even with angel capital, that wasn't going to be enough. So we continued to talk with venture capitalists after we got the angel funding as we built out the beta.

To clarify, did he have the title of co-founder?

Lott: I absolutely gave [him] the title. If I were to look back and think about it, I don't know whether or not that was a good decision, but it was the right decision. If we were going to build something, he was going to work really hard to make that happen, right? And he was coming in so early that, yeah, he was absolutely considered a co-founder. And I gave him equity based on that, which worked out really well. He stayed with us pretty much all the way through, at least four or five years.

I think that's really amazing because a lot of startups actually crumble because of co-founder disagreements.

Lott: And I can understand why. I think there are a lot of things being done much better today, compared to then, in terms of vesting co-founders so you don't inadvertently give away too much of the business. But I do think part of it for us was, we weren't just getting to know each other. We already knew each other, and that worked to our advantage. We could argue and still get up and come back the next day. It was just a good relationship.

What happened leading up to the acquisition? How did you know you were ready?

Lott: I wouldn't go so far as to say that I decided it was the thing I really, really wanted to do. There's something that happens when a founder is that far into the business, heads down. You want to stay with that forever, right? But over time, we had gone from angel investing to where we had a very large customer, which is how we ended up getting a tier-one venture capital investment. So now we're playing a different ball game. Angels are your friends; venture capitalists are fundamentally people who are giving you capital for the purpose of growing their limited earning potential. And when you forget

> Angels are your friends; venture capitalists are fundamentally people who are giving you capital for the purpose of growing their limited earning potential. And when you forget that, you might find yourself not fully aligned with your venture capital partners.

that, you might find yourself not fully aligned with your venture capital partners.

We started this discussion a year, year and a half before the event. We did a major pivot from my original concept to what Bridgestream fundamentally became as a security software component in the identity management world. There were a couple of things going on at the macro level that we did not control, but [that] opened doors for us. One was the regulations around HIPAA [The Health Insurance Portability and Accountability Act of 1996]. The other was Sarbanes-Oxley [a 2002 law designed to help protect investors from fraudulent financial reporting by corporations]. That whole regulatory event was just becoming a big problem for large companies. That forced us to think about the timing related to our value, [which] we really needed to understand.

Once that problem was solved, our value shifted. So we agreed to hire consultants to test our market value. We did that about a year or so before the company exited. In that process, we determined that there was a sweet spot for us coming in the next X number of months. We had also just morphed into a partner sales model rather than direct sales. The downside of that was our product was now fundamentally sold through our partnership with companies like Oracle and IBM, so you no longer fully controlled your sales cycle. Yours is theirs, and that's not a straight-up position of strength for a small software company. It's not something we anticipated, and the reality is, it's more difficult. So our investors were considering both whether or not we could run on our own and whether we needed the partnerships. The answer was that partnerships are necessary.

The market itself was at its peak with respect to what they do, and within the market portfolio, there were a number of companies that were not going to turn a profit in the short term either because of where they were in their development or because, perhaps, they were just going to let go. There's always a percentage of the [market] portfolio that does not go forward, which always happens. And the number of IPO opportunities were few. It was not going to be an IPO. We were a partner.

Because of that, we started pursuing conversations with the likes of Oracle and others. That would not have been my choice. At that point, I did not necessarily think we were done. I thought there were other things we could do. We were looking to add to our original product line. But our investors were at a point where they wanted to recoup the return we'd be able to give them if sold to Oracle. There were many discussions about why and why not. And as much as I'm pleased that we exited—because many companies do not exit at all—I also understand that the timing and the decision around that exit are not always yours. And that has a lot to do with who your investors are and how much capital it's going to take to get you from wherever you are to the next [step].

But I'm okay with it. And, even today, the general partner at the venture fund is still a business associate, so he's still part of the network. He made the right business call. I was on the fence. I would have gone further, but they could trump that book.

It was a good outcome for my team, as they took the company lock, stock, and barrel into Oracle. Almost to a person. When we knew that was going to happen, I was clearly starting to step away and step out because I wasn't going to work for Oracle. That just wasn't something I would do. But I felt good for my team; they all had a nice exit. I think my investors felt that, for an acquisition, they did well. And they did.

I still believe founders don't do this kind of work for money. When you start a business, you expect to get paid at the end of the day for the value you've created. But if it were just about money, I could have done so many other things that are a lot less stressful to make money, right? But that business was different. At the end of the day, I do believe it connects back to where you grew up and what the perception might have been, or what people thought you could do or not. Some part of it was to prove that this venture capital world was something that we could do like anybody else. It was important for me to just see that through.

In retrospect, do you agree with the pivots you made? How would you have examined things differently?

Lott: I don't think it was a hard decision after we had done our due diligence. In figuring out our market, we must have talked to fifty or more chief innovation officers and chief security officers, and [we] found our original model was more of a nice-to-have for large companies. We were getting some interest in the nice-to-have market, but we weren't getting the traction that we wanted. We found that most Fortune 1000 and Fortune 5000 companies did not buy nice-to-have software as often—and not at the price points—as they did the software they had to buy. An application that will make word processing easier is nice, but I have to have finance, I have to have security, etc.

So we threw open our questions to CIOs and security professionals: *What was going on? What are you doing? What are your biggest problems? How do you know? How do they manifest? What would a solution look like?* By asking tons of questions without knowing the answers, we really started hearing a consistent theme around some of the regulatory issues. And when we looked at it, we realized the engine we were building for the nice-to-have was absolutely the thing that would solve the problem for them. So that was a pivot. Once we figured that out, it was easy for me to get moving, to convince my technologists, but very difficult for me to convince my investors. *What are you talking about? You are going from what to WHAT?* So we talked for a very long time to convince them that it was the right thing. And once we got into it, we brought them along.

To address the other part of your question, now, as I sit back and look at it, as an entrepreneur, if there's not a part of you that's always listening for what else is going on in your environment, you're going to make a mistake. You're going to do something, probably, but maybe there's a bigger *there* out there for you.

That's why, when we first started talking about COVID and what that means, that's a really great question. There are probably a ton of people out there right now thinking: *I can do something that's going to be interesting*—not just the solving of the disease issue but all the other implications and unintended consequences of us going through this environmental change. *There's going to be another sea change. I know it; I just don't know exactly what it looks like.* And when an entrepreneur starts seeing something like that, you start thinking: *I wonder what this is going to lead to*, right? And you start paying attention, and reading everything you can read, and listening to people. And mark my words, there's going to be a number of new businesses that you will be able to trace back to what was a very, very difficult time.

In surveying the networks and relationships that you've built throughout your career, who inspired you or really served as a champion, particularly in the early days as you navigated the startup process on your own?

Lott: Yeah, that would be Frank Green. Let me tell you about him. He was one of a handful of the early Intel-esque semiconductor engineers when Andy Grove was just getting started. Frank had a couple of startups of his own, a couple of exits. I think he had an IPO early on. I've forgotten what the product was, but he took no prisoners. Frank could be pretty harsh. Not in a negative way, but harsh in the way he talked about business, in the way he asked questions.

He was on my board after he invested. He and Mike Fields both. And this was early on. At every board meeting, you're telling them about your progress, where your business is going, how everything's going well, and what you're going to do. Frank would say absolutely nothing until the end of the meeting when we'd ask if anyone had any questions.

He asked just one: "So what's your value proposition?"

I'd rattle off what I thought the answer to that question would be. But no, that wouldn't be it. And he wouldn't tell me; he wouldn't help me. So at the next board meeting, we're talking about a *new* set of things. *We've done this and have this new customer, and it's great...*

And at the end of the meeting, we again asked: "Does anyone have any questions?"

To which Frank replied, "Have you figured out the value proposition?"

"Well, Frank, yes."

So this became a thing over months, maybe even a year. It got to the point where I was so angry with him. I went down to his office so we could engage outside of a board meeting.

"What are you talking about? I do not know what you're talking about. What do you mean?"

He looked at me and said, "You still have no idea what your value proposition is, and if you don't figure it out, I don't know."

So I'd leave, and we'd have another interaction like that at the next board meeting. I'd tell Mike Fields, who was always the calm voice of reason, "I can't deal with him. He needs to get off the board. He doesn't know what he's talking about." I'd say to Mike, "You tell him" [*laughs*].

But, long story short, at the end of the day, the most useful feedback I ever received from any source in the seven-plus years I ran that company—my venture partners, my tech people—was that single question. I finally articulated to him the value proposition of what I was doing, and he accepted it.

Not that he smiled, just: "Yeah, okay. Right."

He forced me through the pain, and challenge, and anger. And I realized there was more that he did for me there than the money I raised. That was an important lesson I learned as an entrepreneur. And to this day, when I sit down with young people who are getting started, I say: *Let's talk about your value proposition because, if you don't know what that is, you need to go and work on it.* So, yeah, the most useful thing I ever heard was having Frank give me grief—every quarter [*laughs*].

What impactful advice for you to not only take on your own but, as a result, translate into so much success.

Lott: Well, I hope as this [book] comes together, people can see themselves, and how their path might work, and [take away] the notion that you never know when someone in your network is going to be useful, so you have to constantly look for it. And don't ever throw away a connection.

ERIK MOORE

Founder and Managing Director, Base Ventures

KIRBY HARRIS

Co-Founder and Managing Partner, Base Ventures

Base Ventures is an early-stage venture firm that has raised three seed-stage venture capital funds. It has invested in companies such as Blavity, InDinero, Mayvenn, Modest, Inc. (sold to Braintree), Olly Nutrition (sold to Unilever), Welly, Pigeonly, PlanGrid (sold to Autodesk), StyleSeat, Surf Airlines, World View Enterprises, and more than seventy other companies.

Erik Moore, Founder and Managing Director

E rik Moore is the founder and managing director of Base Ventures, an early-stage tech venture fund. He was one of the first investors in Zappos (sold for $1.2 billion to Amazon in 2009) and an early investor in PlanGrid (sold to Autodesk for $875 million in 2018). Prior to Base Ventures, Erik spent fifteen years in investment banking at Merrill Lynch. He co-founded FlickLaunch, a digital streaming platform on Facebook for feature-length movies.

He recently joined the board of the Common Ground Foundation (founded by Grammy-, Oscar-, and Emmy-award-winning artist, Common), and has been a past board member of Russell Simmons' Art for Life. Erik has also been named to the City of Oakland's Fund Advisory Board with Mayor Libby Schaaf and serves on the advisory board of the Museum of the African Diaspora (MoAD), a Smithsonian affiliate. Finally, Erik serves on the board of Driving Force Group, which focuses on race equity initiatives, and was recently named to the Advisory Council at Dartmouth College. He was recognized as #10 on a list of the top twenty-five most influential Blacks in tech by *Business Insider*—John Thompson, chairman of Microsoft, was ranked #1. In addition, Erik mentors and advises several known professional athletes.

Erik earned a BA from Dartmouth College, an MA in French from the University of Pennsylvania, and an MBA from the Wharton School of Business.

Kirby Harris, Co-Founder and Managing Partner

K irby is a graduate of Morehouse College and was a member of the Kauffman Fellows, Class 21. He graduated with an MBA in finance from California State University, East Bay. An Oakland native, Kirby serves as a formal and informal advisor to several founders and portfolio companies, and is a board member of Space Perspective.

Kirby has invested in more than seventy companies over the course of his career, which began in 2000 as an analyst at Impact Capital Management, a boutique private equity firm. He was the vice president at Impact Capital Management until 2012 when he and Erik Moore formed Base Ventures.

Twitter: @base_ventures, @basevc

Instagram: @erikhmoore

Erik, where are you from, how did you grow up, and how have these experiences influenced the way you do business?

Erik Moore: So I'm from Richmond, California, which is a town near Oakland. And it's an inner-city town. I grew up in the seventies and eighties, so there was a lot of the bad stuff that people always hear about in Black communities—the crack epidemic and gang violence. Those things were happening in our community. There were also people who were influential and going to college as well. So I had the dichotomy. My dad was a civil servant, and my mom was a schoolteacher, both from New Orleans. They moved to California in the sixties.

I went to high school in Berkeley and left the Bay Area to go to college at Dartmouth in New Hampshire. I only knew about Dartmouth because my next-door neighbor had gone there before me, and when I was in high school, I went out to visit when he invited me. He was a mentor and good friend, and in the summers, he'd do algebra with me and teach me a lot of stuff. I'd soon learn that New Hampshire was really different from Richmond.

We'd go around campus, and he'd introduce me to some friends, show me around some of the departments. I remember one time we were going to see some of his friends. We knocked on the door and nobody answered. We just walked into the apartment, and there was money and stereo equipment and TVs just there. It was just so foreign to anything that I'd grown up with—actually, to what most people grew up with. I thought it was unique, and I ended up applying to Dartmouth on early decision and got in.

So I'm at Dartmouth. It's the late 1980s, and if you remember back then, apartheid was strong and kicking in South Africa. We were protesting apartheid by having shanty towns built in the middle of the yard. There was an on-campus publication called the *Dartmouth Review* that was a conservative newspaper, and its advisor was William F. Buckley, Jr., who is known to be the father of neoconservatism. The governor of New Hampshire at the time was John Sununu, who later became a cabinet member for [President Ronald] Reagan. So that was the kind of the environment we were working in. The *Dartmouth Review* people went into the shanty towns and took sledgehammers to them. They said that their goal was to *beautify the green again*, and it was making the green ugly. They wanted to fix that, so they took a sledgehammer to them.

There were a lot of protests, and I was the vice president of the Afro-American Society, so I spoke at rallies about it. But the takeaway for me was that, as important as in-class sessions were, learning about whatever I was learning about in school, the education that I got outside of the classroom was far more relevant and far more significant for me. What I mean by that is, I learned about politics, I learned about culture, I learned about what people actually believe and how they act toward you.

They wrote about me in the paper once, and said that I was an affirmative action student at Dartmouth. Despite the fact that I'd graduated from high school with a 4.0 GPA, was captain of the football team for four years, and all these other accolades I had in high school, they still said I was an affirmative action candidate. That to me was far more enlightening.

They wrote about me in the paper once, and said that I was an affirmative action student at Dartmouth. Despite the fact that I'd graduated from high school with a 4.0 GPA, was captain of the football team for four years, and all these other accolades I had in high school, they still said I was an affirmative action candidate. That to me was far more enlightening.

What did you study at Dartmouth?

Moore: I was a French major at Dartmouth. At one point I taught French in the summer session, and one person in my class was the editor of the *Dartmouth Review*. I taught him, and by the end of the class, we became friends. And we were able to think about our differences differently because we spent time together and got to know each other. So that was the takeaway there.

Because I was the president of my fraternity, Alpha Phi Alpha, I had a relationship with the folks at Tuck Business School at Dartmouth. I spoke to the dean of the business school quite a bit about what I wanted to do after [graduating]. I had a few internship and job offers, and he told me which one to take because it would be unique when I was ready to apply to business school at Tuck.

Before this decision, I had met Dennis Franklin, who worked at Goldman Sachs. He brought me to the trading floor, and I saw the frenetic pace of it, how exciting it was. He told me how much money they made, and there was no turning back at that point. I was singularly focused on getting into the business [of] sales and trading. The one thing he told me I needed was to go to business school. Because I had a liberal arts background, he felt that I needed to go to a quantitative or analytical school. That was Wharton, which is known for being a finance school. So I applied to Wharton and went there.

I got my MBA and a master's in French concurrently, and then spent the summer at Lehman Brothers working in investment banking. I was there when Netscape went public, actually. I ended up in investment banking and spent about fourteen years doing sales and trading.

How was your experience in sales and trading?

Moore: I was perennially a top performer. What I like to tell people is that the bonds I was selling to these big institutions were the same bonds that the people at Goldman Sachs had, the people at Morgan Stanley had, and JP Morgan. But what it boils down to is that I really believe the business—like any other business from my standpoint—is a people business. And I was very good at that. As a result, like I said, I was perennially a top performer. Not because I was the most analytical of my peers but because people like to do business with people they like. As a result, I did well in that.

Fast forward a bit, and I moved back to the West Coast in '98/'99. I had been investing in startups by then [as an angel investor]. When I moved back, it was the tech heyday, and I was around it, but I was content doing my investment banking business. It was still quite interesting to me.

I ended up living in San Francisco in a loft condo that was brand new. I knew a lot of tech folks would be living there, and sure enough that happened. I met a few folks, one of [them was] Tony Hsieh, who had just sold his first company, LinkExchange, to Microsoft in 1998 for 265 million bucks. He and I met on the elevator one night, after having had too much to drink, probably [*laughs*]. We became very good friends, and he later asked me to be on the board of the homeowners' association so he could get the leverage needed to put a hot tub in his unit. It was against the policy, and he had to stack the board. So it was me, his dad, a guy named Alfred Lin—if you look him up, he runs the early-stage fund at Sequoia. So he obviously got his hot tub, and that's how we became friends.

Next thing, after LinkExchange, Tony was working on this other company that was trying to sell shoes online. I used to host these dinners at my house, where people would pitch their ideas. And this kid who had just sold his company for [almost] three hundred million was listening to one of the pitches.

[Tony] walked out early and said, "That's not going to work, Erik. But if you want, I'll let you invest in what I'm working on. We're going to sell shoes online."

I told him I wasn't sure that there was anything crazier than selling shoes online. *I've got a foot that's bigger than the other one, and I'm also not gonna put my credit card online, in short.* But I had gotten to know him very well, and he was special. That company was Zappos. After he and his family, I was among the very first people to invest in Zappos. The first $50,000 I put into Zappos turned into 25,000 shares of Amazon. After [Zappos] was bought by Amazon for $1.2 billion, I ended up investing an additional $450,000 in the company. Around the same time, I also invested in Agencourt Bioscience, which was sold for $100 million—they then spun off another company and sold that for an additional $170 million.

So fast forward. I ended up leaving Merrill Lynch to do a startup that failed miserably, but it taught me empathy for startup founders and how difficult it was to actually do that work and what's required of it. It was called FlickLaunch, founded to help independent films get distributed through social media platforms, starting with Facebook. My initial motivation was my huge desire to be a startup founder. In retrospect, much of it was me being fascinated with the idea of being a founder—the perceived glamour, etc. I was neither passionate about the space, nor was I a domain expert...and what's more, I knew I was not an operator. Nonetheless, I wanted to give it a shot. *You only regret what you don't try.* I quickly found out that I was not good at it, and I didn't like it. But what I did take away was my newfound appreciation for the grit and perseverance that founders must display in order to succeed. And on the heels of that, I just continued investing my own money into startups.

Frankly, that experience as a founder partly informs my investment decisions today. I really just try to get into who the founders are, what their DNA is, and why they are building the company they're building. When I was building a company, I was in it for the wrong reasons, so it was never going to work.

Was there anyone who was particularly helpful at this time? Who is impacting your career at this point?

Moore: As I have done most of my life, I connected with my mentor, Peter Bogardus (now deceased) randomly at a Dartmouth Christmas event. He was this old White dude who graduated from Dartmouth in the fifties and would invite me to lunch whenever I would come home from New Hampshire for Christmas, or any break, really. He would tell me to put a suit and tie on and meet him at this address. I had been doing that over the years, and earlier on, I never knew what it was about. I would just go to this weird, super old, red-leather-chair-library-type place and have lunch with basically, all these old White dudes. And we would have a good time and hang out. Come to find out, our lunch was at the Bohemian Club—one of the premier clubs in the country. Years later, when I started my first year at Wharton, he put my name on the wait list for membership; he and Tony Frank, the postmaster general of the United States, were my sponsors. I was on the wait list for twenty years before I was allowed to join.

George [H. W.] Bush and Ronald Reagan were also members, Mark Twain, Jack London—there's a bunch of artists. You name a CEO of these top corporations, and they're all members as well. And my Black ass, too [*laughs*]. I've been in it for about five years now but I've been going to the club for a long time.

Kirby Harris: Aren't you mistaken for an artist? The Bohemian Club was started by artists. If you're an artist, you don't have to pay as much, and you get fast-tracked in. So a lot of the Black folks there are artists. They asked Erik what instrument he plays [*laughs*]. That's the first question for any new person he bumps into that he doesn't know: What instrument do you play?

Moore: Yeah, versus there's no way I could be in it, you know, as a regular. It's called "regular member," which means a businessperson.

Kirby, where were you born and raised? What was your life like leading up to when you and Erik met?

Harris: I was born and raised in Oakland, California. My parents grew up and lived across the street from each other on Ninety-

Eighth Avenue in Oakland. My dad has eleven brothers and sisters; my mom has eight brothers and sisters. When I'd walk out of my grandmother's house, it's us [*laughs*]. So I have a bunch of cousins around Oakland. Until probably ten years ago, everyone lived in Oakland.

My mother was an Army and Navy brat growing up, so she lived in a bunch of different countries throughout her life. They settled back into Oakland in the seventies. My grandmother is from El Cerrito, actually. My mom and dad were never married. They weren't together, but they were both always actively a part of my life. My mom was a medical records nurse at Highland Hospital, the county hospital in Oakland, which was a wild place to work in the eighties. I saw my mom put herself through nursing school when I was in junior high and high school. She became a nurse, probably my junior year of high school. So I witnessed her for years going through the trials and tribulations of nursing school and doing all that kind of stuff while having two boys.

My dad was a car detailer. He worked at British Motors, which is across the street from Erik's first condo. I'm a few years younger than Erik. My dad always had a side hustle where he detailed cars for clients on nights and weekends. At British Motors they sell Rolls Royces and Jaguars, so a lot of the Warriors [basketball players] at the time, like Fred Jackson, were clients. There were a lot of business owners as clients too. Doctors, lawyers, athletes, and business owners were basically his clientele. So although we lived in an inner-city environment, I basically got to see how the other half lived on the weekends and at night. From the time I could walk, I would help my dad detail cars. There was a department store there called McCaulou's. We'd go to Mr. McCaulou's house, and he had a train like Richie Rich [*laughs*]. He had that actual train in his house. So this was an entirely different experience than where we lived.

I always asked what they did. With Mr. McCaulou, he had three or four cars, so we would spend about two full days there. Of course, as a six- or seven-year-old kid, I was cool helping out for half a day, but by the second day, I was bored. So Mr. McCaulou would take me to his department store, and we'd walk around, and he'd just let me pick out stuff.

I saw what ownership meant, what being a business owner means. And talking to the doctors, the lawyers, and the business owners gave me a reference point. I know how we lived, and I saw how they lived. So I wanted to be a business owner, and would do whatever it took to get to where they were.

I had this thing where I always had money because my dad always paid me to come out and help him work. I was happy to get up at 6:00 a.m. and work until six o'clock in the evening to make forty dollars or whatever as an eight-year-old. So the lure of the streets wasn't that great because I always had money from doing the work that we did.

And my dad was there, and I was a good athlete. I actually played on the state championship team with Jason Kidd. In

'91/'92, we went to a small private high school in Alameda called St. Joseph. I was a decent athlete, but I saw what a professional was like, and it wasn't me [*laughs*]. A lot of the professionals—the doctors and lawyers—who we detailed cars for were Black. A lot of them went to HBCUs.

My dad said, "You know, it's probably a good idea for you to go to an HBCU. All these people we do work for, this guy, that guy, they all went to HBCUs. So it might be something that you consider."

When it came to choosing a college, I applied to Morehouse, Howard, and Georgia Tech. I ended up going to Morehouse, and that was probably one of the best experiences of my life.

Tell us about your experience at Morehouse.

Harris: Well, coming from Oakland and going to Atlanta where everything Black is good [*laughs*], and at Morehouse seeing the full African diaspora, was impactful. In Atlanta, I saw guys who lived on farms in Alabama, in cities [like] New York and Chicago, Tupelo, Mississippi, or whatever. People who are wealthy, third generations of wealth. Black folks that I didn't have an up-close experience with. It was an eye-opening experience. It was a place where you weren't the only smart Black kid. You were just some guy. So I enjoyed Morehouse, but I was focused on graduating.

I went into Morehouse wanting to be an engineer. I love cars, and I wanted to design them. My first semester, I took some physics classes, and didn't think they were fun at all. But

I took an econ class, and that was great, so I changed my major to business and marketing. My second semester senior year, I took a finance class. I was like: *This is the best thing ever. This is what I want to do.*

I talked to my mother and told her that I wanted to stay for an extra semester, and I'd get a degree in marketing and one in finance. She said, "Well, we made an agreement when you started. I'll pay for four years, and you'll graduate in four years."

Needless to say, I graduated, but I wanted to do finance. So as soon as I got home [post-graduation], I was trying to figure out a way to get into finance and the quickest way was to get a degree in finance. So I came back home, started working, and soon entered Cal State Hayward [East Bay] as a full-time MBA student in finance. I left my first semester and did a study abroad program in London, followed by a month in South Africa, which was, again, probably one of the best experiences of my life. And when I got back, I met Erik.

I was halfway through my MBA. I had quit my job before I left London, so I came back home and was trying to figure out what I wanted to do. Well, I knew what I wanted to do, but I was trying to figure out a place. I called my cousin, an executive at Pac Bell who ended up going to work at WorldCom MCI in Atlanta. He had a lot of connections back here in the Bay Area, and he introduced me to someone. She actually connected me to Erik and two Black guys from Richmond and Oakland who started a boutique private equity fund, New Capital Access Group.

What was it like meeting Erik?

Harris: Erik was generous enough to spend, like, a half a day with me. We went to lunch, he showed me around the trading floor. We spent some time together.

He was like: "Yeah, you're probably a little analytical for this job; what else you got going?"

I told him that I was probably thinking about staying in private equity.

"That's probably something you should pursue."

So I ended up interviewing with the guys at the private equity group and began working there halfway through my MBA program. The group was designed to invest in companies in and around Oakland. Though not initially, they eventually grew to a national footprint. *Yeah, I'll cut my teeth there.* I ended up joining them in 2000 and worked there for essentially ten years.

Erik and I stayed in touch. We bumped into each other in 2007 or 2008 and started talking about stuff and spending time. Around 2009 or 2010 we started sharing an office as he was doing his entrepreneurial thing with the startup.

With your journeys aligned, how did your relationship develop from a network connection to a business partnership?

Harris: So in 2008/2009 I was in the process of trying to figure out what I was going to do because we were in the middle of a financial crisis. The partners had kind of bailed, and left to do other things. I was left to wind down the business. I was handling that and negotiating the business with our LPs [Limited Partners]. I think Erik was in a similar position; that was about the same time Amazon had bought Zappos. There was a liquidity event, and he was thinking about what he was going to do. So around 2009 we just started talking every couple of months.

I'm more analytical. I had been running a fund for the last ten years, doing audits, etc. I understood how to develop, and what it meant to manage a fund. But I had no network to raise money; there was no way I could raise capital. Erik, on the other hand, had the network and relationships to raise.

You know, we're kind of opposite personalities. I'm the more introvert; he's more the extrovert. I'm more analytical. I had been running a fund for the last ten years, doing audits, etc. I understood how to develop, and what it meant to manage a fund. But I had no network to raise money; there was no way I could raise capital. Erik, on the other hand, had the network and relationships to raise. So those are our different skill sets and responsibilities as we run the fund and as we started Base.

What are some of the formal and community relationships that helped you all launch Base? Where were you going, and what networks were you tapping into?

Harris: Erik's connection is choppy. I can talk to that. I mean, most of the people who invested are early investors. We did what's called an SPV, a special purpose vehicle. We raised a million bucks and invested in a company that Erik talked about. He invested in a biotech company at the same time he invested in Zappos. That guy sold his first company for almost $300 million and was starting a new company. So Erik was a personal investor in that and was talking to friends about that. We thought: Hey, this might be a good opportunity to gather some money, and we can put some money to work into the guy you're familiar with, who you know.

We spent probably two weeks or something just dialing for dollars, saying: *Hey, we've got this opportunity, do you want to put in? We're doing a vehicle, and the last one we ten-to-fifteen timesed our money. The guys are great. Do you want to get in?*

We raised a million bucks, and most of that was from either Erik's investment banking folks or Wharton classmates. Those were the two communities that were early investors in that opportunity.

I don't know how relevant this is, but one of our first conversations with an investor who's been an investor in everything that we've done, and Erik has done, since the first SPV, he said: "Hey, man, we talked about the opportunity, but I don't understand what you're talking about. I don't know if you understand what you're talking about [*laughs*]. But I'm in for a couple hundred grand, and we can talk later. I'm walking my kid to the park." [*laughs*] I think that was one of Erik's Wharton classmates.

What challenges did you face in raising for the SPV?

Harris: The first SPV was easy because we were just raising whatever we could raise. And whatever we raised didn't matter; it was to put it in the pot of the larger capital raise. Our next raise, though, was a full-on fund. The SPV was in 2011, and we started working on our first fund in 2012. That was a little bit more challenging, where you're trying to get to a number, and you either get there or you don't.

Our first one, we were trying to get to $10 million, I believe, and we got to $2 million. That was just not knowing how to raise capital in a formal manner.

What's different about raising in a formal manner?

Harris: Well, the first time we went out to raise, we literally sat up in an office and dialed for dollars. We didn't go meet anybody or meet with people that Erik knew. The second time, it was people that we knew, but it was a different ask, asking for a blind pool of capital versus a very discrete opportunity that you can put money into. People can understand that opportunity and make a decision, versus you betting on my ability to go raise.

The second time, it was people that we knew, but it was a different ask, asking for a blind pool of capital versus a very discrete opportunity that you can put money into. People can understand that opportunity and make a decision, versus you betting on my ability to go raise.

So, with that, we went out and thought it was a multi-meeting thing; if people are going to write you $200,000 checks, they've got to know you. And that wasn't necessarily the case. So we had outlines of term sheets, but we didn't have docs. We were in New York doing, like, twenty meetings a day, literally, and we'd been there for four or five days, and in twenty meetings we would get five yesses or five: *Hey, what's the next step?*

We just couldn't remember who said yes, who said no, who needed what. We didn't have docs, so we had nothing to send them. We had a pitch, but no docs for them to execute. People were ready to execute because they were only writing $50,000 checks, and for most of these folks, it's not a big ask. They can sign up fifty grand on the spot, but we didn't have docs. Then we would figure out who it was and whatever, and we'd be two or three weeks later, a month later. And they'd lost interest; they'd forgotten who we were.

When a lot of funds talk to us about their first raise, our seminal piece of advice is that people will say yes a lot quicker than you think. So be ready with docs, and try to send the docs immediately because the saying goes: Time kills deals. If someone who says yes does not sign anything soon, the yes turns into a no answer.

So not understanding what the process was, not knowing who our audience was, hurt us in our first raise. When a lot of funds talk to us about their first raise, our seminal piece of advice is that people will say yes a lot quicker than you think. So be ready with docs, and try to send the docs immediately because the saying goes: *Time kills deals.* If someone who says yes does not sign anything soon, the yes turns into a no answer.

How has it felt to be a Black man while tracking this journey through the finance and banking industries, then into startup and venture capital?

Harris: My answer will be quick. I worked for two Black men [when in private equity]. One guy grew up a few blocks from where my parents grew up; we knew the same people. One of his best friends at one time dated my aunt. He had seen me play basketball as a teenager. So my indoctrination was very familial. It was almost like I worked for my two uncles to a large extent. So they were very open, and I got a lot of great experience working with those guys. They showed me a lot and gave me access to everything they were doing. I was able to get a breadth and depth of knowledge that I otherwise may not have been able to get.

My indoctrination was very familial.

Moore: And the experience you got has translated into what our roles are at the fund too. Kirby operated, and knows how to run and put together, a fund, which is why we make a good team.

But to answer your question, there's nothing new under the sun. And as much as it's kind of novel to talk about Blacks in venture, and we have to diversify and get people involved, this is precisely the conversation that was being had when I was in investment banking. The same person who helped get more Black folks in investment banking is the same person who I think doesn't get the full credit, but he'll get more credit for doing the same thing in tech, and that's Jesse Jackson. When he railed against some of the bigger tech companies that put their numbers out about what their hiring looked like and the demographics of the folks who work there, it's the *same* stuff we've been talking about thirty years ago in investment banking, twenty years ago, fifteen years ago, is the same thing we're talking about now in tech and particularly in tech investing.

I have a bit of a different take on it. I'm more of the Reginald Lewis school. He wrote a book called *"Why Should White Guys Have All the Fun?"* and ran a company called TLC Beatrice, the first Black company to do a billion-dollar deal. And he talks about, yeah, that stuff happens, and people are racist. And if you let that prevent you from moving forward or doing what you need to do, then maybe it's not the right business for you. So understand that it happens, deal with it to the extent that you feel is appropriate, but you have to keep moving forward.

So maybe I didn't make as much money in investment banking as my White counterpart, but I was still making a lot. I made it known that I wasn't happy about it, particularly given my performance. But I had also been investing, and I didn't have to be there. So I retired from Merrill Lynch. You know, you can vote with your feet. And this venture/tech investing world, who am I to say I can't? I go to people to get money. If they say no, I don't know if they're saying no because I'm Black, or because they don't like our approach, or if they're saying no for whatever reason. If their reason is valid, I don't get too caught up in it. And if it's because I'm Black, then it's better for me not to have your money because it's going to be a contentious and unpleasant relationship. When an LP invests in your firm, it's a relationship. And if they are racist, it's better for them not to be in your fund. So I don't get too bogged down and caught up in why people are not investing. They don't do it for whatever reason, and that reason is valid.

So does it exist? Do people not want to fool with us because we are who we are? Yeah, of course. But it's not stopped us. It won't ever stop us. We're going to continue to do this. I'm not doing it for them; I'm doing this because we are impactful to the larger ecosystem.

So does it exist? Do people not want to fool with us because we are who we are? Yeah, of course. But it's not stopped us. It won't ever stop us. We're going to continue to do this. I'm not doing it for them; I'm doing this because we are impactful to the larger ecosystem. Take our numbers, and put them up against any other firm, especially a Black firm, and we perform well. We're impactful because we provide access. Ninety percent of our interns have been Black, and quite a few of the other investors in our fund are women, Black women who haven't had exposure to tech investing before. We do an inordinate amount of caring about young Black boys in particular, and girls, too. And we speak at schools in Oakland; we mentor, we do all these things that we don't talk about because it's just who we are. And we don't get a lot of accolades for it; we're not looking for them. We're doing it for a different reason; we're doing it because we can't help it. We can't help ourselves, and this is stuff that's important to us.

It doesn't matter who knows about it, and it doesn't matter if we get any record of it. We rarely talk about this; we only talk about it when people ask us because it's not about checking boxes. We do the work. We help get people

Forty percent of our companies are run by Black and Brown and female founders. So we do the work, and we don't look for an attaboy from folks.

exposure to this business and all aspects of the investing side. Forty percent of our companies are run by Black and Brown and female founders. So we do the work, and we don't look for an *attaboy* from folks.

Given not only your investment focus but your broader community impact across the ecosystem, how have the tone and events of 2020 impacted you as a fund?

Moore: When it [the COVID-19 pandemic] first started happening, we were in the middle of raising, and we took a step back because we thought that it was insensitive and inappropriate to be out fundraising and talking to people about investing in a fund when not knowing if their grandparent, friend, or parent is on a ventilator and potentially not making it. So we just kind of waited and came to find out a little bit later that most people were still out there raising, and it wasn't that big of a roadblock for people to get out and get in front of potential investors. So we took a hiatus, unfortunately.

You know, also, there's a bunch of companies who have found this new religion about how important it is to be diverse and how important it is to invest in Black founders and how important it is to invest in Black VCs [*laughs*]. And we have a somewhat cynical relationship with some of those. I'll say this; the approach by some of them has been insulting. I know it because I've done it. When I was early on in the business, I didn't understand the game, and I remember going to a friend who runs a really big venture fund and [saying]: *Hey man, you know, since we're just starting out, we would love to be able to share deals and get some of your deal flow.*

And this guy, who was a friend, basically laughed at me. He was like: *Yeah, dude—no.* Suffice to say I never got to deal for them. And that happened more than once. I get it now. I understand that you share your deals with your network, people you care about, and people you think can add value. And at that point, I hadn't proved that. I hadn't earned that, so I didn't get that look.

Fast forward to today, and everybody is very interested in and sensitive around investing in *folks*. And they approached us with: *You know, we don't know you. I know [who] you are, but I don't have this relationship with you. I want to spend time with you and get to know you. Would you meet with us?*

Yeah, of course, I'll meet. We met with, I don't know, half a dozen, and the conversations were: *Yeah, give us your deal flow.* Well, what do we get out of it? Give us *your* deal flow or invest in us. I mean, you guys write LP checks. We didn't have that conversation. They just wanted our deal flow so they can go out and be able to make those announcements: *We've got this $100 million, $500 million thing that we're going to start investing out of,* and they get the upside and accolades for doing that. And no one holds them accountable to actually put that money to work, so they don't get the downside of not actually doing the work.

And you know, we can talk about the hard decisions and hard work that comes along with really wanting to make a change. It's not writing $100 million checks, or whatever the number is. It's much harder than that.

It is much harder. So, in what ways would you qualify Base Ventures as an early innovator in that regard?

Harris: We were the first Black fund that was writing seed checks in Silicon Valley. There were some angel investors, and Syncom was on the East Coast doing their thing in the nineties, but writing early-stage checks in Silicon Valley, we were the first.

Moore: And just to qualify, there were other people doing it for impact, right? They were investing with a lens towards impact— and I don't know if it was they, maybe one or two—but not in the same way that we were doing it then, and continue to do it now. As a result of that, you can talk to a few of the folks who just announced big funds; they talk about how they saw us doing it, then us spending time with them, and being helpful translated into them being successful as well. I mean, we don't go anywhere with people not telling us about how we have impacted their journey. We get it nonstop about how impactful it's been just being there

Risk aversion was something else that we were up against. Well, not up against but something we swam against.

among the first to do it. And by the way, we are successful. Our funds have done very well.

Harris: Also, risk aversion was something else that we were up against. Well, not up against but something we swam against. Black folks who were professionals, they were cool with the stock market or money market accounts and CDs and getting people to go out there and put risk capital out there and say: Hey, there's this place where you can five-times, ten-times, twenty-times your money. So we did a lot of educating, especially back in 2012 when we were first starting out. It wasn't widely accepted that people were doing this coming out of the financial crisis. There were very few people seeking risk coming out of the financial crisis.

Is there anything you would have done differently in building Base Ventures? Any nos you second-guessed, or other learning lessons?

Harris: [*Laughs*] There's a lot of those investments that we could have done that we didn't do. But one of the big things we didn't do was that, with our first fund, we probably should have tried to raise more money to set the table, so that from one to two, you're not five-times-ing and from two to three, you're not trying to five-times, ten-times, or something. So starting off with the larger fund, the numbers we raised were so small, people wrote small checks for a small fund.

That and maybe institutionalizing a little quicker. We were working with Carole Crawford [of fincap360] at the time, as an advisor. She was guiding us in our raise and quickly suggested that we become more institutional in our fundraising strategy. We didn't know what that meant. She railed on it to us for six months and finally gave up. It took a year or more before we finally learned what it meant to prepare for and execute an institutional capital raise. So just being institutional quicker, and getting larger faster. I think that the folks who have come after us learned the lesson and got bigger quickly.

Moore: It's a function of what you're saying because I was going to say, write bigger checks, but we didn't have funds [*laughs*], so we couldn't do what we do now. Some of those companies that we invested a small amount in, had we done what we really had the conviction to do, our performance would have been even better.

Harris: Erik was an angel investor in Michael Seibel's first company Socialcam. That was back in 2011/2012. So we were running around together, writing checks even back then.

Erik, you earlier referenced your experience at the Bohemian Club, and Kirby, your experience being mentored by two Black PE executives. Who else has been impactful in your journey?

Moore: I'm hesitant because it's someone who was the reason why I went to Dartmouth and the reason why I am who and where I am now. But he had nothing to do with venture. He just was a mentor in my life and got me from a mindset of growing up in Richmond, where people—especially Black men and young boys—don't do much, to do something great and go to this Ivy League institution three times for an undergrad and two master's degrees. He instilled in me that I was good enough to do it and smart enough to do it. And that I should do it. So it wasn't actually related to venture or investing at all. He passed away in the nineties.

So he and Peter Bogardus, the mentor who got me into the Bohemian Club. He taught me a couple of lessons, but, you know, there were very few Black men in this club, and he took a chance on whatever backlash he would get from his colleagues and friends or whatnot, and put me on this list that I'm sure he thought would be transformational in my life. And he was right. Another thing he did was buy me a suit and told me to pay him back $50 a month, on time. I paid him maybe two or three payments, and he told me to stop paying. But he wanted to teach me the importance of one, keeping your word and two, making sure you always pay your debt.

Specifically around venture, from an investment standpoint, Tony Hsieh, the CEO of Zappos, had some insight that I've lived with for a long time. But also—and I've never voiced this—but Charles Hudson, who runs Precursor Ventures, when we were out first raising, reached out to me and said: *Let's get some lunch.* He was still working at another fund, not his own. I didn't know what he wanted to talk about, but we were friends already, so we got together.

He just said: *Hey, I'm just checking in because I know how difficult it is and how lonely it is to be out there doing this.* That just impressed upon me that business didn't have to be so sharp-elbowed, and you can be helpful and friendly in this. I don't know if that energy is as prevalent now as it was then. I know that when they [Precursor] were starting out, we shared potential investors, LPs, and it's just something that stuck with me. It wasn't something that was huge, but it was impactful.

Who am I missing, Kirby?

Harris: What about Michael Bush or Mitch Kapor?

Moore: Specific to later in this journey of investing, Michael Bush is a friend—a mentor initially—who now runs a publicly-traded company called Great Place to Work. Before that he was the CEO of a publicly-traded company, and he's done a lot of very important and major work. When I was making the decision to leave Merrill Lynch and to do this entrepreneurial thing, my first call was to Michael, and we met. We talked about it a little bit, and he was extremely encouraging. By the way, I'm passing by Kamala Harris' elementary school right now, which is also where I went to elementary school. She was a few years older than me, but not much [*laughs*]. So Michael was encouraging and said I absolutely should do it. And coming from him, I garnered a lot of confidence as a result of those conversations we had. And it wasn't the same answer I got from other peers and friends.

And finally, I'll leave with this. Mitch and Freada Kapor [of Kapor Capital] have been good friends and supporters from the beginning. They really put their money where their mouths are, and they do the work. When they were looking at potential funds to invest in, it really needed to have an impact lens, an impact focus. And he knew that our fund wasn't that—or we didn't call ourselves that. I remember calling him and relaying: *Man, I know what you guys are doing, so if it doesn't make sense for us to meet with you about this, I totally understand since we're not really an impact fund.*

He took me aside and said: *You guys aren't, but you and Kirby are more impactful in this space than people who claim to be impact funds, and it would be a problem if you didn't come in and talk to us about getting money.*

He and Freada were generous enough, and they doubled the allocation to our fund.

Harris: I didn't come from a space of early-stage. The private equity fund I worked with didn't invest in tech. We did some early-stage, but we did a lot of control investing where we would just buy the whole company or buy enough of it to control it and bring management along. A lot of me learning how to do early-stage investing was watching Erik and spending time with Erik when we initially started. So from him, I could see what it was all about and talk about it. And maybe I didn't get what they were doing, but Erik would share: There's something about this person; there's something about them, whether it was Michael Seibel or Tracy Young of PlanGrid. So I learned a lot about early-stage tech investing from Erik.

Then spending time with guys like Chris Redlitz at Transmedia Capital, and seeing how he invests, and seeing the work he did after he invested. Spending time with Mitch, reading and talking about his journey—all these experiences were helpful. I'm also a student of more traditional investors like Joel Greenblatt and Warren Buffett. I've spent a lot of time studying and reading and understanding, and applying some of those tools to early-stage ventures.

So, what's next for Base Ventures? What are you all looking forward to?

Harris: We're excited to grow the family tree of fund managers, several of whom got their start working for or interning at Base. We're also looking forward to our next intern's billion-dollar exit and, more generally, continuing to lift the tide of Black fund managers.

DELANE PARNELL

Founder and CEO, PlayVS

PlayVS is the official high school and college esports league, dedicated to inclusivity, teamwork, and sportsmanship. PlayVS partners with the National Federation of State High School Associations and twenty-three state associations, enabling students to play competitive games, earn a varsity letter, and compete for state championships.

Delane Parnell is the founder and CEO of PlayVS, the venture-backed startup building the infrastructure for amateur esports, starting with high school and college leagues. Before PlayVS, Delane was the youngest Black venture capitalist in the US as a

Senior Associate at IncWell Venture Capital, and an early employee at Rocket Fiber, which raised over $31 million to build a gigabit Internet service provider. A lifelong entrepreneur, Delane started his entrepreneurial journey at age thirteen, and now leads a top gaming startup that has raised over $100 million since its founding in 2018.

Website: http://www.playvs.com/

Editor's Note: Delane Parnell grew up in the Jeffries Homes, a public housing project located in Detroit, Michigan. He later moved to other neighborhoods of Detroit before relocating to Los Angeles to launch PlayVS. He was raised by a single mother; his father was murdered before he was born. By thirteen, he worked forty hours per week while a full-time student. He owned his first business at sixteen, and soon expanded his entrepreneurial footprint to own three cell phone stores and a car rental company with multiple locations across Michigan. Choosing business over college, Delane's pursuits built a historical career in venture capital before dominating the future of esports.

What inspired you to take risks early on, especially those that propelled you to where you are today?

Delane Parnell: For me, there wasn't another option. Working for someone was never really in the plans. Not because I thought that was beneath me, or I didn't think I could attain value from working for someone, but because I'm the type of person that really likes to bet on myself. I believe I have the opportunity to generate the largest return in almost anything in life, whether it's something as simple as a sport or learning something new, or betting on making a shot into a waste bin. I'm going to take myself in every scenario, even if I've never done something before. And when it comes to my career, that is the thing I'm going to spend the bulk of my time on. Maybe eight to twelve hours a day sometimes—if not more—at least five days a week. I figured if I wasn't putting myself in a position to bet on myself and generate outsized returns for myself, that wasn't in

Not only do I belong at the table, but the table sits in the building that I own. That's always been the mentality I've carried.

my best interest. Even as a kid, I recognized—obviously with some mentorship to get there—it otherwise wasn't in my own best interests.

So I just started betting on myself and trying to find people who could give me an opportunity (through partnership) to build businesses together. At the cell phone store, I found some people, [and] we did that. With the car rental, we did that. At every other moment in life, I just don't really believe in asking for a handout or having to be invited to the table. Not only do I belong at the table, but the table sits in the building that I own. That's always been the mentality I've carried.

And ownership is important. Every step of the way, everything that I'm a part of, I want to have ownership in. The things that I spend my time on are things that I own. And because I believe so much in myself, that gives me the highest leverage and opportunity to win in life, to set myself, my family, and my family's families up for, hopefully, an easier life one day. It's not even about having all sorts of materialistic stuff like cars and money, but just a life of no financial stress. I think that's something that many of us deserve—frankly, all of us deserve it, if we're willing to put in the work and make the sacrifices to get there. I happen to be in a position to do that. And I want to make sure I accomplish that.

Let's talk about your journey to PlayVS. How did your previous career in VC impact its inception?

Parnell: So there was a long gap of time between working in VC and starting PlayVS. When I worked in VC, I just worked in VC. I actually didn't know anything about esports—or had really heard of the space. Obviously, I was a gamer, but we had looked at literally zero gaming companies during my time in VC. The closest thing was fantasy sports. We spent a lot of time digging into that, and we even made some investments. There were some that I obviously didn't personally support. They didn't do well, but not because of that. But because they were bad companies. But we looked at the space nonetheless.

It wasn't until I worked at Rocket Fiber that the concept came about. Rocket Fiber was the job I took right after VC. And the reason I took that job was, at the time, I thought that I wanted to be a career VC. But I also wanted to do so in Michigan. And I learned a ton about running a venture fund, in making investments, and in supporting the investments in the hope that they become successful. The people I happened to do that work with, I didn't have the greatest pleasure working with them. Not only were there cultural differences—being the only Black person every time there's a room of people. Most of the time there's a room of ten to twenty people. And then also they just didn't do things that were norms in the industry. They basically moved into the space from the auto industry, and at the most corporate level of the auto industry. So they operated a fund that's a lot more lax from an industry perspective, just as they would an auto company. I recognized that a lot of the things they were doing from a best practices standpoint and process standpoint were abnormal, and I decided that I wanted to separate myself from that.

While doing so, I recognized that, not only did I have empathy for entrepreneurs and want to support them, but potentially I wanted to be an entrepreneur myself. And so I joined a startup during its early days with a founder I admired, Marc Hudson at Rocket Fiber, so I could actually learn from him and go through the experience of taking an idea from concept to business, from an entrepreneur to a CEO, because they're just two different things. Luckily Marc Hudson thought I could add some value at that time, and [he] invited me along the journey. It was a pleasure. And there, fortunately, I fell in love with esports.

It actually happened by happenstance. The vice president of client experiences at Rocket Fiber, Christina Fair, had come to Marc and me one day, and said: *There's this guy who keeps hitting us up about using our Internet for these things called esports tournaments.* Marc and I both were gamers, and he knew my love for the space, so he said to me: *You should take it.* So I did.

I met with the guy and we spent a ton of time together. I fell in love with the space, and it ended up consuming my day, even at work. I was fully invested in esports and figuring out what our position in esports could be. I think Marc and I both decided that Rocket Fiber may not have a place in esports that fit naturally, and maybe I did. So during that time while at Rocket Fiber, I also started a team called Rush Esports, and I sold that team right around my second to last, or my last week, at the company. From there I was full-time in esports.

The idea for PlayVS didn't come until the year after that, 2017. Toward the latter half of that year, I met Peter Pham at SXSW [South by Southwest], and we started to talk at the Culture House about esports. I shared ideas I had, and where I saw the most opportunity in the space, in addition to where the challenges existed that we would need to solve to unlock those opportunities.

Peter said, "Hey, give me your info. I want to reach out to you."

I gave him my info, and he called me the next day. He said he'd been thinking about my idea, and [he] suggested I come out to LA and build this thing with him and his partners. He and I stayed connected, and I came out to LA a number of times over the next few months, from March to June, then moved there full-time in June. From July 1 through October, there wasn't a set idea, but I had a vision that I wanted to build a platform for esports, and it means a lot of different things because we experience sports in a lot of different ways. But I was going about entering the market by building out the high school experience first—like if you're a high school student and want to have a team, what does that look like?

From an idea standpoint, that didn't come together properly until about October of that year. Then, through December, I spent a lot of time validating and invalidating contingencies to that idea while also trying to put deals together to firm up the viability of that. Then, in January 2018, I started the company with a little bit more traction.

With Peter Pham, the first investor?

Parnell: It's hard to actually say from a timeline perspective. Peter and Science Venture Capital were the first institutional investors, but when I first started the company, there were a few good friends who believed in me, even before I knew what I was doing. And they had given capital before January 2018, before I'd even started the company. Bryan Smiley was one. He's also the president of HartBeat Productions, which is Kevin Hart's company. Before that, he was an executive at Sony, Fox, and New Regency. He's from Detroit, and he's ten-plus years older than me. We met a long time ago through a mutual connection, and started talking on the phone, and just never stopped talking. He believed in me from the very start, so he gave me some resources well before I formally started the company.

And then my best friend—I have a number of best friends, but this is my ultimate best friend of the five—his name is Eugene Donald, but we just call him Gene. He owns a company called Fresh Baked Prints, which is one of the biggest print shops in Michigan. They print banners, cards, signs, and T-shirts for a lot of companies and independent Black creators in the state. So I told him about the idea, and he was like: *Yo, pull up on me.* He was in LA but staying in the [San Fernando] Valley, so I pulled up on him. He handed me a little brown bag full of, like, $5,000 or $10,000. I'm like: *Dude, I can't take money like this. Let's do some paperwork and figure out a vehicle.* So we had a number of steps to get his capital, but he was actually the first person to extend cash to invest.

Then Bryan Smiley, and the third person was Hajj Flemings, an entrepreneur in the branding space, based in Michigan. Hajj and I worked together on a number of things, like events, before I became an entrepreneur. Hajj is the person who told Tom LaSorda at IncWell, the venture fund, that he should hire me. Hajj and his wife, Cassandra, had never made an investment before, but they really wanted to be a part of what I was doing—whatever it was. I mean, I didn't know, so they didn't know. I think Hajj gave me $15,000.

So, basically, with Bryan's capital, Gene's capital, Hajj's capital, and my own capital, I had enough money to buy the domain and register the trademarks associated with the domain, which I didn't buy for, like, $2. I had to spend thousands of dollars because someone else owned it. I had to buy the trademarks associated with the domain that were, like, tens of thousands of dollars. And after registration and other startup costs, we had a little bit of capital remaining to do some other stuff.

It was a big investment to get the company started well before we took in any outside capital. When we did take outside capital, we did so in a sort of institutional round. I don't know if I would even call Science Ventures the first institutional investor because the lead investor—that was EA [Electronic Arts]—set the terms, and then Science obviously participated in that. Without Science, the company wouldn't have come together. So I think there are a number of people who deserve the credit for supporting the company from a finance perspective: those three Black men I mentioned who are friends of mine and wanted to support me even before I knew what I was doing; obviously Peter Pham from Science Ventures who, from day one, saw talent in me and urged me to relocate to LA to be able to unlock that talent and fulfill my potential; and then New Enterprise Associates, one of the greatest venture funds of all the time. The first meeting I had with Rick Yang and Jon Sakoda, we talked for an hour. Thirty minutes into it, they looked at each other and said: *We should invest in this.* Literally, that's exactly what they said to each other. And they've been great partners ever since.

After you closed your first round, what were the next steps? What were your main priorities?

Parnell: Well for one, $15.5 million is just a lot of money. It's crazy because, at the time—and I don't know if it's been broken since—PlayVS's Series A funding round was the largest ever raised by a Black founder in the consumer Internet industry. It's kind of crazy to think about that, you know, not only from an impact perspective but just within the journey to have such a mega-fundraise the first time around.

I think we spent that money mostly on the team. I don't know how many other ways you can spend money building the company, but the biggest investment comes through the team. We hired people to support a number of things; they built the product, they supported customers. We ended up hiring sixteen people in the first year, and a good amount of those people are still with the business today. For some of them, we outgrew or they outgrew the business. We didn't really spend any money on office space or anything like that, but we were in the Science Ventures office, so we did a slight overhaul, but it was very inexpensive. But our biggest investment was in the team.

What previous operations and management experiences influenced your first years of leadership at PlayVS?

Parnell: The first years of building at PlayVS I was just winging it. While there were a ton of things I learned from watching Marc build Rocket Fiber, and working with the guys at the venture fund, and learning from them things to do and things not to do, nothing will ever prepare you for the moment that you're the captain of your own ship. Especially when it's a hundred-foot yacht to start. So I had to figure everything out on my own. Luckily, I had some good partners to give me advice. But I was just winging it.

Nothing will ever prepare you for the moment that you're the captain of your own ship. Especially when it's a hundred-foot yacht to start.

The journey in the first four months of the first year, we weren't even a public company. No one knew that we existed or that we were three people working behind the scenes. The first guy I hired was Sean Yalda in January, and I hired another guy in March named James Kozachuk. Then we announced the company publicly on April 18, 2018. So James, Sean, and I were basically just kind of winging it from January to April. In May, we started fundraising. In June, we closed it and announced the fundraising, I think on my brother's birthday, June 4. Within that time, we hired my brother. And then, over the summer, I hired a number of other people, but I'm also trying to close my first publisher, and the first group of states that will actually allow us to roll out esports.

At that time, while we had this deal with the NFHS [National Federation of State High School Associations], which basically said we're going to be the exclusive partner to operate esports on behalf of the NFHS for their state associations, we hadn't actually gotten a group of states to agree to support esports. We also didn't have a game to actually roll out in order to be the first high school esport. So I spent a significant amount of time trying to gain a publisher to partner with me, and then trying to get a group of states to work with me, while also building up a product.

Until that point, we had a demo of the product, but we had to actually build the first version of the product. So I was hiring, trying to build a product, and trying to get a game publisher to work with us— which is a quarter of our business— getting states to be part of our go-to-market strategy. So that was all a process.

I would say that most businesses probably don't have a launch goal at launch. It should be more common, but I think most businesses just want to make it go live and hope it works, but not with a number of people that they actually want to reach. For those who do launch with actual numbers associated with it, kudos to you guys. We were so green; we didn't have any number. We were just like: It should be big.

Eventually, I started to get some of those things done by September. We got a game. We were going to roll out in five states, and we'd organized on the product side with the first versions of how the league was going to look for that first season, which was supposed to start October 30. Right before the season, we started getting a lot of inbound interest from investors who had missed out on the first round and wanted to do another round, sort of a pre-Series B. So now I'm trying to launch a season, finalize hiring, go to market, and now also [do] fundraising.

Truthfully, we didn't set any goals that year. Most businesses launch and say: *Oh, we want to have this.* I would say that most businesses probably don't have a launch goal at launch. It should be more common, but I think most businesses just want to make it go live and hope it works, but not with a number of people that they actually want to reach. For those who do launch with actual numbers associated with it, kudos to you guys. We were so green; we didn't have any number. We were just like: *It should be big.*

Was there an initial pushback? If so, what aspect of your idea did investors have reservations about?

Parnell: There wasn't pushback because we got the rounds done quickly. People wanted to support it. We raised $46 million before we ever launched. When people invest in a company early, they're betting on the talent of the team, mostly a CEO, founder, or founders, if it's multiple people. Then they're betting on the vision and the market. So between those three things, they're taking the bet to say: Hey, can this person, with the team they have, execute their vision, and is the market big enough so, even if they get halfway there, it'll get a big win? I think all those things check yes for us, so we were able to get it done. But I didn't know how to run the business. I knew I was an entrepreneur. I know how to get things done. I have a checklist I'm going to get done, but I didn't know how to organize that within an actual organizational structure to drive outcomes and then manage the business versus just doing shit. So the first year, I just did shit. And luckily it worked out for us.

We went from our first season, we set real goals, and we measured those goals, iterated those goals in terms of focus areas. I stopped doing everything. So I think now I'm not even an entrepreneur. I'm a CEO. Or I'm not a founder in the sense of when you first start the company. Now things are filtered to me, there's way more process, there's an entire team of executives plus leadership at the company.

And then, the second year, I began the first phase of actually being a CEO, adding more depth and maturity to the organization. We rebuilt the product, but we did it with more process, more effectively this time. We went from our first season, we set real goals, and we measured those goals, iterated those goals in terms of focus areas. I stopped doing everything. So I think now I'm not even an entrepreneur. I'm a CEO. Or I'm not a founder in the sense of when you first start the company. Now things are filtered to me, there's way more process, there's an entire team of executives plus leadership at the company. Leadership being, like, senior directors, VPs, C-level executives, and a broader group to keep the ship afloat. It's a lot of people, and a lot more is getting done than I could manage on my own. We're only twenty-something months old, too, so we're still fairly young, but, luckily, I was able to transition and learn very quickly. But it's definitely been a journey.

What were some of the mistakes that you made or learned from as you transitioned from entrepreneur to CEO?

Parnell: I don't know if there are mistakes, because it still worked out for us, but had I not done it that way, I would have never learned. If I could go back and think through what things I would have done differently, one would be to hire a CTO and COO from the very beginning. I would have made two hires right after we raised capital. That CTO would have managed the product build. Instead, what ended up happening is that we built the product one way without strong leadership in that area. And then, the next year when we hired strong leadership, we had to rebuild it. So from a product standpoint, while we have the best product in the market, and it's certainly more advanced than anything within the space, we still lost at least a half year of development because we've basically been re-platforming. That would have saved me a lot of time, and the product would be a lot further along had I invested in that talent from day one.

Then, I'd say, a COO. For some time, we couldn't operationalize the vision and grow at scale because we didn't have ops talent. We were a product-driven organization for the first eighteen to twenty months. And, just recently, I added a COO, who has now added thirty to forty ops talent across marketing, central ops, and regional ops. He's basically taken the learnings we had over the last four seasons, and while there's been positive growth organically, he's now building a growth plan with teams, testing and iterating to hopefully find some sort of repeatable framework for growth for us. Had I done that earlier, our velocity would have been different.

Third, I would have hired someone in talent from day one. I would have hired a recruiter or head of recruiting. While a lot of my time early on was going to hiring talent, it gives you more leverage to do other things when you have someone else managing the process and building the pipeline. So if I could do anything differently that would've changed the trajectory of the business, while fundraising or shortly after, I would've hired talent in those three areas.

Did you experience founder's dilemma? Was it difficult for you to delegate and trust others to lead operations as PlayVS started to expand?

Parnell: No, people will tell you [that], if I'm hiring you, I'm not hiring you to do your job. I'm hiring you to teach me and also execute the role that I've hired you for. I have no problem trusting people and giving them responsibility. And I do so, I think, in a really effective way, especially for executives that come to work for me. During onboarding, I organize a document that's called CEO–[insert new executive hire]

> People will tell you [that], if I'm hiring you, I'm not hiring you to do your job. I'm hiring you to teach me and also execute the role that I've hired you for.

Expectations, for example, CEO–COO Guide. It's only nine slides: the cover, an agenda that lays out what we're going to talk about, which is (1) the company vision, (2) my expectations of you in this role, (3) my top concerns/the things that I'm stressing about as it relates to your job, (4) what I'm going to focus on as it relates to what you do, (5) my operating style, and (6) questions.

So when it comes to the vision, I'm talking through how I want to grow the business, in this order. If we win, here is a sentence that people would use to describe our business, and then here is the ideal exit size for that business, and here's how many people I want associated with that business—basically how to be both talent- and capital-efficient.

For expectations, I want you to complement other executives, serve as a business partner, promote this sort of culture, and grow the business [in a way that is] evident by these actual metrics. The next thing I present are my four top concerns, followed by my focus as it relates to what you do. Then, the last thing before Q&A is my operating style. Like, I take action items really seriously, and I expect you to make sure your team hits your goals—always, full stop. I'm okay with renegotiating priorities and deadlines, but I'm annoyed if you don't do so in advance of the deadline. I prefer to make decisions with data, not anecdotes. I like to see things as early as possible; any time things are a work in process, show them to me. I'm happy to be involved. If you come to me with something, bring it to me organized in a document, in a deck, in a spreadsheet. Don't just spill out a bunch of stuff to me; let me digest it and provide feedback. Don't add stuff to my calendar. Go through my [executive assistant] always. I don't make decisions based on what competitors or investors think; I make decisions based on what I and the team believe. I read every email or Slack sent to me, but I only respond if it's clear that I have to. If you want a response, tell me. Don't send me long emails. Don't be offended if I send you a short response to a long email.

Stuff like this is really important in terms of who I am and how I operate. It provides leadership with clear expectations of their role, how things are going to be measured, and how I work so you can best align with that. And that allows the talent that I hire to be best in their role.

How did you develop this leadership style? Was there a particular mentor or experience, or has this been through trial and error?

Parnell: Well, look, I'm not a manager. I'm not a great manager. I do think I'm a really great leader. I'm a great organizer of people. I have a strong ability in spotting great talent, validating or invalidating that talent, and convincing them to join the vision and be part of the tribe, and then empowering them by removing blockers, and supplying them with the talent and resources they need in order to be successful. Giving them the confidence to tackle the things in front of them. In many cases, that's like a coach's position or the leader of any team, a captain of the team.

So I'm really good at that. And maybe I learned those skills from team sports. Any time I played team sports, and we had to draft teams right on the spot, people would always say: *Delane, be the*

Maybe I learned those skills from team sports. Any time I played team sports, and we had to draft teams right on the spot, people would always say: Delane, be the team captain. I was always evaluating all these different talents and understanding, based on the opponent, how I could structure my team to best beat them. I was able to learn those skills very early on, and that carried me on to my business career.

team captain. I was always evaluating all these different talents and understanding, based on the opponent, how I could structure my team to best beat them. I was able to learn those skills very early on, and that carried me on to my business career. So in the role of a CEO, where I don't have to manage a lot of people, just my EA, my chief of staff, and my executive team, that's a small enough group for me to be really effective. I try to hire great managers and great leaders, people with strong depth and experience in their particular area. If you can check those boxes, I think we can work really well together.

Though I don't have a style I've modeled my career off of, I've certainly learned strategies and tactics from really great CEOs and founders like Michael Ovitz, co-founder of Creative Artists Agency, Dick Costolo, former CEO of Twitter, and many others I've been graced to experience on a one-to-one basis.

Most people will tell you, I'm just me. I don't try to be something or someone else at any time. I run the business in a way that aligns best with the life that I want, and who I am. And in many cases, I'm really intense, and we're really aggressive, and we move really fast [*laughs*], but that's because of who I am. And I try to find people who align with that.

What's the tone of your team now?

Parnell: We've got seventy to eighty people who work at the company now; it will be a hundred-something over the next couple of weeks. Maybe 120–130 over the next year. And the people who work at the company are amazing. They believe in not only me but our mission. They are passionate about the problems that we're solving every single day. We're doing something new, and our investors believe in us and put their money where their mouths are with respect to that support.

While I appreciate all the love and support, I also recognize the position I'm in. And I'm going to do my best to make sure I get a win for all of us. And I hope that that has a compounding impact on all those areas where our investors can invest in more people of color.

I just feel extremely grateful and privileged. I also feel a responsibility to the generation of young Black entrepreneurs who look up to me and know that it's possible. So from a personal level, I just want them to know that, while I appreciate all the love and support, I also recognize the position I'm in. And I'm going to do my best to make sure I get a win for all of us. And I hope that that has a compounding impact on all those areas where our investors can invest in more people of color.

Our community is filled with millions of kids and adults who are being able to unlock their passion and build lifelong friendships, and even take their lives to the next level. If they want to pursue esports professionally, they're able to come in, learn a bunch of new things, and take their career to the next level. I hope my success inspires thousands of other young Black and Brown entrepreneurs to move into not only gaming, but into other spaces, and there's a roadmap that I've laid to help them find their way.

What's something that you're learning now, or someone who you're learning from?

Parnell: Well, I'm learning a ton now. I'm learning everything. I'm learning how to build a business. We're past product–market fit now, and we're well-capitalized. We've made money, we've validated that our product works, we've validated that our business works, we have strong partnerships, we have a sense of how to grow. But we're trying to take the growth that we've had and turn it into a $100 million-plus per year business. That is my focus and my next milestone. And that's a different skill. Zero to one, one to ten, ten to one hundred—you have to keep leveling up.

MICHAEL SEIBEL

CEO and Partner, Y Combinator

Y Combinator (YC) provides seed funding for startups. Twice a year, they invest a small amount of money in a large number of startups with a goal to create an environment where founders can focus exclusively on building product and talking to users. As of September 21, 2020, YC's Black-founded companies have a combined valuation of $2.08 billion and have raised $483 million (101 companies, 64 US-based). YC's Latinx-founded companies have a combined valuation of $13.5 billion and have raised $3.9 billion (153 companies, 67 US-based).[7]

---

[7]   Gené Teare, "Y Combinator Releases Data on Black, Latinx and Woman Founders," *Crunchbase*, September 21, 2020. https://news.crunchbase.com/news/y-combinator-releases-data-on-black-latinx-and-woman-founders/

Michael Seibel is thirty-seven years old and has lived and worked in the Bay Area since 2006. Currently, he works at Y Combinator as a full-time partner and CEO of the YC startup accelerator program. Previously, he was a co-founder and CEO of Justin.tv from 2007–2011 and the co-founder and CEO of Socialcam in 2012. During 2012, Socialcam participated in Y Combinator, and raised angel financing from a group of amazing investors, and sold to Autodesk Inc. for $60 million. Needless to say, it was a busy year. In 2014, Justin.tv became Twitch Interactive, and under the leadership of Emmett Shear and Kevin Lin, sold to Amazon for $970 million.

Before getting into tech, Michael spent a year as the finance director for a US Senate campaign, and before that, he graduated from Yale University with a bachelor's degree in political science. Today he spends the majority of his free time cooking, reading, traveling, and going for long drives. He lives in San Francisco with his amazing wife, Sarah, and their son Jonathan.

Website: https://www.michaelseibel.com/

Twitter: @mwseibel

Tell us about your personal background. What experiences were influential in you becoming an entrepreneur and founder of Justin.tv?

Michael Seibel: Okay. So I was born in Brooklyn in 1982 to two young parents—twenty-two and twenty-three. I grew up [there] for about nine or ten years [before] the family moved to the suburbs in New Jersey, where my sister and brother were born, fifteen and ten years younger than me. I'm still figuring out how the difference between growing up in the suburbs and growing up in the city really affected us. I think that weirdly shaped me.

The one thing that always stuck in my mind is that, in the fourth grade in Brooklyn, you can get a permission slip to go off campus to eat lunch. In the suburbs, you got that same permission as a senior in high school. How much more parents and institutions have to trust kids earlier when they grow up in cities just stuck with me throughout the whole path.

I would say I got serious about high school during my sophomore year. I started doing AP classes and worked pretty hard my junior and senior years. At the time, all my friends were going on these crazy college tours. My dad basically said that he wasn't taking me to any college that I hadn't already gotten into; it just seemed like a waste of time and money. And it was so funny [*chuckles*]. It was such a good argument, I had no comeback. I love my dad, and I was just like: *You got it; I don't think I would do that for my kids. So I totally understand.*

I applied to a bunch of schools because I had no idea, right? And I ended up getting accepted into a bunch of schools. So I started at Yale in 2000 and was pretty quickly disappointed with it. I think I believed the hype around Ivy League schools, this idea that everyone's going to be a genius there. I went to a good, very competitive high school. And any of the top thirty kids—maybe even top fifty kids there—could have gone to Yale, and, like, only three of them got in. That broke the illusion.

The second thing that happened was, I was always a goody-two-shoes. Like, I didn't drink in high school, and always went to [class]. When they told me you didn't have to go to class in college, I [thought]: *Oh, shit. Well, if I don't have to go to class, why would I go to class?* I got disillusioned with the whole academic thing and with this idea that school should be producing academics. It never really occurred to me that being a professor or an academic was something I should ever aspire to.

So, although I quickly got disillusioned, I invested a lot of time and energy into clubs. I ended up working with three: the Black Student Union; the *New Journal*, which published a magazine on campus; and Focus, a community service program that worked in New Haven. It was through those clubs where I got the most enjoyment out of school.

Needless to say, not coming to class eventually caught up with me. I got kicked out of school my senior year. Well, at Yale, you don't get kicked out; I was "invited" to leave for a year, and had to get my life back together. I had this kind of very cushy plan where I was going to live with my grandparents and, yadda, yadda. I love my parents because, when I told my mom I got kicked out, she was like: *Fuck you. You're going back to New Haven. You got to get a job and figure shit out.* So I had to get a job and figure out my shit.

I ended up getting one of the most Yale jobs imaginable. I worked at the Office of Public Affairs reading newspapers to look for Yale mentions that I then had to turn into clips, which were given to the president of Yale every morning, so he could drink his coffee and read about where Yale was coming up in the news.

But then the summer came, and I had to get a *real* real job. And I ended up in an amazing job at UPenn, working for an NPR program there called *Justice Talking*. It was this debate program talking about legal reform and social justice reform. And it really changed my path.

I think if you'd asked me before going into that job what I was going to do, I probably would have said: *I'm going to be a lawyer*, or at least, *I'm going to go to law school*. The woman who ran the program, Kathryn ("Katie") Kolbert, was one of the most important people in the fight for abortion rights. I remember talking to her about whether I should go to law school, and she spent about five minutes describing what a lawyer does.

And then she said, "Do you want to do that?"

I said, "No."

"Then, why the fuck would you go to law school?"

That was loud and clear. It was all I needed, and [it] made perfect sense to me [*chuckles*]. That really helped me. And, as an aside, I always joke with UPenn kids that I also got to TA her class. So I was kicked out of Yale, but I was a TA at UPenn, which I really love. Anyway, I went back to school and took it seriously. I became really good friends with this guy named Justin Kan, one of the more popular kids in our 2005 class. He accepted me and opened his friend group to me, so it made my second senior year of school so much more enjoyable than my first.

I knew I didn't want to be a lawyer, but I still generated this life plan over the course of school, which was: in my twenties, I'd make money; in my thirties, raise a family; and in my forties, do politics, retire, and teach.

I knew I didn't want to be a lawyer, but I still generated this life plan over the course of school, which was: in my twenties, I'd make money; in my thirties, raise a family; and in my forties, do politics, retire, and teach.

I read the autobiography of Bill Clinton, who mentioned that he'd worked at a campaign very early when he was a student. That clicked for me. *While I'm really young, I can basically live in a shitty place, not make a good salary, and that's probably the best time to work for a campaign.* So, after school, my plan was to get a job with a campaign.

It was a crazy path that basically involved interviewing for a couple of campaign jobs I was not qualified for. And then some random Yale grad, this older dude, [who] was, like, an expert in setting up campaign staff, was hired by Kweisi Mfume [Representative for Maryland's Seventh Congressional District, 1987 to 1996, and again since 2020] to set up his Maryland campaign staff. And the way he did it was crazy. They invited a bunch of people to this office in Baltimore, Maryland, and basically said: *We're going to teach you all how to be a fundraiser, and at the end, based on how smart we think you are, four of you will get the job. And the rest won't.* At the end of the day, I was told: *Okay, you're going to be a fundraiser in this campaign, and you're going to focus on national fundraising.* I'd never done anything like that in my life.

Justin and [another college friend] Emmett Shear told me that they had gotten into this program. The way they described it was, there were a bunch of recent college grad dudes in this program, and once a week, they would go over to this other guy's house, where he cooks them dinner, and they talk about their startups.

I'm like: *This sounds a little weird* [*laughs*]. But Justin and Emmett are like: *No, no, no; it's totally cool. We loved it. It's awesome.* So I'm like: *Okay, awesome.*

Maybe about six, eight months later they ended up selling their YC [Y Combinator] startup on eBay for about $258,000. I remember being in the campaign office, and I had told everyone that my friends were selling the company on eBay, so I'm refreshing the page, and the price went up as people were bidding on it. That was pretty fun.

Well, I was not a great fundraiser [*laughs*]. My candidate, Kweisi Mfume, was very proud, and I would say that he was very nervous about asking rich people for money because of the quid pro quo that might involve. So we only raised about a million dollars in the primary. Our number one competitor, Ben Cardin, probably raised about $4 million, and we lost the campaign by three percentage points. In Maryland, whoever wins the Democratic primary, wins [the election].

And so I had this great experience, but I was super tired. At the same time—this was 2006— Justin and Emmett had sold their company, and they were going to start a new company. Instead of doing it in Cambridge, they wanted to do it in San Francisco. They emailed our whole friend group from college and said: *Hey, we're doing a road trip from Cambridge to San Francisco.* I think they perceived it as an announcement; I

I think they perceived it as an announcement; I perceived it as an invitation [laughs]. I'd never been to California. I'd never been west of, like, Kentucky. I was: Oh, this sounds cool. I always wanted to do a road trip! Can I come with you?

perceived it as an invitation [*laughs*]. I'd never been to California. I'd never been west of, like, Kentucky. I was: *Oh, this sounds cool. I always wanted to do a road trip! Can I come with you?*

They were building an online reality TV show where Justin was going to stream his life through a camera on his head, which—I told him to his face: *This is the dumbest idea I've ever heard in my entire life.* So [there was] no plan whatsoever to work at their company, but I thought it'd be a great vacation. They said: *Sure, come along.* What they didn't tell me was that they had packed up Emmett's Honda Civic with all their stuff to drive across the country. To give me a seat in the car, they had to throw away a quarter of their stuff [*laughs*]. I was like: *Okay, what's the plan?* And they were like: *Well, we're just going to get on Route 80 and drive until we feel like we're going to fall asleep then stop.* I'm like: *That sounds like a horrible road trip. Let me plan the trip.*

So we drive across the country and visit a bunch of people on the way. And this is one of these things where there's so much luck. We arrive on Treasure Island [in San Francisco] a week before my birthday, and it's Fleet Week. And the fucking Blue Angels are flying over the city. It's early October and warm! I'm like: *This is the coolest place I've ever seen in my entire life* [*laughs*].

But we're not staying in San Francisco. Justin's cousin lived in a condo in Mountain View, so we drive for another hour. We're staying in the basement of this condo, and they're starting to work on their company. And I'm getting this week of vacation, just twiddling my thumbs, so [I thought] I might as well help them. I helped them find an apartment. And I helped them open a bank account because they were carrying around these two crumbled $25,000 checks for, like, a month and a half.

The weekend before I left was my birthday. So we went wine tasting with a couple of friends. Justin bought me a birthday gift—an iPod. I had mentioned at some point that I always wanted an iPod, but I never felt like I could buy myself one because they always improved. I don't really exchange gifts with any friends, right? I was like: *This smells fishy.*

When he was driving me to the airport for my flight back to Baltimore, he said, "I want you to be a co-founder of Justin.tv."

I straight up said no.

"Well, just think about it."

He was my best friend, so I said I'd think about it. I fly back to Baltimore, and we're in the process of closing down the campaign. Justin and them send me an email: *Hey, we've recruited this fourth guy named Kyle, and he is going to build this camera that's going to power this company. Here's this PDF of the technical drawings he's done on this camera. He's going to build it in the next couple of months. It's happening.*

But when your best friend tells you: I'm starting a startup, and I want you to join me? That seemed like the unique thing; the campaign thing was always going to be there. So I said: Let's go do new things.

Two things happened in my mind. One was smart, and the other was stupid. I think to start a company, you have to be stupid. There has to be something irrational going on. And the stupid thing that went through my head was: *Well, they have $50,000. They've got this [guy] Kyle to build the camera. This could work.*

Which is, like, no [*laughs*]! That's nowhere near enough to do *anything*.

Then, the smart thing that went through my mind was: *This is a one-time moment.* My plan was to go work in the presidential campaign circuit. I didn't know Obama was going to be running. I would have had a very different life if I had done that. But when your best friend tells you: *I'm starting a startup, and I want you to join me?* That seemed like the unique thing; the campaign thing was always going to be there. So I said: *Let's go do new things.* I had to get out of my lease. I could only bring a couple of suitcases, so I left a bunch of stuff in some basement in Baltimore. It's still there. And I had a girlfriend at the time. This wasn't the most mature thing, but I said: *We need to break up. I'm moving to the other side of the country* [*chuckles*].

And two weeks after leaving San Francisco, I was back in San Francisco, sleeping on a futon in the living room of the apartment that I had found for Justin and Emmett. And that was the beginning.

That's the hustle of starting up a new company. How did Justin. tv evolve from there?

Seibel: The first big leap was that Kyle built the first version of the camera, and it worked. Suddenly we had an MVP [Minimum Viable Product] version of the site. We had our first moment when we invited maybe ten or fifteen friends to a little private beta. And they happened to be watching when Justin and our friend Steve Huffman, who's now the CEO of Reddit, went to this bar where they ended up getting arrested. They called us and were like: This is awesome! And we realized: Oh, maybe, like, maybe there's something here.

The next moment was launching the full version. That happened somewhere in April 2007. We raised a little bit under $200,000 in angel funding, plus the $50,000 we'd gotten from Paul Graham and YC. And it blew up—at least initially. Justin was on the *Today Show*, the front page of the *Chronicle*, the *New York Times*. Everything started looking like something was going to happen.

Fast forward three months. We have what's called the *trough of sorrow*. The novelty factor is off, and we realize that our lives are not that interesting. Justin's life certainly isn't that interesting, and people don't want to watch. So it got down to the point where, on a typical day, there might be six to ten people watching.

I don't know how we did this, but during that time, we both made the plan to open up the platform so that anyone could stream live video. We raised a Series A, [which] back then, though, looked a lot more like angel rounds now. We raised $2 million on an $8 million valuation, and to this day, I don't know why Stewart [Alsop of the venture capital firm Alsop Louie] gave us that check. It didn't seem smart [*chuckles*]. And I think one of the reasons why [he did] was that we had a very technical team. Emmett, Justin, and Kyle were engineers. Kyle and Emmett were two of the four best engineers I'd ever worked with. So I think that helped. That October, we opened up the platform and allowed anyone to stream live video. That was very exciting. But we were not really taking off.

Early-to-mid-2008, people start realizing they can stream not just people's lives on Justin.tv, but they can stream other content. The first time that happened was with a dude in Morocco. He was watching a local Moroccan soccer league game, and his friends in America wanted to watch it. So he pointed his laptop at the TV screen and broadcast a soccer game on Justin.tv. That was the biggest channel we've ever had on the site. That begins a year and a half of crazy growth with content we had no rights for. And so we were kind of stuck.

I think if you would put a polygraph on me, the entire time I was running Justin.tv, I was not convinced it could be a real business. It was making money, but if I define real business as the potential to become a billion-dollar business, it wasn't a real business.

The numbers on the site were big: Thirty million people came every month. We were making $750,000 per month, but spending $1 million per month, so it wasn't looking to be a successful business. We raised a little bit more money, thank God, right before the 2008 [economic] crisis. But, by 2010, it became clear that no one was going to give us more money, and Justin.tv wasn't going to work.

I think if you would put a polygraph on me, the entire time I was running Justin.tv, I was not convinced it could be a real business. It was making money, but if I define *real business* as the potential to become a billion-dollar business, it wasn't a real business.

Then Gideon Yu [former CFO of Facebook and YouTube] came in one day and basically said: *Your company sucks. What you guys have done thus far is basically worthless, and if you keep going down this path, your company will die within three years, and everyone will forget that you ever existed.*

Because we felt like we had our own fate in our hands, we could finally accept this truth that we knew the whole time. So we started thinking about what we should do differently, and basically came up with two ideas. One of those ideas ended up becoming Twitch, and the other idea became Socialcam. That really sparked the beginning of when we started being successful.

What kept you motivated to keep working on it?

Seibel: This is something that I've talked to a lot of founders about. And the way I describe it is, I think there has to be something that irrationally motivates you to work on your startup when things aren't going well because it won't go well. In my life, I've seen three things that can work. One is you're really passionate about the problem. Oftentimes, it's a personal problem. The second is you're really passionate about your co-founders. The third is some combination of ego and hatred of big companies.

I had the second and the third. I really liked my co-founders, and I really enjoyed working with them, and I internalized this idea that the only thing I had ever done in my life at that point was Justin.tv. And if Justin.tv failed, my life would get a failing grade. That's not healthy, but it is motivational. And then the other thing is that [I believed] the four of us, the co-founders of Justin.tv, we're just better than everyone else, so we're going to win—which is not true [*laughs*]. We're not better, but part of this thing is being dumb enough to convince yourself of things that have no evidence of truth.

What was the process like getting into YC back then?

Seibel: I went through YC twice, but I never applied, and I never interviewed, so I don't have normal YC stories. I feel, like, really bad, but my path is not a normal path because Justin and Emmett were in the first class. When they sold their company, then went back to [Paul Graham], he was like: Sure, we'll fund you to do it again.

When I went through with Socialcam, Justin.tv was already something. So [Paul] and Jessica [Livingston of Y Combinator] were: *Oh, you should come back and do YC with Socialcam!* So I never had the normal experience, unfortunately. It's really embarrassing because there are a lot of people that have asked me for advice on applications and interviews. I know now, but I didn't know back then at all.

It points to something we try to communicate to the HBCUvc community: how important relationships—especially strong relationships—are to your entrepreneurial journey. Being in different places to build relationships is so important. You can't put a dollar amount on it. What were some of the reasons you believe the team was successful in raising funding, despite some of the business challenges you experienced?

Seibel: It's really hard for me to say. There are a couple of things about the fundraising experience that are tricky. With a lot of Black founders that I speak to, the fundraising experience is where they perceive and feel the most discrimination and the most disadvantage. For me, here was the problem: I was pitching this very dumb idea, and I had no experience raising money. So it was really, really hard to tell why everyone was saying no, because it was completely logical that they were saying no, because I told them we're making an online reality TV show as opposed to some Black founder today saying they're making a payment processor, which is not weird. That's normal. Look at these billion-dollar payment processors, and I'm doing it this way.

During the fundraising process, I never felt that I could specifically pinpoint that I was being treated differently. With that being said, I got tons and tons of nos, [but] we had to raise money, so I was going to keep on pitching, [and] we got a little lucky. There's so much luck involved.

During the fundraising process, I never felt that I could specifically pinpoint that I was being treated differently. With that being said, I got tons and tons of nos, [but] we had to raise money, so I was going to keep on pitching, [and] we got a little lucky. There's so much luck involved.

I remember we were all living in an apartment together, and Stewart came by to talk to us. He wanted to meet everyone and see where we were working. I think, in Stewart's mind was: *Here are some young technical folks just working really hard.* It didn't look like an MBA startup [with] a fancy office. It looked like a bunch of scrappy young kids, which is a pattern that investors like.

We had [also] written the term sheets on a whiteboard in the office/apartment that we *thought* we could get. And we didn't erase them. We hadn't gotten either of those term sheets. But Stewart saw those written on the board, and I think he thought those were deals we had in our hand. And within a day or two of that meeting, he gave us a term sheet. I never asked Stewart if that was a thing, but now, knowing VCs a lot better, I bet it was a factor. So I never want anyone to think that *my* skill got anything done. There were so many moments where things just had to break the right way [*laughs*].

And once enough lucky breaks broke, we started to get the feeling that, if we worked really hard, something good would happen, because it always had, which is funny. Because if you look at our company, there was a time where Justin.tv was seen as a pirating company, straight up, illegal content, parody Internet—worse than BitTorrent. And we just kept working it until it got better.

The second thing was that their fund re-upped in our series B. They had some irrational belief in us that we couldn't even quantify. We thought we were the shit, but we knew we hadn't proven it [*chuckles*]. So we had no idea why anyone else would think that we were good.

But I will say that none of us thought seriously about giving up. It seemed *inconceivable* to us that we would give up. And once enough lucky breaks broke, we started to get the feeling that, if we worked really hard, something good would happen, because it always had, which is funny. Because if you look at our company, there was a time where Justin.tv was seen as a pirating company, straight up, illegal content, parody Internet—worse than BitTorrent. And we just kept working it until it got better.

Do you see parallels between the Justin.tv community and the Reddit community? And congratulations on your recent appointment to the board at Reddit.

Seibel: I have to be honest; I am a Reddit lurker, not a Reddit community member. One of the reasons why I was excited about the role at Reddit was because we definitely had to deal with a lot of community issues at Justin.tv. But I don't know that they're the same issues. One, Reddit is a lot more political than Justin. tv ever was, and more political than Twitch and Socialcam. And two, Reddit's path was weird, where it was a startup, and then it was part of a company, and then the founders weren't there. I feel like, in a weird way, there was a chunk of time where Reddit was neglected. And I think that neglect created a lot of badness no one took responsibility for. And that just didn't happen at Justin.tv. There wasn't a time where we were neglecting the company.

Jumping from Justin.tv, Twitch, and Socialcam to YC, what does it mean to be the CEO and partner of YC?

Seibel: Sure. So now, I'm the CEO of a startup accelerator, but YC has got more parts than the accelerator. There is the Growth Program, which is their startup school. But the accelerator is where I work with a bunch of early-stage partners to try and make the biggest impact. I joined YC in 2014 after being what we call a part-time partner for the year before. At the time, YC was basically transitioning from a family business into an actual company, and it was struggling to do that. In my mind, I had perceived YC as this perfect job to do when raising a family. I'd made some money in my twenties, so this was the next thing on the list. And then it turned out that it wasn't exactly that. I ended up seeing YC struggling, and wanting to step up and do more, and then being given more responsibility—now my schedule is destroyed [*laughs*].

It doesn't have the stress of an early-stage startup. There's the fear of death in the bottom of your stomach 24/7, but it certainly is, like, not a retirement job by any means. My responsibility is basically to make the accelerator as great of a program as possible. And then also to help encourage other services for YC companies' other programs, whether Startup School before, or the Series A program after. I think there are a lot of [YC] alumni who are now a part of running YC, and we have a lot of things that we wished YC [had] provided us that we can now help YC provide to others. Almost all of us are doing this job more as a community service job than a money-making job. Our lives do not resemble the normal investor's life. Our payback period—the time where I'm going to get my first meaningful check from YC—is probably twelve years from when I started. So it's not this money-making thing. It's far more that this organization gave me a unique opportunity to get into tech, and I want to help it give other people that opportunity.

As a visible Black man at a prestigious accelerator, do you feel Black community pressure to make changes to the investment community? If so, how do you balance those expectations?

Seibel: YC is set up structurally in a way that I think is fundamentally better than other investment firms. Specifically, the reason why is that you don't have to know us. You don't have to network into us. We actually do accept companies from the application process. We don't have an email on our website and then never check the inbox. I always felt the credential matters. Demo Day works. The advice is good. It had the format that could help a lot of people who didn't have access to the [Silicon] Valley get access. I had an advantage because a lot of people saw me doing YC, and therefore decided to apply, who otherwise wouldn't.

The second thing that was challenging is that startups got more popular—in a bad way. It's almost like the startup world consumed the small business world and the entrepreneurship world. Basically, everyone who wanted to be an entrepreneur thought they wanted to do a startup, and raise money from VCs. It became really frustrating having to continually tell people: This is a perfectly great business, but it's just not something that VCs are set up to fund.

Interestingly enough, my job when I got in, was an information job. Before YC existed, if I wanted to help people do startups, I had to use my network. After YC was created, I just had to teach people how to get into YC, and the YC machine would do a lot of the additional work. At first, when I thought about that, for sure, I wanted to increase the number of underrepresented founders doing YC, and doing that was hard. I realized that no matter how much work I did to recruit people for this batch, I had to start all over again next batch [*chuckles*]. There was no feeling like I was building off my previous work. It felt like every time it was this new challenge.

So that was the first thing. The second thing that was challenging is that startups got more popular—in a bad way. It's almost like the startup world consumed the small business world and the entrepreneurship world. Basically, everyone who wanted to be an entrepreneur thought they wanted to do a startup, and raise money from VCs. It became really frustrating having to continually tell people: *This is a perfectly great business, but it's just not something that VCs are set up to fund.*

And, once again, it felt there was an information gap; like some people have more information than others. So my tactic wasn't sophisticated: Reply to my emails, and do things that don't scale. We didn't institute a bunch of new programs or yadda, yadda, yadda. I just started trying to help Black people get into YC. Five years later, it's this weird mixed bag.

Looking back, I would have said, on one hand, if this were my sole responsibility at YC, I probably could have gotten more people in. On the other hand, very quickly it became just one of many responsibilities. But, as Black people started getting into the program, there became this flywheel, where you could talk to a Black person who'd been through YC, and they could tell you about it. I wasn't the only one who had to speak for YC, which was helpful. So looking back from 2015 to today, we funded about 190 or so Black founders, about 240 Latinx founders, and about 440 women.

And it's this complicated track record, right? I simultaneously want to be yelled at because that is a small percentage of the total people who did YC during that time. But I also want to be acknowledged. Point [out] anyone else—anyone—who funded that number of underrepresented people. There are very few on that list. When I think about the next five years of my work on this front, I now have this community that I can rely on. When I'm thinking about what I want to do over the next five years, it's about how to leverage the alumni communities that we have.

And what I hate about the pipeline problem conversation is that inevitably someone [says]: The root of the problem is kindergarten. And then goes into: Well, if you do these things over twenty years, we can solve it. No startup person wants to hear that argument.

The other thing that I'm starting to really dive deep into, that everyone talks about, is a pipeline problem. This is, like, the hilarious third wheel of talking about diversity: *Oh, it's a pipeline problem, is it not? Blah, blah, blah.* And what I hate about the pipeline problem conversation is that inevitably someone [says]: *The root of the problem is kindergarten.* And then goes into: *Well, if you do these things over twenty years, we can solve it.* No startup person wants to hear that argument.

One of the things that clicked for me, and was always in the back of my head, was that at Yale, one of the ways Black people got into Yale was they were good at math and science; that was a fucking core way they got into the school. So many people I knew were good in math and science, but did not major in computer science (CS). They may have been pre-med, electrical engineering, or they did mechanical engineering, or they did econ, which was a *big* driver into finance. Part of me was: *What is going on in these CS programs that is making them unattractive?*

So I started digging into some of the programs and realized how hostile they were to people who didn't know how to code before they came in. Being a business founder, I never went through CS, so I never experienced this. But the more I learned, the more I was distressed because this is a clear path to economic freedom for a lot of people, and the school was not incentivized to do anything about it. The professors in this program were not incentivized to have better programs. You're giving someone the key to a six-figure job when they graduate college. When I graduated from Yale, the CS class had ten graduates. So in the back of my mind, I was trying to figure out what it would take to get those kids to do CS.

There have been two projects I've gotten really excited about recently. One was a company that went through YC in the last batch, named Edlyft, and I met [co-founder] Erika [Hairston] when she was a sophomore CS student considering dropping out. It's so hilarious because I basically yelled at her to not quit—*yelled* is a strong word—I *encouraged* her to not quit. I'd never done CS; I had no idea how hard it was [*laughs*]. But I was: *No, you can't quit.* That started, like, a four- or five-year relationship with Erika that turned into her starting a company and doing YC *that* much longer afterward. But her company was basically trying to formalize all the support systems that she created informally to get through the major. And, to me, that was really exciting because 90 percent of what you need is there at the school. If someone can just do the last 10 percent—that the school clearly doesn't want to—maybe there's a game.

And then the second thing was even more recent. Makinde Adeagbo started /dev/color, that we funded at YC. Makinde was like: *You can help out [Jehron Petty], [who] is trying to do this nonprofit, [ColorStack] for Black and Hispanic CS students at Cornell. And, over the course of running this student organization for a year and a half, he more than doubled the number of Black and Hispanic CS majors at Cornell.*

That's exactly what I was looking for. And so it was funny because I thought to myself: *This is where me putting my finger on the scale can make something happen.* So we set up a unique situation with him where he's actually going to be employed by a YC company named Triplebyte, which is a great company that tries to give a test for engineering credentials to people who don't work at Google or go to a good school, which is really important in order to let a wider group of people get access to this world. So he was going to work [at Triplebyte], but his full-time job is to work on [ColorStack]. So that company is almost incubating his nonprofit.

And, after two years, he's going to have the ability to just work on a nonprofit. They're not going to own any part of it. So, I thought it was really cool for Triplebyte because it wasn't like the standard *hire-a-head-of-diversity-and-put-them-in-a-corner-and-ignore-them* play. It was, like, a very unique play, and it was really cool for him because he can expand the program that he built to other schools.

The last thing I really loved about it was that he ran the program profitably because, of course, employers want access to groups like this. It [won't] be something where [he has to] rely on foundations and philanthropic giving, which I think is very hard. He's actually going to be able to run it sustainably, which I really liked.

So, whereas I think the first five years was about doing things that don't scale, I feel like the next five years [are]: Are there any ways that I can push some levers for people who might create solutions that can scale? That's my thought on it.

Knowing what you know now, and having mentored so many companies through YC in addition to building your own, what, if anything, would you have done differently with Justin.tv and Twitch?

Seibel: I get this question constantly. Let me describe how my ears hear this question. Okay, so, seven years ago, you won the lottery. If you could go back and tell yourself ten years ago, would you do anything different? It's like: God forbid I change something and don't win the lottery [*laughs*]! So no, no. I got very, very lucky, and I got to work with amazing people.

We ask because HBCUvc puts a strong emphasis on reframing risk calculations within our community. We've noticed patterns among first-gen college students or wealth creators in how, when, and what they risk—and understandably so. Despite the setbacks, though, your journey played out in the best way possible through consistent bets on yourself and the ability to jump.

Seibel: I will tell you something, though; this isn't the conversation that happens publicly. I think the conversation that the Black startup community doesn't have enough is that there are so many socioeconomic challenges that, in the public conversation, are pushed under the rug. But in the private conversations I have with founders, they are front and center. I never had to worry that, if everything didn't work, I couldn't crash on my parents' couch. I never had to send a check home. I never had to give my couch up for a relative to crash on, or help during the period of time when I had a lot of focus on my startup. There was never a family crisis that I had to be a part of handling. I never had to be any part of the social safety net of my family until after I made money.

I never had to worry that, if everything didn't work, I couldn't crash on my parents' couch. I never had to send a check home. I never had to give my couch up for a relative to crash on, or help during the period of time when I had a lot of focus on my startup. There was never a family crisis that I had to be a part of handling. I never had to be any part of the social safety net of my family until after I made money.

I think there's a hard question that people don't ask. I've been told that I should go around to high schools with Black students and tell them all to start companies. The odds of being successful when you do a startup are like the odds of getting into the NBA or being successful as a musician. I would be hard-pressed to go around and tell a bunch of young Black kids that they should try to be a rapper or a basketball player. I think there's a set of those kids who are growing up in a stable "enough" set up, where they're doing the risk–reward math wrong. They need to be taught the right math. But I actually think there's a larger set of those kids who are doing the math exactly right. And if they want to make the jump, I'm happy to help them, but I never want to *push* them.

There are so many people I talk to who are very talented, who are the safety net for their whole family, and I can't look them in the eye and tell them it's going to work. I tell everyone the first day of YC: It's probably not going to work [*chuckles*]. That's our message. So it's tricky. And the other dangerous part of these conversations is equating the diversity conversation in tech with the diversity conversation in startups. Like, those kids should want to work for Google and not Lockheed Martin, or Fidelity, or Goldman, right? And Google should be trying to hire them. But whether those kids should be basically risking the livelihood of their families in order to do a startup so that we can all feel good about ourselves and how we're diversifying the tech-startup world? That is, in my mind, dangerous, and it's hard to have that conversation. It's really, really hard.

I've noticed when I've tried to twist people's arms to do startups, it does not work. Like, if the coach is twisting your arm to practice free throws for two hours after practice, it doesn't work, right? They have to be encouraging you; they can't be *forcing* you to do it. That's this world that we live in, which is, if you're a Black CS grad, I probably don't mind forcing you to apply to Google [*chuckles*]. I *do* mind forcing you to start a company. Happy to encourage, but the force thing? That's tricky.

DR. GLEN TONEY

---

*Pioneering Silicon Valley business
executive and educator*

By Nicole Hickman

G len grew up in Oroville, California. The son of Alice and James Toney, he graduated from Oroville High School in 1957 and went on to attend Chico State University where he received his BS in philosophy. After graduating, he served in the military from 1962–1964 in the US Army missile division where he attained the rank of Private First Class. Upon completing his military service, Glen settled in Silicon Valley and began his career as a computer programmer at Lockheed Missiles and

Space Company. During this time, he attended San Jose State University, where he earned a master's degree in instructional technology and a bachelor of science in mathematics.

At his core, Glen was always interested in using education to improve social justice for people of color, and that interest is woven throughout his career. Inspired by Reverend Dr. Martin Luther King, Jr., Glen was committed to advancing civil rights and improving opportunities for the next generation of students of color, particularly in the area of technology. After many years at Lockheed, he pivoted to education and served as assistant superintendent of schools in Ravenswood City and Palo Alto School Districts. Glen went on to earn his doctorate in organizational behavior and higher education in 1975 from the University of Southern California and also earned his teaching and administrative credentials.

In 1979, Dr. Toney returned to the technology sector as a senior executive, launching a twenty-three-year career with Applied Materials, Inc., the largest supplier of products and services for the global semiconductor industry. Before his retirement in 2002, he was a key part of the executive team that led the company in growing annual revenue from $42 million to $10 billion while earning frequent recognition for its management, performance, diversity, and success. While at Applied, he served as chair of the 21st Century Education Initiative, was Chairman President of Applied Materials Global University, and was a trustee for the Noyce Foundation.

"Glen was an exceptional and inspirational man," said James Morgan, Chairman Emeritus of Applied Materials. "He was a transformative figure whose insights, integrity, and wisdom will have a lasting impact on Silicon Valley."

Glen was a member of the California State University Board of Trustees. In the early 1990s, Glen was invited to be a founding member of CSU Chico's College of Engineering, Computer Science, and Construction Management advisory board. His deep community roots and passion for student success were tremendous assets. He had a particular interest in CSU Chico's MESA Schools Program, which promoted engineering and technology to underrepresented students. His contributions included funding a summer science and engineering camp, and funding the Multicultural Engineering Program Blue Chip Scholars, which established scholarship funds to recruit outstanding first-generation underrepresented students interested in technology. In 1995, the College of Engineering, Computer Science, and Construction Management at CSU Chico honored Glen as a distinguished alumnus. The CSU Board of Trustees and University followed suit by awarding him an honorary doctorate of humane letters—one of the system's highest honors—in 2004, to pay tribute to his personal and professional achievements and meritorious service to society. He was honored by Chico State once again in 2011 with the Distinguished Alumni Service Award. In addition, Glen was granted an honorary doctorate degree from Santa Clara University.

Glen's legacy is characterized by his reputation as a transformative and outstanding business leader and an inspirational voice to young people, helping them better understand the career opportunities in the tech field and what it takes to succeed. He truly led by example. He used his voice to ensure that accomplishments by people of color in the tech sector were known and acknowledged.

HANK WILLIAMS

Tech entrepreneur and diversity advocate

By Chrystal Cantrelle

I n the words of Wayne Sutton, "Everyone knew Hank's story." Hank was a tech founder who, in 1998, during the dot-com bubble, raised $40 million from investors, including Merrill Lynch and Philips Electronics, in order to launch an early Internet music provider, ClickRadio. Through ClickRadio, Williams sought to deliver uninterrupted and high-quality music. ClickRadio allowed consumers to download and listen to songs without an Internet connection. His product design shaped many of the concepts that have become the standard in the music streaming industry.

And his outspokenness helped channel attention to diversity in technology startups.

Henry "Hank" Williams was a Harlem-raised technologist who had a vision for a truly inclusive innovation economy. He spent his nearly thirty-year career pioneering the Black tech ecosystem by creating spaces and opportunities for Black founders to make an impact. He is most remembered for his persistence in holding the industry accountable for its lack of diversity at a time when diversity wasn't yet a part of the conversation. He did this not because it was the right thing to do but because it made smart business sense.

Williams' drive to cultivate the representation of minorities and women in the innovation economy was driven by his unique perspective and impressive career as a technologist. He established a career in tech at a time when Black people in the industry were few and far between, making every move more integral to future tech opportunities for people of color. Feeling this sense of responsibility, he forged his own path and made an impact at every turn in his career.

Williams grew up in Harlem, New York. The son of Elaine Williams and Judge Henry Williams, Sr., he spent his formative years at the St. Bernard's School before completing his secondary education at the Taft School, a boarding school in Connecticut. He went on to study computer science and engineering at the University of Pennsylvania. His entrepreneurial career began in the mid-eighties when he designed and launched hardware that doubled the processing speed and tripled the memory capacity for early Macintosh computers. As President and Chief Executive of Paster Development Corporation from 1988–1994, he also developed a highly-regarded personal information management program for Newton and Macintosh called DayMaker. During the mid-nineties, Williams co-founded the technology consulting firm Cybersonic. Working with most of the major music labels, he provided broadcasting and Internet development services, while pioneering in the industry of large-scale cybercasts.

In 2008, Williams pivoted to launch Kloud.co, a startup developing a new cloud information management platform for organizing and managing email. Simultaneously, Williams participated in the first class of the Silicon Valley–based NewMe accelerator program. NewMe was created to help founders launch sustainable businesses through an online platform, a residential boot camp accelerator, and an equity portfolio. Incidentally, Williams and his NewMe cohort were integral in exposing Silicon Valley's resistance to change.

CNN featured Williams and the cohort's seven other minority entrepreneurs in the 2011 documentary *The New Promised Land: Silicon Valley*. While following the entrepreneurs as they pitched for venture capital funding, the project sparked a much needed conversation about the lack of diversity in Silicon Valley— specifically the absence of Black employees at some of the largest tech companies, and the lack of capital for Black founders. It provided a new framework for engaging people on this previously avoided issue. In Williams' view, "Silicon Valley is very, very White." It is this view coupled with his passion for changing the tech landscape that led to the conception of his next project, Platform, a not-for-profit organization dedicated to increasing the participation and success of underrepresented minorities in the innovation economy. The organization's first endeavor, Platform Summit, launched in July 2013 at MIT Media Lab in Cambridge, Massachusetts.

In just three years, Williams and Platform shifted the narrative about diversity in tech. During a new phase, when diversity and inclusion were becoming the attractive talking point for many organizations, Platform differentiated itself by actually bringing disadvantaged groups together to forge meaningful connections and create an inclusive ecosystem. The annual event featured entrepreneurs, speakers, and investors from different gender and cultural backgrounds, and gave people of color space to increase their visibility in the industry. The initiative was supported and funded by many organizations, including Google for Entrepreneurs, Credit Suisse, Kapor Center for Social Impact, Shahara Ahmad-Llewellyn Family Foundation, Knight Foundation, Bill and Melinda Gates Foundation, Twitter, Ford, Genentech, Morehouse College, Georgia Tech, and Cox Media Group.

Williams was a connector, a builder, and a highly regarded visionary. He longed for an entrepreneurial community that embraced diversity and inclusion of everyone irrespective of race, gender, and ethnicity. When he didn't see space for people of color in tech, he created his own platform just for us. He became one of the first Black tech bloggers in the mainstream conversation through his blog, *Why Does Everything Suck*, where he shared candid and impactful thoughts on what he believed in. His work shaped ecosystems, and his legacy built foundations that continue to catalyze Black tech innovation today.

References:

Snider, Mike. "Tech Entrepreneur, Diversity Advocate Hank Williams Dies at 50." *USA Today*, November 16, 2015. https://www.usatoday.com/story/tech/2015/11/15/tech-entrepreneur-diversity-advocate-hank-williams-dies-50/75841942/

Sutton, Wayne. "How Hank Williams Lead Us... In Tech, Diversity and Life." *Medium*, January 6, 2016. https://medium.com/@waynesutton/how-hank-williams-lead-us-in-tech-diversity-and-life-333b17bd7942

Talbert, Marcia Wade. "NewME Hank Williams Launches Platform." *Black Enterprise*, April 8, 2013. https://www.blackenterprise.com/newme-hank-williams-launches-platform/

Tinuoye, Kunbi. "Industry Heavyweights Pay Tribute to Tech Trailblazer Hank Williams." *UrbanGeekz*, July 8, 2020. https://urbangeekz.com/2015/11/industry-heavyweights-pay-tribute-to-tech-trailblazer-hank-williams/

Zaal, Mayida. "The Hank Williams Tech Trailblazer Award." *All Star Code Spring Celebration*. Accessed November 26, 2020. https://www.allstarcodespring.org/hankwilliams

———

H BCUvc builds pathways for the underestimated investor and founder. Since 2017, HBCUvc has operated programs to engage over 185 university students, entrepreneurs, and emerging venture capital professionals, with the view that venture capital and related roles in technology startups are the linchpin for accelerating access to wealth in Black and Latinx communities. We support a community of emerging investors and founders by providing equity-free micro-investments, mentorship through peer communities and leadership development, culturally-affirming investment curriculum, and access to paid internships in venture capital and technology companies.

Our mission prioritizes Black and Latinx students and professionals who are impacted by systemic social and economic oppression. We root our work at one of the most overlooked institutions for Black innovation—Historically Black Colleges and Universities (HBCUs)—and extend to cities where stark inequalities and implicit biases continue to widen the racial wealth gap.

Learn more and connect with us:

 HBCU.VC

 @HBCU.VC

DELORIS "DELA" WILSON

D ela Wilson is the Founder and Principal of Axle Impact Studio, a social impact design firm repositioning economies, institutions, and human behavior for equity, as well as Due Goodies, a company for mission-driven merchandise. As a strategist and writer, her work seeks to decolonize development efforts through an intentional redirection of capital, influence, and opportunity.

She has worked across eight countries to maximize corporate impact, seed innovation in post-colonial states, and design strategies that reallocate resources for Black and Indigenous entrepreneurs, innovators, and nonprofit executives. Her strategies for entrepreneurial ecosystem development, culturally-relevant approaches to public health, and transnational racial equity span Georgetown University's Institute of Technology Law and Policy, the Ash Center for Democratic Governance and Innovation at

Harvard University, and the *Harvard Journal of African American Public Policy* (previously as Editor-in-Chief). As a graduate of Spelman College (BA, *summa cum laude*, political science), Georgetown University Law Center (JD), and Harvard Kennedy School of Government (MPA), she is also a Global Fellow of the Atlantic Institute and Senior Fellow for the Atlantic Fellows for Racial Equity.

 DWILSON.CO | AXLEIMPACTSTUDIO.COM

 @ADOSEOFDLO

HADIYAH MUJHID

Hadiyah Mujhid is the Founder and CEO of HBCUvc. Previously, Hadiyah co-founded the nonprofit Black Founders in 2011. Black Founders was one of the first organizations to focus on supporting Black technology entrepreneurs. Its nationwide conferences and events reached more than 500 entrepreneurs, and its programming has been successful in introducing many Black entrepreneurs to their first investors. Hadiyah has spent fifteen years as a software engineer with experience ranging from flight system software at Lockheed Martin to developing software prototypes for a mobile helicopter booking startup. Hadiyah holds an MBA from Drexel University and a BS in computer science from the University of Maryland Eastern Shore, an HBCU. She is a strong advocate for leveraging technology and entrepreneurship to address economic inequality. She is recognized as a 2019 Echoing Green

Fellow and 2019 Praxis Fellow. Her work has been featured in *Forbes*, Blavity, *TechCrunch*, *Business Insider*, *Black Enterprise*, and *Handelsblatt*.

 HBCU.VC

 @HADIYAHDOTME

GLOSSARY

Accelerator: A program that provides the mentorship and capital necessary to accelerate the growth of young startups. Typically, the program will provide some capital and, in exchange, will take an equity stake in the startup.

Accredited Investor: An individual or institution that meets certain wealth criteria (as defined by regulators), and is therefore deemed to be sophisticated enough to participate in private, non-public investments. There are many ways to qualify. For the most up to date definitions, visit www.irs.gov

Anchor Investor: The first investor in a fund and/or the largest investor in a fundraising round; can be also referred to as the lead investor.

Angel Investors: Wealthy individuals who invest in startups in early stages of development or during the seed round of fundraising. Due to the inherent risks of loss of capital or significant dilution in subsequent fundraising, angel investors typically pursue investments that they believe may have the potential to return multiples of the initial investment.

Annual Revenue Run Rate (ARR): The revenue for the last month multiplied by 12 as an estimate of the total revenue rate for the year.

Assets Under Management (AUM): The total market value of assets that an investment company or financial institution manages on behalf of investors. Assets under management definitions and formulas vary by company.

Bootstrapping: A business strategy by which a startup self-finances, eliminating the need for seed or angel investment. Typically achieved through lean operation and a product that generates revenue early in the company's life cycle.

Burn Rate: The rate at which a company consumes cash to cover expenses. Typically expressed monthly or weekly. Usually applied to a company with no revenues in order to give a metric of financial health and fundraising needs. A company with a low burn rate can theoretically operate longer without new injection of capital.

Business-to-Business (B2B): A form of transaction between businesses, such as one involving a manufacturer and wholesaler, or a wholesaler and retailer, rather than commerce between a business and an individual consumer.

Business-to-Consumer (B2C): A form of transaction in which businesses sell and market products or services to consumers.

Business-to-Government (B2G): A form of transaction in which businesses sell and market goods and services to federal, state, or local agencies.

Capitalization Table (Cap Table): A spreadsheet or table that shows the capital structure of a company, including how the specific ownership level aligns with each investor. It is generally used to view the percentage that each investor or employee owns in a certain company.

Carried Interest (Carry): The General Partner's (GP's) share of any profits realized by the fund's investors, after limited partners (LPs) have made back their invested capital.

Common Stock: A type of equity security, contrasted with preferred shares (or preferred stock). Common stock is most frequently issued to founders, management, and employees. In a liquidation event, preferred shares generally take priority over common shares.

Convertible Debt or Convertible Note: A loan that allows the lender to exchange the debt for common stock at a predetermined ratio instead of recollecting the principle as cash.

Customer Acquisition Cost (CAC): The total overall cost associated with convincing a customer to buy your product or service. The CAC includes research, marketing, and advertising costs, as well as the cost of producing, storing, and shipping the items that a customer purchases.

Customer Lifetime Value (CLV): A dynamic measurement of how valuable a customer is to your company, not just the value of a single purchase.

Due Diligence: The process performed by prospective investors to assess the viability of an investment and confirm that the information provided by the company is accurate.

Earnings Before Interest and Taxes (EBIT): An indicator of a company's profitability. EBIT can be calculated as revenue minus expenses excluding tax and interest. EBIT is also referred to as operating earnings, operating profit, and profit before interest and taxes.

Elevator Pitch: A concise presentation given by an entrepreneur about an investment or partnership opportunity. The presentation should be concise enough to be shared on an elevator ride.

Exit Event or Liquidity Event: When an issuer engages in a transaction that allows investors to sell their shares, which generally happens through a tender offer (sale) or an IPO (initial public offering).

Fiduciary: Someone who owes special duties to another person and who has liability if they do not perform that duty.

First Refusal Rights: The right to purchase stock in future offerings by the company on the same terms as other investors.

Founder's Dilemma: An experience shared by many founders who may be convinced that only they can lead their startups to success. They later need to give up control in order to allow their venture to grow.

Friends and Family Round: Capital provided by the friends and family of founders of an early-stage startup. This is typically the first outside capital when the startup is generally too early to raise capital from angel or seed investors.

Fund of Funds: A fund created to invest in private equity or venture capital funds. This entity is often referred to as a Limited Partner to the venture capital fund.

Fund Manager: A role within a venture capital fund. A fund manager is responsible for identifying investment opportunities, innovative business models, or technologies with potential to generate high returns on investment for the fund.

General Partner (GP): A role within a venture capital fund. A GP is responsible for all fund investment decisions and normally invests their own capital in the fund.

Growth Equity: Private investments in late-stage companies which aim to finance revenue growth through market expansion.

Incubator: A collaborative program for startup companies—usually physically located in one central workspace—designed to help startups in their infancy to succeed by providing a workplace, seed funding, mentoring, and training.

Investment Syndicate: A venture capital fund created to make a single investment. They are led by experienced technology investors and financed by institutional investors and sophisticated angels.

Lead Investor: The first investor in a fundraising round, also likely the largest. In early stages, they typically take on more responsibilities than other investors, including negotiating the investment terms, doing due diligence, and monitoring the company after closing. The lead investor usually invests more than other investors who participate in the round. They are often located near the company or specialize in the company's industry.

Limited Partner (LP): High-net-worth individuals, institutional investors (e.g., pension funds, foundations, endowments, finance companies), and family offices that invest in a VC fund. The word "limited" asserts their passive role in fund operational activities.

Managing Director/Managing Partner/General Partner (MD/GP): The leader of a venture capital fund who is compensated through management fees and receives direct carry in the funds. They are responsible for day-to-day operations, engage in fundraising, and vote on the deals the firm considers executing.

Milestone: An event that triggers another investment by the venture investors.

Minimum Viable Product (MVP): The most basic version of the product that delivers its main and core value to the consumer. The MVP is designed to collect feedback from early adopters.

Preferred Shares or Preferred Stock: Shares of a company's stock with dividends that are paid out to shareholders before common stock dividends are issued. Preferred stock takes preference over common stock in the event of liquidation.

Venture Capital: A form of private equity and a type of financing that investors provide to startup companies and small businesses believed to have long-term growth potential.

Venture Capitalist (VC): A person or company that invests in a business venture, providing capital for startup or expansion. They can work independently but are more commonly a part of a venture capital firm that pools money from multiple members/investors. They obtain investment capital from pension funds, university endowments, foundations, finance companies, and high-net-worth individuals.

Venture Capital Fund: A type of investment fund that invests in early-stage startup companies that offer a high return potential but also come with a high degree of risk. The fund is managed by a venture capital firm, and the investors are usually institutions or high-net-worth individuals.

INDEX

Index entries for particular companies contain featured founder names in parentheses. Example: Base Ventures (Erik Moore & Kirby Harris).

H

I

R

CPSIA information can be obtained
at www.ICGtesting.com
Printed in the USA
LVHW052258060621
689421LV00008B/53

9 781736 952108